COLLECTING IN A
CONSUMER SOCIETY

THE COLLECTING CULTURES SERIES
Edited by Susan M. Pearce

COLLECTING IN A
CONSUMER SOCIETY

Russell W. Belk

London and New York

First published 1995
by Routledge
11 New Fetter Lane, London EC4P 4EE

Simultaneously published in the USA and Canada
by Routledge
29 West 35th Street, New York, NY 10001

© 1995 Russell W. Belk

Typeset in Stempel Garamond by
Florencetype, Stoodleigh, Devon

Printed and bound in Great Britain by
T J Press Ltd, Padstow, Cornwall

British Library Cataloguing in Publication Data

A catalogue record for this book is available from the British Library

Library of Congress Cataloguing in Publication Data

A catalogue record for this book has been requested

ISBN 0–415–10534–X

CONTENTS

— ·•· —

3319

SERIES EDITOR'S PREFACE

———— •◆• ————

Nearly one in every three people in North America collects something, and this figure is unlikely to be very different for most of northern and large parts of southern Europe. Some 30 per cent of this population are therefore willing to define themselves as collectors, and to see collecting as a significant element in their lives. "Collecting' is difficult to define (and its scope is an important issue which the books in this series address), but clearly the gathering together of chosen objects for purposes regarded as special is of great importance, as a social phenomenon, as a focus of personal emotion and as an economic force.

In the past, the study of collecting has concentrated upon the content of collections, usually viewed from the perspective of a traditional discipline such as the History of Art, Geology or Archaeology. In this, of course, study was in line with characteristic modernist approaches to understanding, of which the disciplines themselves were also a major part. New work in the field has opened up new and fruitful ideas which are concerned with collecting as a process in itself, and with the nature of collecting as part of our effort to construct an intelligible world-view.

Collecting seen from this angle will be the topic of the volumes in this series. The books will explore issues like: the social context of collecting in both the historical long term and the medium term of single lives; the relationship of collecting to consumption; and the ways in which collecting can contribute to the creation of identity in areas like the dimensions of time, space and gender. Particular studies will draw also on debates concerning the nature of material culture and our response to it, and the nature of the museum as the institution concerned with collecting.

Collecting lies near to the hearts of many of us, and close also to our social mind and our ability to understand ourselves and the world we live in. This series is the first to explore this significant and fascinating area of human experience. Objects are our other selves; the better we understand them, the closer we come to self-knowledge.

Susan M. Pearce

TO KAY AND AMY

CHAPTER ONE

THE RISE OF CONSUMER SOCIETY

—— ·◆· ——

The world is so full of a number of things
I'm sure we should all be as happy as kings

(Stevenson 1905)

ON BEING AS HAPPY AS KINGS

Written during the rise of the age of consumerism, Stevenson's couplet contemplates the abundant things of the world with a child's sense of wonder. The happiness of kings is seen as a happiness that comes from having things. If this happiness was once restricted to kings it was because only they could command any thing they wished. But in a democratic consumer society within a market economy, the consumer is king. Given sufficient resources, any of us can now have our most regal material wishes fulfilled. The belief that such unbridled access to things should lead to unbridled happiness is the central premise of a consumer society.

The development of contemporary consumer societies has had a profound effect on the way we view the world. Stated most simply, we have come to regard an increasing profusion of both natural and human-produced things as objects to be desired, acquired, savored, and possessed. Both individuals and social institutions have enthusiastically, if sometimes guiltily, embraced this world view. Perhaps the most prominent manifestation of such consumerism is in the proliferation of individual and institutional collections. For collecting is consumption writ large. It is a perpetual pursuit of inessential luxury goods. It is a continuing quest for self completion in the marketplace. And it is a sustained faith that happiness lies only an acquisition away. But while collecting may well be the stylized and distilled essence of a consumer orientation toward life, the conceptual relationship between collecting and consuming remains largely unexplored.

This investigation of the interplay of collecting and consuming attempts to understand the interdependence of these phenomena both historically and in contemporary cultures. The primary focus is on collecting as a consumption activity that is shaped by the same cultural processes that affect other types of consumption activities. The dramatic growth of mass production, mass distribution, and mass communication is found to parallel the similarly dramatic growth of mass consumption, mass individual collecting, and

I

massive museum collecting. More importantly, collecting is found to be a key activity that articulates our sometimes conflicting values concerning work and leisure, science and art, male and female, high culture and popular culture, us and the "other," and production and consumption. These values are socially constructed and accordingly differ over times and cultures. My focus will be mainly on the phenomenon of collecting and on contemporary Western collecting. But before narrowing the focus too much, it is important to situate the development of consumption and collecting more broadly.

THE DEVELOPMENT OF CONSUMER SOCIETIES

Consumer society

We humans have consumed non-necessary luxuries for a very long time. A collection of interesting pebbles found in an 80,000-year-old cave in France may mark the beginning of collecting (Neal 1980). As the climate warmed, these collections became more extensive, and during the Upper Paleolithic era collections of shells, iron pyrite, fossils, quartz, and galena were assembled in Cro-Magnon caves (Pomian 1990). Cave paintings, sculptures, and grave goods found in these caves from about 30,000 BC have suggested to some a "creative explosion" in human evolution, that may mark the first time we invested extra-utilitarian symbolic meanings in objects of human creation (Halverson 1987; Pfeiffer 1982). If so, this was the beginning of a long path toward contemporary consumer societies in which a large portion of the world passionately desires a variety of luxuries ranging from the momentary services of purchased travel, entertainments, and exotic foods to more durable automobiles, televisions, and fashionable clothing.

There were vast accumulations of art, books, and other luxury goods among the rulers and wealthy elite of many early civilizations, including those of China, India, Egypt, Sumeria, Assyria, Persia, and Babylonia (Rigby and Rigby 1944). But the luxury consumption by kings, gods (in temples managed by priests), and the elite is not sufficient for a consumer society to exist. According to one definition (Rassuli and Hollander 1986), a culture of consumption requires four conditions:

1. People (or some very substantial segment of the population) consume at a level substantially above that of crude, survival-level subsistence.
2. People obtain goods and services for consumption through exchange rather than self-production.
3. Consumption is seen as an acceptable and appropriate activity.
4. People, in fact, tend to judge others and perhaps themselves in terms of their consuming lifestyles.

(Rassuli and Hollander 1986, p. 5)

Although the characterization of life in a subsistence hunting and gathering economy as "crude" displays a sometimes unwarranted prejudice (Sahlins 1972) and although there is a lack of recognition of the non-utilitarian hedonic nature of a consumer culture (Campbell 1987; Hirschman and Holbrook 1982), this definition usefully stipulates that the existence of a consumer society depends on more than economic conditions. The last two requirements suggest that consumption values are also intimately involved.

A key value change in the development of a consumer society is the change from envy avoidance to envy provocation. A related shift is the change from being a "limited good" society (in which it is perceived that there is only so much good to go around and one person's gain is another's loss) to an "unlimited good" society (in which it is perceived that society is not a zero-sum game and through a multiplier, spillover, or trickle-down effect another's gains may even contribute to our own gains). In small-scale societies where all are known to all, the limited good perspective is thought to apply (Foster 1965). The threat of provoking envy by having more than others is dissipated in these societies by foregoing unusual consumption, by sharing, hiding, and denying consumption, or by institutionalizing ceremonial gifts (Foster 1972). Widespread belief in the evil eye of envious others, held at bay with various amulets to protect against this malevolence, is another form of envy avoidance (Maloney 1976; Schoeck 1966). For example, among the Muria Gonds of India, even though many have acquired considerable wealth, Gell (1986) found a great reluctance to spend it on possessions beyond the locally accepted standard of a wristwatch, bicycle, and radio. But as a consumer society develops, envy avoidance gives way to competitive display of possessions aimed at envy provocation (Belk 1988b). This fundamental value shift may be facilitated by division of labor, multiplication of social roles, employment outside of the home, the growth of cities, increases in economic wealth, greater social mobility, and the rise of individualism, but it is doubtful that it depends upon any of these factors. Nor is such a shift to envy provocation through conspicuous consumption inevitable. Rather, it is a value that emerges from the confrontation of available consumer goods with the social construction of norms regarding acceptable and desirable consumption patterns. Among the Muria, Gell (1986) found that acceptable consumption includes traditional cloth, jewelry, traditional foods, and household collections of brassware, all of which help to reinforce Muria identity, Hindu caste, and, in the case of jewelry, act as a store of wealth and security for women. Feasts and drinking parties are the other major ways in which extra Muria wealth is spent (both of which are envy-reducing forms of sharing and ceremonial gift-giving). Thus envy-reducing public luxury has not given way to envy-provoking private luxury and a consumer society has not yet developed. Nevertheless, the acceptance of the status symbols of wristwatch, bicycle, and radio suggest cultural changes in this direction.

Besides changing values regarding conspicuous consumption and envy, the other major value change entailed in the development of consumerism is the adoption of what Campbell (1987) terms modern hedonism. Campbell begins with Scitovsky's (1976) distinction between need-satisfying necessities (which produce comfort) and desire-satisfying luxuries (which produce pleasure). The initial response of the traditional hedonist, Campbell suggests, is to strive to acquire more necessities (e.g., the Roman practice of purging to allow the consumption of more food and drink) and more luxuries (e.g., more exotic foods and wines, a harem, art works). Braudel illustrates such traditional hedonism in describing the courtly dining of pre-fifteenth-century Europe as involving:

> fountains of wine, set-pieces, and children disguised as angels descending from the sky on cables. Ostentatious quantity prevailed over quality. At best, this was a luxury of greed. Its striking feature was the riot of meat – a long-lasting feature of the tables of the rich.
>
> (Braudel 1973, p. 127)

The modern hedonist by contrast concentrates more on emotions than sensations. Here the key to pleasure is the imagination and fantasies that create or expand desire. Desire is ironically seen as an enjoyable state of discomfort or pain which eventually gives way to the pleasure of realizing the fantasized object of desire. But both because the object seldom lives up to the fantasy expectations that we have daydreamed and because it is the state of desire itself that provides the opportunity to enjoy heightened emotions, this cycle of desire is likely to be rapidly reinitiated by focusing on yet another object. In this sense, the modern hedonism of consumer culture is self-illusory. That is, it is produced by an illusion that we participate in creating. Consumer culture is also, Campbell insightfully argues, tied to the early-nineteenth-century rise of romanticism in Europe. Romanticism is the enemy of utilitarianism which valorizes the rational evaluation of goods according to their need-satisfying potential rather than according to their emotional potential to inflame desire. Among the legacies of romanticism is romantic love, which Campbell unromantically concludes leads to the same cycles of fantasy–desire–disappointment characteristic of consumerism. The relationship of romantic love to collecting will be developed in the concluding chapter of this book. It is also significant that although Campbell does not address the phenomenon of collecting, it appears to be a vehicle for modern hedonism *par excellence*. It is a renewable source of pleasure and desire, a target for our fantasies, a focus of cyclical quest and romantic yearning, and is often a conspicuous luxury provoking the envy of competing collectors. Before pursuing these contentions in the historical development of collecting, it is necessary to consider the historical development of consumer culture. The reason for doing so is that the historical development of collecting parallels and derives from the historical development of consumerism.

Historical moments in the development of consumerism

An investigation of consumer culture in ancient civilizations has yet to be written, with the assumption generally being that the expansion of world trade with the European discovery of the New World and the massive changes precipitated by the Industrial Revolution were the major impetuses to the creation of consumer societies. Yet it is clear that the earliest moments of pervasive consumerism were in ancient civilizations and that the early development of consumerism is not restricted to the West. One imperfect but useful index of the change from a rigid aristocratic society to a more democratic mass-consumption society is the sumptuary laws that often emerge during the transition period. These laws attempt to stem the changes taking place in consumption through legislation restricting luxuries, either by outlawing them or limiting them to certain ranks of society. Appadurai (1986) notes that such laws are common both when the status quo is threatened from within by developments such as capitalism, and when it is threatened from without as with a rapid influx of foreign goods. Miller (1987, pp. 135–136) observes that when rigid social hierarchies begin to break down, sumptuary laws are an attempt to keep goods as signs of status rather than allowing them to become directly constitutive of such social status. However, sometimes sumptuary laws have been enacted as reactions against consumption extravagance in general rather than being aimed at parvenus. Regardless of whether they are general or class-specific, the passage of sumptuary legislation may be taken as indicative of a reaction against the rise of consumer culture.

In ancient Athens the laws of Solon of about 594 BC included sumptuary laws aimed at curbing conspicuous consumption. They included outlawing extravagance at funerals and fixing the price of animals sacrificed in public ceremonies (Vincent 1934). Women were singled out as potentially more extravagant and were forbidden from bringing more than three sets of clothing into a marriage and from traveling with more than this much clothing or more than a fixed amount of baggage (Lindeman 1950). The sale of perfume was also prohibited, presumably because it was seen as excessive and unnecessary consumption (Freeman 1976). Early in the fourth century BC, further legislation restricted the number of wedding guests in Athens to no more than thirty in an attempt to curb wedding-celebration extravagance (Oakley and Sinos 1993). These sumptuary laws appear to have crumbled in the Hellenistic age with Alexander the Great's conquest of the Greek city-states in the late fourth century BC.

The first sumptuary law in Rome was passed in 215 BC and restricted extravagance in dress and jewelry. It was repealed 20 years later due to difficulties in enforcement (Phillips and Staley 1961). As with Solon's laws in Greece, women were singled out in the areas of dress, transport, and jewelry, with attempted restrictions on food and entertainments applying more broadly. Roman laws that were aimed at curbing conspicuous consumption included the Lex Orchia (187 BC) limiting the number of guests at a feast and the Lex Fannia (161 BC) regulating the cost of entertainments (Hurlock 1929). Unlike Greece, sumptuary laws in Rome were often specific to rank, with rank-specific limitations in such features as the color and fabric of clothing and the use of gold in jewelry. Additional sumptuary laws were passed in Rome through the first century AD. However, even by Cicero's time in the first century BC, such laws were so seldom obeyed and enforced that they were regarded as "merely funny" (Cowell 1964).

In Europe sumptuary laws proscribed foods and drink that could be publicly consumed and types of carriage, but they primarily concerned clothing and jewelry. In Genoa a law banning the use of rich furs was passed in 1157 and repealed in 1161 (Hughes 1983). Sumptuary laws of both Genoa and Venice peaked in the mid-sixteenth century. They precluded lavish weddings and baptisms as well as extravagant clothing, and they also fined tailors, embroiderers, and designers who created lavish dress for commoners (Braudel 1982, pp. 491–492). In France the earliest sumptuary legislation was by King Louis VIII in 1229 and was addressed to permissible clothing for nobles (Hughes 1983). By the end of the thirteenth century rank- and income-appropriate furnishings were also prescribed. Other French sumptuary laws were aimed at curbing conspicuous consumption. A flurry of six different sumptuary laws passed in France between 1563 and 1577 restricted extravagance through limiting meals to three courses and prohibiting meat and fish at the same meal (Farb and Armelagos 1980, p. 155). This was during the reign of Charles IX who also promulgated the greatest number of rank-specific sumptuary laws of any French monarch (Hurlock 1929). These laws remained in place until the fall of the Bastille, when one of the first acts of the new General Assembly was to abolish all sumptuary laws. In England the earliest sumptuary legislation was a 1337 law forbidding wearing clothes of foreign cloth (Mukerji 1983). Although this law was repealed a year later, it became a model for subsequent laws that reached their peak in England in the sixteenth century. In addition to stipulating what the lower classes might wear, it distinguished different classes of gentlemen, knights, and merchants. Furs, velvets, and clothing colors other than natural fabric or solid blue dye were also restricted to the elite. This was followed by a 1362 law specifying that grooms, yeomen, and craftsmen could not wear "precious stones, cloth of silver, silk, girdles, knives, buttons, rings, brooches, chains, etc. of gold or silver or embroidered silken clothing" (quoted in Mukerji 1983, p. 180). In the Netherlands it was in the mid-seventeenth century that the strongest sumptuary laws were passed, limiting the extravagance, size, and duration of feasts, including funeral and wedding celebrations (Schama 1987, pp. 186–187). This timing followed the shift of the center of the European economy to Amsterdam at the beginning of the seventeenth century (Braudel 1977). The rise in the power of the merchant class is evident in that some of the Dutch laws were aimed at restricting the consumption of the elite rather than curbing encroachments by the emerging middle class.

While most of the Italian and other European sumptuary laws were concerned with proscribing forbidden pleasures in consumption, some were concerned with prescribing required clothing or jewelry to mark stigmatized social or ethnic groups. Such was the case for instance with prostitutes and Jewish women whom a number of fifteenth-century Italian cities required to wear such marks as ear-rings, bells, insignia of yellow or red circles or stripes, headbands of yellow, or veils (Hughes 1986). In the case of Italian Jews, hatred of them arose not only from envy of their wealth and fine dress, but also from resentment of the practice of usury to which Jews were also marginalized (Hughes 1986; Hyde 1983; Shell 1982). While mandated dress requirements were used to identify and further stigmatize Jews and prostitutes, another strategy was to mandate that prostitutes wear certain finery in the hope that it would discourage other women from adopting these same fashions. However, as Freudenberger (1963) observes, this merely reinforced the tendency for marginal members of society to be its fashion leaders, much as hippies, punks, and gays have been in more contemporary societies (McCracken 1988).

The American colonies enacted sumptuary laws regulating clothing during the first half of the seventeenth century. As in the Netherlands, much of this legislation was aimed at curbing luxurious clothing of the elite as well as enforcing class distinctions (Schmidt 1989). For instance, in Virginia in 1621, a law was passed prohibiting ostentation in dress, including the use of gold clothing by all but high government officials. In New England after 1634, anyone wearing embroidered caps, hatbands, belts, ruffs, beaver hats, or garments with slashes in the sleeves could have their clothing confiscated (Worrell 1980). Much of the American sumptuary legislation was in the Puritan colonies and was intended to curb the sins of pride and envy. As North (1974) notes, there was a paradox here in that the Puritan virtues of hard work, thrift, and discipline, coupled with the free land and free economy of the New World, created wealth and social mobility that contradicted other Puritan beliefs in humility, modesty, and a fixed social order. The sumptuary laws were an unsuccessful attempt to reconcile the "intolerable excess" of consumption among some Puritans with these basic beliefs. At a more general level, this problem has been termed the paradox of the Protestant Ethic: hard work produces wealth which leads to a consumption ethic that undermines the work ethic (Albee 1977).

Japan, like Europe, had numerous sumptuary laws concerning clothing during the Tokugawa period which lasted from 1603 to 1868 (De Mente and Perry 1967). These laws prescribed dress by class and occupation. In some cases a worker's employer was also evident in the symbols with which work outfits were emblazoned. The highest clothing privileges went to the imperial court and samurai warriors who could wear silk. However, during the late Tokugawa period merchants and their wives sometimes circumvented these laws by lining their cotton garments with expensive silk (De Mente and Perry 1967, p. 92). Japanese sumptuary laws also prescribed class-appropriate umbrellas, prayers, and housing. For example a farmer with a large income could build a house 60 feet long but with no alcoves and no roof tiles (Hurlock 1929). Enforcement of these sumptuary laws was difficult in Japan as it was elsewhere, and fashion-conscious consumers also found ways around them. For instance, when red (benibana) garments were restricted to the court in the eighteenth century, commoners turned to red undergarments (Berthe 1992). While the benibana red helped to connote status in Japan because of the high cost of the dye, red was also a color reserved for the upper classes in medieval Europe (Stuard 1985).

Clunas (1991a, 1991b) finds striking similarities between China and Europe between 1550 and 1650 (the late Ming dynasty), not only in terms of consumer culture, but in terms of sumptuary legislation. The earliest of this legislation was passed in China in 1393. It was also much more inclusive than the European laws, prescribing not only appropriate dress, but also carriages, sedan chairs, parasols, horse trappings, seals, buildings, and utensils. One such law stipulated that:

> Dukes, Marquises and officials of the First and Second Ranks might have wine pots and wine cups of gold, and for the rest use silver. Officials of the Third to Fifth Ranks might have pots of silver and wine cups of gold, while those of the Sixth to Ninth Ranks might have pots and cups of silver, for the rest making use of porcelain or lacquer. Items of woodwork should not make use of cinnabar, gilt or painted gold decoration, or of carvings of dragons or phoenixes. The common people should have pewter wine pots, wine cups of silver, and for the rest use porcelain or lacquerware. Couches, screens and window lattices of variously colored and decorated lacquer belonging to officials should not be carved with dragon designs or be of vermilion lacquer decorated with gold. Military officials and officers should have bows and arrows of black lacquer, while bow cases and quivers must not employ vermilion lacquer or painted gold decorations ... officials of the First and Second ranks might not use vessels of jade, but only of gold. Merchants and practitioners of craft skills might not use vessels of silver and were in all respects to be as the common people.
>
> (Clunas 1991a, p. 149)

But these laws were similar to the European and American laws in another respect: they were only sporadically and ineffectively enforced. This was a result not only of the difficulty of enforcement, but of an eventual resignation to the forces of consumer culture.

The power of consumer desire to thwart sumptuary laws is seen in the strategies developed to legally circumvent these laws as well as in their outright disregard. This is true even when the penalties for violating these laws were imprisonment or death (Freudenberger 1963). When buttons were outlawed, studs were substituted. When gold and silver fabrics were prohibited in Europe, garments began to be lined with such fabric and slashes made in sleeves so that these linings would show (Hughes 1983). When a limit was placed on elaborateness of cloth sold, women began to embroider plain cloth to make it more elegant (Hurlock 1929). Each time a new sumptuary law was imposed to stop such circumventions of the old law, new means of circumvention were found. As a result, in the 400-year period between 1300 and 1700, Phillips and Staley (1961) found a total of 472 sumptuary laws passed in Italy, Germany, Switzerland, France, England, and America. The same analysis concludes that the three major purposes of these laws were to maintain class distinctions, to protect morals, and to limit extravagance and thereby keep money in the country that might otherwise be spent on foreign luxuries. Not only did the European sumptuary laws rise with the development of commerce, the economic rationale behind them grew in importance as governments sought to protect their home industries during the sixteenth century. At the same time the moral concern of sumptuary laws seems to have shifted from the evils of consumption to the evils of sexuality associated with women's extravagant and fashionable dress (Hughes 1983, 1986). The general shift then was from discouraging extravagant consumption to encouraging it, at least as long as it benefitted the local economy. By the end of the eighteenth century, unless excise taxes, luxury taxes, prohibition, and "sin" taxes on products like alcohol and tobacco are considered sumptuary in nature (Hollander 1984), the sumptuary laws had either been repealed or were no longer enforced.

Sumptuary laws were a futile attempt to stem the initial swell of consumer culture. Their demise reflects a shift in the social treatments of envy and fashion. Braudel (1979, pp. 489–492) notes intermediate stages in Venice and other Italian city-states. Conspicuous luxurious gowns in bright colors were first worn under more modest dresses. Later such fashions were worn more openly, but the owner's face was hidden in public behind a mask like those used during Carnival. Eventually discretion gave way to display and private luxury and envy avoidance gave way to public luxury and envy provocation. Rather than outlawing conspicuous fashion consumption or making it a rigid function of hereditary social class, growing consumer cultures began to embrace novelty and seek the latest fashions. Increased demands for luxury consumption also led to increased production and merchandising to meet growing consumer desires. Sombart (1913) argues that the awakened consumer desire for fashionable goods led to capitalist production organization. Freudenberger (1963) suggests that fashion lust also led workers into the routinized work force in order to earn wages to facilitate the purchase of these luxuries. Still, the decline of government opposition to consumption via sumptuary laws did not mean the immediate acceptance of fashions and conspicuous consumption. Critiques of luxury consumption are another expression of the lack of full acceptance of consumer society (see Belk 1983). In order for consumer society to become as entrenched as it is today, additional developments had to occur to overcome both personal and social concerns with getting caught up in the perpetual quest for happiness in the marketplace.

FACTORS PRECIPITATING THE DEVELOPMENT OF CONSUMER SOCIETIES

Bringing Asia and the Americas to Europe

One such development was European contact with Asia and the Americas. The flow of both knowledge and goods from these distant lands to Europe served to stimulate the desire of Europeans for more. The detailed chronicles of Marco Polo and others as well as the imaginings of more fanciful writers first created images of an enchanted world in the East. Ashworth (1991), Mukerji (1983), and Welu (1991) trace the development of such geographic information in the construction of maps and natural-history encyclopedias. As in China at about the same time (Clunas 1991a), knowledge itself became a commodity for the first time – something that could be purchased on the market rather than only passed on orally. From the sixteenth through the eighteenth centuries, Europeans read and enjoyed new travel accounts of "discoveries" in the Americas, China, Africa, India, and the Middle East. As one such work in Portuguese began, paraphrasing the Bible and foreshadowing Stevenson's couplet, "Today we are witnessing wonderful things" (Defert 1982, p. 15). The excitement and amazement at these wonderful new things also led to their avid collection. The European discovery of the New World stimulated both early anthropology and Renaissance collecting habits, epitomized by highlighting exotic materials in *Wunderkammern* serving both ends (Hodgen 1964). Like the "wonder books" of the sixteenth and seventeenth centuries, the desire for owners of these "wonder cabinets" was not only to know the world (Hooper-Greenhill 1992), but to know it as an enchanted place (Park and Daston 1981; Schneider 1993). Kenseth describes the period from about 1550 to 1700 as one in which

> European culture was marked by an intense fascination with the marvelous, with those things or events that were unusual, unexpected, exotic, extraordinary, or rare. The word marvel (*meraviglia* in Italian, *merveille* in French, *Wunder* in German) was widely applied to anything that lay outside the ordinary, especially when it had the

capacity to excite the particular emotional responses of wonder, surprise, astonishment, or admiration.

(Kenseth 1991a, p. 25)

Kenseth goes on to define the possible characteristics that were seen at the time to constitute a marvel:

1 Novelty or rarity.
2 The foreign or exotic.
3 The strange and bizarre.
4 The unusually large and the unusually small.
5 Demonstrations of supreme technical skill or virtuosity; the triumph over difficult problems and the achievement of the seemingly impossible.
6 Vividness and verisimilitude.
7 The transcendent and the sublime.
8 The surprising and unexpected.

These properties help account for the large number of both natural and artificial objects that made their way into the *Wunderkammern* and *Kunstkammern* of the period. It is also a list of properties that continues to have an impact in many contemporary collections and consumer-goods promotions.

Helms (1988) suggests that material goods from relatively unknown foreign territories have not only magical fascination but also the lure of material gains from lands regarded as dangerous or morally and intellectually inferior. The period from the middle of the fifteenth century to the late seventeenth century was one not only of discovery but of acquisitiveness. Parry sketches the basic format of this period of European expansion:

Land, and the labour of those who worked it, were the principal sources of wealth. The quickest, most obvious, and socially most attractive way of becoming rich was to seize, and to hold as a fief, land already occupied by a diligent and docile peasantry.

(Parry 1963, p. 19)

And if native labor was not enough, slave labor was soon brought from Africa as little more than another foreign commodity to be exploited in producing wealth. Not only land and labor, but other goods were among the riches to be gained, as Greenblatt elaborates:

The European dream, endlessly repeated in the literature of explorations, is of the grossly unequal gift exchange: I give you a glass bead and you give me a pearl worth half your tribe. The concept of relative economic value – the notion that a glass bead or hawk's bell would be a precious rarity in the New World – is alien to most Europeans; they think that the savages simply do not understand the natural worth of things and hence can be tricked into exchanging treasures for trifles, full signs for empty signs.

(Greenblatt 1991, p. 110)

Christopher Columbus vividly exemplified this view in 1492 claiming possession of New World lands and returning from his first voyage with five "Indians" (the survivors of seven he had set out with) who became immediate curiosities. A similar *terrae nullius* possession took place when Captain James Cook claimed Australia for the British in the 1770s. Goods from Asia and the Americas that fascinated Europeans of this period included calicoes from India (Mukerji 1983), tobacco and sugar from the Americas (Goodman 1993; Mintz 1985; Schivelbusch 1992), tea from Asia (Evans 1992), and coffee from the Middle East (Goodman 1993; Hattox 1985). Besides their foreign origins, the fact that many of these substances had the added cachet of being forbidden pleasures, that they tend to be addictive stimulants, and that the stimulation they provide quickly dissipates, helped in no small measure to develop their repeated consumption.

World's fairs

Another important development in legitimizing consumer culture in both Europe and America was the world's fair and international exposition. The first of the modern expositions was the "Great Exhibition of the Works of Industry of All Nations," or Crystal Palace exposition, held in London in 1851. The huge glass "palace," with its indoor trees and Follet Osler's 27-foot crystal fountain made of 4 tons of crystal glass, was a dazzling setting for a display of the machinery of the industrial revolution and the new consumer goods it produced. Its contents were equally impressive:

> it seemed as though in an immense Aladdin's cavern the whole world had contracted into a glorious riot of spectacle and colour. There were silks and satins, furs and feathers, jewelled weapons and saddles, gold and silver ornaments of every kind, clocks, cabinets, couches and chairs, thrones in ivory and zebra wood, adornments in jet, jasper and jade, tapestry, embroidery, lace and brocade, fine linens, leatherwork, gold and silver filigree, perfumes, tobaccos, exotic foods and drinks, pottery, jamolica and terracotta, porcelain from Wedgewood, Worcester, Derby, Sèvres, Delft and Dresden, marble and metal statuary, furniture in onyx and carvings in a hundred different woods. These and thousands of other articles, were scattered in extravagant profusion as if they had been spouted from Osler's magic fountain.
>
> (Beaver 1986, p. 47)

The full catalogue of the exposition's 100,000 objects is contained in three 500-page volumes that visitors could buy as a souvenir in order to memorialize their visit and to be instructed by these fabulous objects at home. By drawing together the latest luxury goods and ingenious gadgets from around the world, the Crystal Palace formed a "monument to consumption" to which people made a "commodity pilgrimage" (Richards 1990, pp. 3, 18). During the six months the Exhibition was open more than six million pilgrims toured it (Howarth 1951). Mounted in a period of rising wages and declining costs of living, the fair helped to nourish and appeal to dreams of consumer abundance. The Crystal Palace was a lavish spectacle that for the first time brought consumer luxuries into a museum setting with monumental architecture and extravagant display. Unlike the more staid museums of the day, but like the world's fairs that would follow, the Great Exhibition also used sex to draw crowds, relying in this instance on "deliberately titillating" nude female statuary on ancient Greek themes (Beaver 1986, p. 57). The fair was, as a prize essay in the official fair catalogue suggested, "a lesson in taste" (Wornum 1851), but not only the refined aesthetic taste and implicit class distinctions the author had in mind. The fair presented the elegant alongside the vulgar and it was a mixture of the two that attached to the new mass-produced objects displayed there.

The 1851 Great Exhibition provoked an "exhibition mania" (Breckenridge 1989) and was followed by numerous subsequent expositions including the 1853–54 World's Fair of the Works of Industry of All Nations in New York, the 1855, 1867, 1878, 1889, and 1900 Exposition Universelle exhibitions in Paris, London's International Exhibition of 1862, the 1876 Centennial Exhibition in Philadelphia, the 1893 Columbian Exposition in Chicago, the 1904 Louisiana Purchase Exposition in St. Louis, the 1915 Panama–Pacific Exposition in San Francisco, the 1925 Exposition Internationale des Arts Décoratifs et Industriels Modernes in Paris, the 1929 Exposición Internationale in Barcelona, the 1933 Chicago World's Fair, the 1935 Exposition Universelle et Internationale in Brussels, the 1935–36 California Pacific International Exposition in San Diego, and the 1939 New York World's Fair. Although there continue to be world's fairs and they continue to heroize consumption (Ley and Olds 1988), with competition from films, television, and faster communications it has become increasingly difficult for fairs to create profitable consumer spectacles to lure an increasingly jaded public, although in many respects Walt Disney's EPCOT Center has become a permanent world's fair that is far more economically viable than a temporary fair (Nelson 1986).

Several consistent features of the world's fairs and expositions refined the spectacle and consumption celebrations pioneered by *Wunderkammern* and embellished by the Crystal Palace exposition. Besides monumental architecture and museum-like displays, the world's fairs used theatrical techniques of presentation, including giganticism, miniaturization, redundant quantities, emphasis on cultural icons, and borrowing prestigious motifs from around the world (Benedict 1983). Starting with the 1867 Paris exposition they featured re-creations of exotic foreign locales such as Turkish mosques, Swiss châlets, Swedish cottages, American Indian tipis, Irish castles, and villages of Africa, Patagonia, Java, Lapland, native America, or the Philippines (Tenkotte 1987). Displays of the artifacts of these lands were also prominent and a variety of ethnic and foreign restaurants were also included in each fair. As Bean (1987) recognizes, collecting and exhibiting were the main occupations of nineteenth-century anthropology, and museums and world's fairs were its primary institutional homes. Starting with the 1878 Paris exposition, "native villages" were included involving living exhibitions of the "exotic" foreign people moved to live in them during the course of the fair. In displaying tribal peoples as commodities for the gaze of the curious, the colonialist and imperialist vision of the world was emphasized and the concurrent commoditization of people and fetishization of objects of which Marx warned was made vivid (Benedict 1983; Benjamin 1970; Hinsley 1990). The same was true of the fairs' carnival midways which became a central focus. They included sideshows of "human oddities" as well as increasingly risqué shows of female flesh ranging from Little Egypt at the 1893 Colombia Exposition to Sally Rand in the 1933 Chicago World's Fair and Zoro's Nudist Gardens in the 1935–36 San Diego exposition (Rydell 1984, 1993). Thus the sensual pleasures of sex and consumption were never far from one another. The emphasis on sex, distant cultures, and the strange and unusual is all part of the exoticism that was created by these fairs. Of these emphases, only sex was absent from the *Wunderkammer* of preceding centuries.

One further feature that these expositions had in common was the increasing participation of corporate sponsors of exhibitions and pavilions. They provided a key opportunity for consumer-goods companies to link their products to an atmosphere of abundance, exoticism, entertainment, and spectacle as well as reach large numbers of people in an excited and enthusiastic frame of mind. In Williams's view, the expositions helped corporations realize the "new and decisive conjunction between imaginative desires and material ones, between dreams and commerce, between events of collective consciousness and of economic fact" (1982, p. 65). For many, the fairs introduced them to electricity, automobiles, flush toilets, telephones, cameras, bicycles, foreign foods, and a variety of foreign goods. But besides new *types* of products, the fairs also built consumer images of the *brands* of consumer goods that began to emerge in the decades around the turn of the century. Brands first introduced at world's fairs included Fleishman's yeast (Philadelphia, 1876), Coleman's mustard (Paris, 1878), and Goodyear rubber (Philadelphia, 1876). Quaker Oats distributed a free souvenir book at the 1893 Columbia Exposition, and at the 1904 St. Louis World's Fair it introduced its Puffed Rice by shooting it from eight bronze cannons and by handing out free four-color prints of American landmarks suitable for framing (Strasser 1989). Collecting small color advertising trade cards was a popular hobby in the 1880s and 1890s and many companies handed theirs out at the Columbia Exposition. Displays by corporations grew from moderate-sized entertainments, displays, and demonstrations of products like Singer sewing machines and Heinz foods at the turn-of-the-century expositions, to full pavilions by General Motors, Ford, Sinclair, General Foods, General Electric, Westinghouse, Eastman Kodak, Southern Pacific Railroad, IBM, and AT&T at the 1933 Chicago World's Fair and 1939 New York World's Fair (Zukin 1991). The majority of these exhibitors are now represented at EPCOT Center. The difference between the carnival barkers on the fair midways and the advertisers in its pavilions relates more to the amount of capital invested than to the nature and enthusiasm of their presentations. At the Chicago fair alone, Ford Motor Company spent nearly $14 million on its exhibitions in the middle of the Great Depression (Rydell 1993). Twenty corporations built pavilions at the Chicago fair versus nine in the 1893 Columbia exposition. Anthropomorphized brands were also presented at these fairs, including Planters' Mr. Peanut, Aunt Jemima, The Little Sunshine Bakers, and The Talking Plymouth (Nelson 1986; Strasser 1989). As a result, says Robert Rydell (1989) with intentional irony, "Fairs had the effect of making advertising seem as 'true and natural' to the American way of life as midway exhibitions of roller coasters and Ferris wheels and ethnological ghettos of Africans, Asians, Latin Americans, and native Americans" (p. 204).

The department store, merchandising, and advertising

Consumption requires distribution as well as production, but this is too functional a description to account for the emergence of consumerism. Thus it is significant, for example, that in the second century BC when Greek consumption was ascendent, the most splendid of the Athenian Agora buildings, the Stoa of Attalos, was built (Dixon 1994). It housed the most exclusive shops that sold perfume, jewelry, textiles, and art works. Anticipating the arcades of Paris, its effect on consumption must have been profound. "With the erection of the Stoa commerce presented a splendid and dignified facade; the colonnades in front of the shops provided elegant promenades. The ramshackle bazaar district was masked and kept in the background" (Thompson and Wycherley 1972, p. 172). Mass production, mass distribution, and mass communication worked jointly to precipitate mass consumption. As mass production provided both reduced prices and increased wages, the availability and affordability of former luxuries became democratized. As Thirsk (1978) finds in England, the rise of production and wages was not always well synchronized or smooth, but "by the end of the sixteenth century goods that had been deemed rich man's luxuries in 1540 were being made in so many different qualities and at such varied prices that they came within the reach of every man" (p. 179). But it would take another three centuries before the market mechanisms were found to turn commodities into fetishes. Three important mechanisms of fetishization were the department store, merchandising, and advertising.

In 1878 a young woman from San Francisco named Hattie Crocker visited Paris with her mother for twelve days in July, and returned in September for another seven weeks. Her diary shows that she visited the department store Bon Marché on her first day in Paris and that year's Exposition Universelle on her third. During just over two months in the French capital Hattie's diary recounts how she "went shopping as usual" at least thirty times and "went to the Expo" sixteen times (Davis 1989). Like the fair, the department store proved to be a source of delight and fantasy that was significant to the development of consumer culture. The first such store was the Bon Marché which opened in Paris in 1852, just a year after the Crystal Palace exposition. The overlap of the fair and the department store is evident in Bon Marché's exhibitions at the Chicago and St. Louis fairs and its separate pavilion at the 1900 Paris fair (Miller 1981), and in the remodeling of Chicago department stores to emulate the displays of the Columbian Exposition (Lewis 1983). The store in Zola's novel *Ladies' Delight* (1883) was based on the Bon Marché, and Williams's summary captures the period in which it emerged:

> Denise is the heroine of Émile Zola's novel *Au Bonheur des Dames* (1884), which opens with [an] account of her arrival in Paris. Her initial encounter with a department store dramatizes the way nineteenth century society as a whole suddenly found itself confronting a style of consumption radically different from any previously known. The quantity of consumer goods available to most people had been drastically limited: a few kitchen utensils used to prepare a sparse and monotonous diet, several well-worn pieces of furniture (bed, chest, table, perhaps a stool or bench), bedding, shoes or clogs, a shirt and trousers or a dress (and sometimes one outfit for special occasions), some essential tools. That was all. Moreover, these goods were obtained mainly through barter and self-production, so that the activity of consumption was closely linked with that of production. Money was rarely used by the average person and credit was haphazard and scarce. Only the better-off spent much time in stores; for most, the activity of shopping was restricted to occasional fairs.
>
> (Williams 1982, pp. 4–5)

The department store changed all this. It borrowed from the world's fair the spectacle of dazzling display, exotic merchandise, and expanses of glass, and added deferential salespeople, fixed economical prices, credit (eventually), and a variety of services from restaurants to writing rooms, all designed to make consumers feel pampered and free to browse. While Charles Baudelaire and Walter Benjamin focused on the *flâneur* who felt newly empowered to stroll the shops and arcades of Paris merely to look at the cornucopia of merchandise they contained, it was the *flâneuse* to whom the department store was primarily directed (e.g., Bowlby 1985; Gordon and McArthur 1985; Saisselin 1984). Palatial department stores similar to the Bon Marché followed rapidly in Europe and America. In rural towns smaller stores, fairs, and catalogue selling reminiscent of the Crystal Palace catalogues did similar missionary work in promoting new consumer desires (Schlereth 1989).

The protagonist in Dreiser's *Sister Carrie* (1900), like Zola's Denise, comes from the country to the big city (Chicago) and is completely captivated by the merchandise she sees in an 1889 department store that Dreiser modeled on Marshall Field's:

> Carrie passed along the busy aisles, much affected by the remarkable display of trinkets, dress goods, shoes, stationery, jewelry. Each separate counter was a show place of dazzling interest and attraction. She could not help feeling the claim of each trinket and valuable upon her personally and yet she did not stop. There was nothing she could not have used – nothing which she did not long to own. The dainty slippers and stockings, the delicately frilled skirts and petticoats, the laces, ribbons, hair-combs, purses, all touched her with individual desire, and she felt keenly the fact that not any of these things were in the range of her purchase.
>
> (Dreiser 1981, p. 22)

So ignited by consumer desire, Carrie's downfall begins when she allows the traveling salesman Drouet to give her twenty dollars so that she may buy a jacket that has caught her eye:

> There is nothing in this world more delightful than that middle state in which we mentally balance at times, possessed of the means, lured by desire and yet deterred by conscience or want of decision. When Carrie began wandering around the store amid the fine displays, she was in this mood. . . . She came upon the corset counter and paused in rich revery as she noted the dainty concoctions of colour and lace there displayed. Ah, if she would only make up her mind she could have one of those now. Where the jewelry was, there also she lingered. She saw the earrings, the bracelets, the pins, the chains. What would she not have given if she could have had them all.
>
> (Dreiser 1981, p. 67)

This is precisely the state of delightful anticipation that Campbell (1987) diagnosed as indicative of contemporary imaginative hedonism. Feeling guilty Carrie goes to Drouet to return the money, but having already been seduced by the merchandise gives in to her material desires, only to be subsequently at the mercy of Drouet's sexual desires. The exchange of male power and money for female youth and beauty is a commodification theme similar to that of the expositions' entertainment midways. In a larger sense it also is illustrative of Gail Reekie's (1993) cogent metaphor of department-store selling as a seduction of women by men. The sexist and sexual aspects of much sumptuary legislation have by no means disappeared. Consumer desire has much in common with sexual desire. Consumer temptation has strong parallels in sexual temptation (Duncan 1965, p. 121; Laqueur 1992). And as with the statuary in the Crystal Palace and the erotic dancing featured at subsequent world's fairs, the department-store windows and merchandise displays are meant to stimulate consumer desires and fantasies. The success of this commercial seduction is evident in the rise of shoplifting among middle-class Victorian women (Abelson 1989; Miller 1981).

Given the goal of stimulating consumer fantasies and desires, it is perhaps fitting that L. Frank Baum was writing *The Land of Oz* (1904) as he completed another book on *The Art of Decorating Show Windows and Drygoods Interiors* (1900). In his window-dressing text Baum emphasized the theatrical creation of fantasy in order to bring alive the magic of consumer goods (Culver 1988; Leach 1984, 1989). Subsequent window displays followed this advice, often with the aid or influence of top artists of the day (Marcus 1978). Consider the terminology used by one writer in describing the effects of department-store windows in the Chicago Loop just before the turn of the century:

> In this plutocratic realm there were no formal or informal sumptuary laws determining who could wear what kind of adornment. For the first time in history, all, regardless of rank, sex, race, religion, age, or birth, were urged to buy. These tableaux of slender, immaculate gods and goddesses of plutocracy, with their "heiress look," standing before rich draperies parted like clouds opening to paradise, communicated the mystery and wonder of wealth to the thousands of young Chicagoans who poured daily and hourly into the Loop.
>
> (Duncan 1965, p. 114)

Early department stores have been called cathedrals (Gardner and Sheppard 1989), temples (Hutter 1987), dream worlds (Williams 1982), and palaces of consumption (Benson 1979). They extend the lavish display and magical atmosphere of the exposition to everyday consumer goods and the simultaneous development of these two forms of spectacle involved imitation in both directions (Lewis 1983). A third interdependent institution is the museum, as is discussed in Chapter Four.

One last significant influence on the development of consumer culture is the growth of advertising and mass media. Prior to 1900, outside of France where outdoor advertisements often covered the entire sides of urban buildings (Varnedde and Gopnik 1990), advertisements consisted mainly of newspaper advertisements composed of text and sometimes simple drawings.

Because of the "agate rule," the type size in newspaper advertising was the same as that used in editorial features, until companies anxious to draw greater attention to themselves began to use patterns of small letters to create larger letters forming a headline or announcing the company's name (Presbrey 1929). Although France had used large-print newspaper advertising since the early 1850s, U.S. newspapers continued to run only classified advertising until the late 1860s and early 1870s. The branding of products like those promoted at the world's fairs was also an infrequent practice at the beginning of the nineteenth century, but was becoming widespread by the century's end (Strasser 1989). This allowed manufacturers to take advantage of new mass-media possibilities, to promote their merchandise without benefitting competitors, and to decrease reliance on retailers who sold their product either as a generic good or under the retailer's own name. Between 1870 and 1900 the volume of advertising in the U.S. increased from $50 million to $542 million per year (Trachtenberg 1982). By the end of the century mass-market magazines were also becoming popular and carried advertising as well as editorial content that often instructed readers about what and how they might consume. By the mid-twentieth century radio and television advertising became dominant and consumer magazines became more specialized and targeted at specific audiences (Leiss *et al.* 1986).

Both advertisements and media depictions of consumer life created an image of the good life as involving an expanding and escalating set of consumer goods. This is true not only of the products being advertised or discussed, but also of the models depicted and the background products and settings in which these products are shown (Belk and Pollay 1985). As one observer noted, these portrayals "teach people how to dress, to furnish a home, the wines to put away, the cheeses to cultivate – in short, the style of life appropriate to new middle class status" (Bell 1957, p. 283). As a reminder that consumer culture is not a solely Western phenomenon and did not begin to stir only in the nineteenth and twentieth centuries, it is worth noting a Chinese book published about 1620 by Wen Zhenheng entitled *Treatise on Superfluous Things*. Like the etiquette manuals and consumer magazines of the West, the *Treatise* was an instruction manual of how to consume in the same way as the elite of Chinese society. Written during the late Ming era when status mobility into prestigious civil-servant and scholarly ranks (through examinations) was increasing, it instructed new arrivals in such areas as the teahouse, the studio of the literati, tables and couches, vessels and utensils, clothing and adornment, boats and carriages, and incense and teas (Clunas 1991a; Watt 1987). But advertising provides more than information about the good life for aspirational social classes. It also touts the benefits arising from such consumption. American advertising during the twentieth century has been found to decreasingly emphasize practical and functional aspects of the goods advertised in favor of luxury, pleasure, and other desirable intangibles associated with consumption of the advertised brand (Belk and Pollay 1985). Chinese advertising since its reappearance in 1979 has begun to follow an apparently similar path (Tse *et al.* 1989).

While the impact of advertising at an individual brand level falls far short of the manipulative potential that it is sometimes feared to have (see Schudson 1984), the cumulative impact of advertising on consumption aspirations has unarguably been to advance the spread of consumer culture. Where department-store displays attempt to create a dreamlike world of fantasy through theatrical staging techniques, advertising draws on techniques from fiction, painting, and (later) film to deliver its fantasies. The effect has been likened by some to creating in consumers a childlike sense of wonder (Lears 1984). When advertising is able to evoke this state, we suspend disbelief and project ourselves into the fairytale worlds of wealth, glamour, success, ease, and delight. Besides emphasizing fantasies of prestige, luxury, sexual appeal, novelty, and the good life, branding and advertising can infuse successful brands with a non-religious numinous character (Belk *et al.*, 1989). It makes these products secular icons by invoking "the imagery of the sublime" (Marchand 1985). As tobacco was transformed into branded and advertised cigarettes, it became something more than a mere utilitarian commodity (Braudel 1973, p. 190; Goodman 1993). Cigarettes came to be seen, if briefly, as vehicles of transcendence (Klein 1993; Zuckerman 1991). In the view of Lears (1983), consumer societies have abandoned belief in religious salvation for belief in self-realization through goods. It may even be that sharing common brands becomes a part of the fabric of what it means to be a community (Boorstin 1973; Friedman *et al.* 1993).

SUMMARY: THE BIRTHDATE AND BIRTHPLACE FOR CONSUMER CULTURE

The sumptuary laws and their periods and place of concentration mark the earliest indices of the development of consumer societies. As the differing timing of these laws in the ancient world, Asia, Europe, and the Americas reflects, there was no single point at which consumer culture emerged and then spread elsewhere. Rather, as McCracken (1988) notes, there were numerous explosions of consumer culture, which in Europe and America became more sustained and on-going revolutions by the nineteenth century. Significantly, the start of the nineteenth century also marks the end of sumptuary legislation and its enforcement. But the demise of sumptuary laws does not mean the end of opposition to consumer culture. Throughout the nineteenth and twentieth centuries religious and philosophical objections to the growth of consumer societies have continued to be heard (e.g., Belk 1988b; Flynn 1993; Horowitz 1985; Tucker 1991). This may be partly due to the displacement of religion as a source of the extraordinary and transcendent in our lives. During the Age of Discovery the quintessential shrine became the *Wunderkammer* full of natural and artificial exotica. These cabinets show a vestigial trace of interest in religious objects and miracles as well, but it is clearly giving way to the new religion of science. The period since the end of the seventeenth century has been one of the ascendence of consumption as the latest locus of wonder and sacredness (Belk *et al.* 1989). Kenseth says of the passing of the cabinets of curiosity in Europe:

> One of the interesting ironies in the history of the marvelous was that as cabinets of curiosities and *Wunderkammern* proliferated all over Europe, the *naturalia* and the *artificialia* in them lost their capacity to excite wonder. As Baxter Hathaway [1968] has observed, "the concept of the marvelous presupposed a contrast to what is expected in everyday life." But when exotic and wonderful objects came into the possession of a great many collectors and when their specific types were displayed in large numbers, they no longer could be regarded as marvels. Indeed they became commonplaces and a familiar part of human experience.
>
> (Kenseth 1991a, p. 54)

It must be regarded as an even more interesting irony then that it is precisely the familiar everyday consumer goods of contemporary experience that have replaced the objects of the cabinet and become prominent among contemporary objects of marvel and wonder. A literally graphic illustration of the shifting locus of the sacred from religion to non-commercial objects of art and nature to commercial branded objects is found in the changing subject matter of art. Medieval religious paintings contrast sharply with the mimetic detail of Dutch still lifes (Barthes 1988; Foster 1993) and Dutch and American *trompe-l'oeil* paintings (Baudrillard 1988b; Drucker 1992; Maine 1991; Wheelock 1991), which in turn are strikingly different from the advertising collages of the Cubists (Varnedde and Gopnik 1990), and even more so the blatant depictions of everyday consumer objects of Pop Art (Kunzle 1984; Mamiya 1992; Schroeder 1992). In order to appreciate how this shift in emphasis from sacred to secular has happened and how it has affected collecting, the next critical focus is on collecting history as it relates to the development of consumer culture.

CHAPTER TWO

A BRIEF HISTORY OF COLLECTING

—— •◆• ——

ANCIENT GREECE AND ROME

Not every assemblage of rare and valuable objects constitutes a collection. For instance, during the Middle Ages in Europe, many treasure hoards acted as stores of wealth and were melted down, broken up, or sold as the need arose (Alsop 1982; Hooper-Greenhill 1992; Wittlin 1970). Neither shall I be particularly concerned with royal or temple collections during periods when general poverty and the flow of treasured objects from the people to the crown or the church effectively precluded the people from collecting. The first widespread collecting outside of these contexts appears to have been in ancient Greece. In a pattern typical elsewhere as well, Athenian sumptuary laws were a harbinger of both consumer culture and popular collecting. Only after Greek unification by the Macedonian Alexander the Great in the fourth century BC and the subsequent introduction of foreign objects and influences did collecting become a popular habit in Greece. Rigby and Rigby's (1944) thorough research suggests that along with "far more luxurious" living, Hellenistic Greeks' collecting enthusiasm changed the form of Greek art from the public frescos and symbolic statues of gods, typical of earlier eras, to secular paintings (on wood) suitable for the home. Realism also came into fashion in both painting and sculptures and portraiture became common. Artists who formerly toiled as mere craftsmen or laborers became celebrities:

> Fashion held the reins, and – ah, familiar bone of contention! – a work of art signed with a famous name could command a higher price than an anonymous piece of equal quality. The minor arts also were increasing in popularity. People now began to collect engraved gems, fine pottery and embroidered textiles; and when a new hobby was born – collecting or copying the letters of famous men – we find our first Greek autograph hound.
>
> (Rigby and Rigby 1944, p. 118)

Also newly in vogue as collectibles in Hellenistic Greece were rediscovered early Greek statuary and newly imported luxuries from the East, especially Persia (Taylor 1948). Oriental carpets, wall hangings, and sumptuous furniture joined paintings and statues in private homes. The city of Sicyon became the central location for artists and art dealers. All of this was made possible by the new wealth of the era:

> the amount of gold and silver that poured into Greece was phenomenal. No comparable influx of precious metals has ever been seen except in the sixteenth century when American and Indian gold poured into Spain. The adventurers brought home with them large fortunes and the traders and purveyors of the army increased their own already considerable wealth.
>
> (Taylor 1948, p. 15)

It was the newly wealthy traders who were most prominent among the new collectors.

In ancient Rome, as in ancient Greece, sumptuary laws were a precursor to the rise of popular collecting. Roman plunder from Greece and elsewhere began to flow into Rome when Marcellus brought cartloads of cult images, temple dedications, and other artwork from the Second Punic War with Syracuse in 212 BC (Alsop 1982). He gave all except an astronomical globe to the Temples of Honor and Virtue on the Appian Way. Since the Romans worshipped the same gods as the Greeks this protection of the sacred was even guaranteed in advance by Roman generals (Taylor 1948). But such religiously oriented public collecting eventually gave way, first to treatment of temple plunder as public wealth and then to private collecting. Rigby and Rigby (1944) place the critical juncture in 133 BC when Attalus III willed his art-rich kingdom of Pergamum to the Romans. As Romans began migrating there, they acquired an appreciation of Greek art, just as the Greeks had been stimulated earlier by the novelty of Asiatic art. Roman rulers were the first collectors, but by the middle eighties BC Sulla is credited with becoming the first great private collector (Rigby and Rigby 1944). By the time of the start of the Roman empire (27 BC), Rigby and Rigby (1944) observe, "everyone who could possibly manage to do so was collecting something" (p. 128). Various concentrations of dealers emerged in Rome to capitalize on this collecting frenzy, with the most famous being the art dealers, booksellers, and antique dealers of the Villa Publica. So too did forgery emerge and the tendency to sign minor objects with a famous name like Praxiteles (Rheims 1961). The artist's signature is the equivalent of a consumer-product's brand name, and forged artwork is equivalent to the counterfeit product or currency; within a system based on the object's aura and authenticity it is less than the real thing – a false idol. Sicyon became a center for defrauding the gullible as Roman visitors were shown the clothing of Odysseus there and were likely to return to Rome with silver cups that had belonged to Achilles (von Holst 1967). It was an era of luxury, extravagance, snobbery, envy, and vanity, which lasted until the fourth century AD.

Among the objects collected, in addition to sculptures and paintings, were Corinthian bronze statues and vessels, bronze tripod tables, silver-ware, ceramics, carpets, tapestries, embroideries, books, jewelry, gems, and fine furniture. Those who could not afford to collect original art collected copies as well as coins, fossils, and natural curiosities such as insects trapped in amber (Rigby and Rigby 1944). Fads and fashions in collecting came and went, as did unscrupulous collector–thieves like Gaius Verres and boastful nouveau-riche collectors like Trimalchio in Petronius's *Satyricon*. Petronius himself was a collector of bowls and drinking cups. Both Verres and Petronius reportedly met their deaths because of their collections and died in a similar manner. When Verres was asked by Mark Antony to give him some of his Corinthian bronzes, he refused despite knowing the penalty. Poison was soon sent to him in Antony's most valuable mur-rhine cup. Verres drank the poison and promptly smashed the cup to bits (Taylor 1948). Similarly, when Nero wanted Petronius's valuable murrhine bowl, Petronius drank the hemlock Nero sent from the murrhine and similarly dashed it on the floor (Rigby and Rigby 1944). The passions elicited by these objects suggest that collecting can stimulate extreme degrees of acquisitiveness, covetousness, and possessiveness. Both the character and timing of Roman collecting affirm a clear link to consuming tendencies in the several senses of this term.

EDO JAPAN AND MING CHINA

While the spread of collecting in Japan and China tends to coincide with periods of economic growth by either internal or international trade and roughly parallels the spread of collecting in Europe, many of the objects collected lack parallels in ancient Greece and Rome or in the collections of Europe and North America. Unique objects include tea sets, funerary bronzes used in ancestor ceremonies, incense burners, calligraphy (which shares more in common with Islam where representational paintings were banned as sacrilege), zithers, ink stones, lacquer furniture, textiles, rare woods, kosodes (predecessors of kimonos – see Dalby 1993), scroll paint-ings, landscape rocks, and "amateur" (unpaid patronage) paintings, which were all prized by collectors. Some collectibles were similar to those of the West, however, including other kinds of paintings, books, sculpture, ceramics, jewelry, weapons, armor, and decorative objects of rare metals and precious stones.

As Rigby and Rigby (1944, pp. 145–146) specify, royal collecting spread from China to Japan as early as the first century AD, but it was not until the rise of a wealthy bourgeoisie under the Tokugawa Shogunate in the Edo era (1603–1868) that collecting spread beyond royalty, aristocrats, and the temples. Chinese objects as well as some Korean objects were also popular in Japan (e.g., Hayashiya and Trubner 1977). Not only art objects, but also social traditions were influenced by China during this period, and all educated men were expected to paint, do calligraphy, perform music, and write poetry (Guth 1989), paralleling the literati tradition in China. The artwork, ceramics, utensils, and etiquette of the tea ceremony were also matters of great social importance, and those who could afford it had a tea master to help them learn the ceremony and select the proper art and implements. So valued were the proper works of art for the ceremony that they could be used as rewards, tributes, and even as collateral for loans should crops fail (Guth 1989). Chinese paintings from the Song and Yuan dynasties, especially those with a celebrated provenance, were especially prized. Certain tea masters also encouraged the use of amateur paintings made by Japanese Zen monks and scrolls with calligraphy rather than painting. Tea masters also helped popularize the collection of certain painting themes and certain poetry verses and themes (Guth 1989). Although members of the merchant class were theoretically beneath members of the artisan, farmer, and warrior classes, newly wealthy merchants became prominent patrons of lacquerers who produced the lacquer furnishings so important in signaling wealth and power. Although owning such works was proscribed by sumptuary laws, enforcement of these laws was impractical and would have involved constant inspections of every household (Yonemura 1989). Wearable art in the form of kosodes, especially for women, became another significant collection used in displaying wealth. For a time both males and females would change clothing several times during a day-long kabuki performance in order to display their collections to maximum advantage (Gluckman and Taked 1992). These garments replaced the European dress, including velvet hats and crucifixes, that had been adopted by all classes of Japanese men after contact with Europeans just prior to the Edo period (Gluckman 1992). In Europe clothing would not be treated as collectible, but in Japan it is clear that the status of kosodes as valuable wearable art and calligraphy placed them in a special category of collectibles. Relatively ineffective sumptuary laws still applied to such garments, but the Edo period was nevertheless one of unrestrained luxury and indulgence. Besides collecting tendencies, this luxury was also evident in the many entertainments of theater, travel (relying on published travel guides), and legal brothels in Tokugawa Japan. Plays of the day addressed these luxurious changes and often dealt with themes such as the delights and dangers of hedonistic pleasures and the conflict between desires and traditional obligations (Hauser 1992).

In China the comparable period of economic boom and the spread of collections was the late Ming period of roughly 1550 to 1650. There had been some earlier short-lived expansions of collecting, as with the growth of luxury and ostentatious consumption during the Han dynasty (206 BC–AD 220; Powers 1986), when merchants and pilgrims brought back relics from India during the T'ang dynasty (618–907; Rigby and Rigby 1944), and during the economic growth and amateur archeological unearthing of ancient bronzes and other antiquities during the Song dynasty (960–1279; Rawson 1993). But it was during the late Ming that the democratization of collecting (through the open meritocracy applied to government positions as well as through rising merchant wealth) became most widespread and most similar to European collecting during the same period (Clunas 1991a, 1991b). Sumptuary laws of the period were at least as comprehensive as those in Japan and were equally unenforceable. As is true elsewhere, art connoisseurship was a means to claim status and the nouveaux riches were those who tried hardest to gain such knowledge (Clunas 1991b). As pointed out earlier, in China they were helped by guide books such as the *Treatise on Superfluous Things*. The potential effectiveness of mastering this knowledge is suggested by the important collections of paintings and calligraphy by Xiang Yuangian, an owner of a chain of pawnshops during the sixteenth century, and his subsequent acceptance by traditional landowning aristocrats (Clunas 1991a, pp. 15–16). It was an era of individuality and romanticism that Watt (1987) characterizes as embracing three principles: the need to escape the everyday world, the search for true and unadorned art, and the elevation of the concept of "interesting" as an artistic ideal (pp. 3–4). Further parallels to the principles that Kenseth (1991a) found to underlie the European *Wunderkammer* are seen in some of the elements suggested as desirable in antiquities during the late Ming period: finely printed books, strange rocks, imported spices of a subtle kind, rare and beautiful foreign treasures, rare and delicious food from overseas, and mysterious colored pottery (Li 1987a, pp. 15–16). Wen Zhenheng's *Treatise on Superfluous Things* also suggested that women who would be social climbers keep parrots "taught short poems and harmonious phrases," fish, golden pheasants, peacocks, and turkeys (Clunas 1991a, pp. 41–42). With the increased demand for art treasures, authenticity grew to be more of a concern. A poem by Shao Changheng (1637–1704) called "Bogus Antiques" describes some of the methods of faking various collectibles found in the antique stores:

> Previously, fakes were mixed with the genuine;
> Now it has become cleverer in recent years . . .
> Calligraphy by Su [shi] and Huang [Tingjian] were copied by filling
> out the shapes delineated with double outlines (kuotian).
> Tang and Song stelae are ground and cleaned.
> Sutra papers are made to look old by smoking,
> Xuanhe collection is documented by "imperial seals."
> The bigger the name, the easier the sale . . .
> People in high places are so proud of their connoisseurship,
> They will keep on buying with all the money they have.
> How many authentic antiques can there be?
> No wonder the market is filled with forgeries.
>
> (quoted in Ho 1987, p. 31)

Clunas (1991b) notes that forgers put very little effort into producing good imitations of artwork and much effort and skill into producing good seals and inscriptions, since these were precisely the sorts of reassurances sought by nouveau-riche purchasers. The existence of these seals and inscriptions from prior owners and the artist is almost totally absent in Europe with the exception of books. By the late Ming period most works of art were signed by the artist, but these too were frequently forged. Fakes were so common according to one late sixteenth-century estimate that only one of ten paintings owned by collectors was genuine (Clunas 1991a, p. 114). Because the life of the literati was based on producing art to present as gifts and was not focused on material gain, they might seem to have been above the clamor for collectibles. This was not the case however. As Li (1987b) points out, the literati required considerable wealth to pursue the simple life, in order to create their collections of books, paintings, calligraphy, and the other objects that filled their studios. As a result, many of these scholars' collections were more impressive than those of the nouveaux riches.

MEDIEVAL EUROPE

During the Middle Ages in Europe, collecting outside of royal treasure chambers was largely confined to the Church. As Braudel (1973) describes it, even a well-off European peasant's material belongings before the eighteenth century consisted of little more than cooking equipment, a few work tools, simple bedding, a few old clothes, and perhaps a bench, stool, table, and chest. And "A nobleman who possessed three leathern garments qualified as a rich man. A bed was a luxury. How then could one bother with such pleasant *divertissements* as books or antiques?" (Rigby and Rigby 1944, p. 137). The one active area of collecting was the pursuit of relics – bits and bones of saints and holy artifacts – by churches (Mackay 1932; Sumption 1975). Not only was the possession of relics a source of prestige and power for local churches that came to own them, they provided a source of hope in miracles for the masses. Through contagious magic such relics, even though they might consist only of a toenail, a piece of wood from the true cross, or a drop of martyr's blood, were believed to have the power of a saint – someone who was a special friend of God (Geary 1986). Since each church needed relics for its altar, the demand for relics soon outstripped supply. As a result a lucrative market in fraudulent relics arose as well as a practice of theft of relics from other locales (Burns 1982; Muensterberger 1994). Mackay (1932, p. 696) notes that the number of pieces of the true cross in circulation could have built a cathedral. The ultimate theft, notes Geary (1986), was the pillage of Constantinople's relics during the Fourth Crusade in 1204. But although a few relics found their way into private hands, the Middle Ages saw little of either consumer culture or private collecting. All this changed dramatically with the waning of the Middle Ages.

Important collectors during the transition from the Middle Ages to the Renaissance included Duke Jean de Berry and the Medici. De Berry was the son of the King Jean le Bon of France who died in 1364 when the younger Jean was 24. As with many prominent collectors the death of his father (and later of his own sons) seems to have been an impetus to the collecting of Jean and his brothers. Jean de Berry is a significant figure in the history of collecting because he was among the first to collect many of the types of objects that became common in Europe in *Wunderkammern* and related curio cabinets two centuries later (Muensterberger 1994). We know this because his collection is well inventoried. Besides paintings and sculptures, among the objects that de Berry collected were precious stones, objects made of precious metals, illuminated manuscripts, cameos, coins, medals, games, perfumes, animals, vases, tapestries, wall hangings, embroideries, religious relics, crucifixes, and footwarmers (Bazin 1967; Meiss 1969). His collection is significant also because it marks the transition from the medieval treasury to objects collected solely for their own sake with no thought to their acting as a store of value. The Duke's passion for collecting was contagious and a number of other nobles of late-fourteenth-century France also became collectors as the fashion spread (Chastel 1963).

Another prominent part in the transition from medieval treasure chambers was played by the Florentine commercial family of the Medici. They were the first of the "princes of commerce" thanks to the banking empire developed by Cosimo de' Medici (1389–1464). The Medici were not alone in collecting in Italy during the time of Cosimo, but they were the clear leaders, imitated to varying degrees by other princes of commerce as well as popes. The oldest remaining inventories of the Medici collections were drawn up by Cosimo's son Piero in 1456 and 1463. These inventories omit the paintings and sculptures commissioned by Cosimo because they were considered part of the impressive decor of the Medici palace rather than a collection. The inventories instead listed silver and gold medals, cameos, musical instruments, Cordovan leathers, Byzantine icons, and Flemish tapestries. Cosimo's grandson Lorenzo de'Medici was not a patron of living artists but dealt exclusively in historical paintings (Materer 1988). This was an important step toward making art a commodity, even though there was not yet an art dealer in Florence. By the time Lorenzo ("the Magnificent") died in 1492, the Medici collection had grown considerably and the inventory conducted listed paintings and sculptures, sometimes noting the artist. But the paintings were still considered less significant than the jewels, gems, books, intaglios, and such oddities as a "unicorn" horn (Bazin 1967). Two years later much of this collection was dispersed as the Medici fled from the advancing French army. While it is not a new pattern in the history of collecting, the Medici, and Piero in particular, made clear that the fascination of the objects collected included their acting as emblems of power and status, providing magical protection in the case of certain objects, and providing sensual delight (Hooper-Greenhill 1992). Notably, the medieval justification of collections as being testimony to the glory of God was diminishing in favor of a more secular ethos of pleasure.

The examples of Jean de Berry and the Medici should not imply that collecting in this period was the sole province of the nobility, the Church, and merchant princes. The bourgeoisie were also becoming collectors. An illustration is the collection of the Frenchman Jacques Duchié in about 1430. In one room of his town house in Paris were paintings as well as instructive scriptures on the walls. One room contained musical instruments while another contained a collection of games. Rare furs were stored in another room, while yet other rooms contained fabrics, rugs, metalwork, weapons and suits of armor (Bazin 1967). While the concept of cabinets of curiosity did not yet exist, Duchié's collections, like those of Jean de Berry, are a part of the growing interest in what Mullaney (1983) called "strange things, gross terms, [and] curious customs." In the case of high art, the demise of the Medici not only put much of their collections onto the market, it also robbed the patronage system of some of its greatest patrons and provided artists with a new incentive to produce "ready-made" art for the market of newly rich collectors (Hooper-Greenhill 1992). A number of art dealers, antiquarians, and auction houses sprang up also determined to seize the resulting opportunity and speculators began to buy for investment purposes (Bazin 1967). Another impetus to collecting was the unearthing of ancient Rome between 1450 and 1550 (Hogden 1964). One collector in 1507 observed, "The moment an object is dug up, a host of buyers miraculously appears. They give eight or ten ducats for rusty medallions which they resell later for twenty-five or thirty" (quoted in Bazin 1967, p. 52). An art market had existed for some time in Italy and Flanders with workshops producing small inventories of standardized works such as Virgins and Child and Crucifixions for amateurs and other chance customers (Chastel 1963). But in the period that followed the Medici, artists gained a new independence and patronage was replaced by the rise of art as a commodity. In addition a new type of collector consisting of professionals including doctors, lawyers, and scholars emerged. The result was a huge swell of collecting activity in sixteenth- and seventeenth-century Europe, an age of collecting and an age of curiosity (Pomian 1990).

SIXTEENTH- AND SEVENTEENTH-CENTURY EUROPE: COLLECTING THE WORLD

The Renaissance interest in amassing the world in a cabinet of curiosity was spurred as well by discoveries of foreign lands, European population growth following the plague, new inventions such as the clock and the printing press, and the rise of capitalism (Major 1970). It was a period of substantial economic growth and rising consumer expectations. Mullaney (1983) cites a cabinet established in Vienna in 1550 as the first, but there were clearly forerunners. The sixteenth and seventeenth centuries were the primary periods in which the thousands of European wonder cabinets emerged, most commonly referred to with the German conjunctions for cabinets of wonder and art, *Wunderkammern* and *Kunstkammern*. The excitement of finding new things in the world during the age of discovery in Europe produced not only explosions of consumer culture and fashions, but explosions of interest in collecting and displaying wondrous objects (Mason 1994). As Pomian (1990, p. 53) insightfully interprets them, these collections made visible the growing desire or passion for things. Based on the evidence of the things acquired for *Wunderkammern*, this desire was imaginative and nearly boundless. For instance a visitor detailed the partial contents of the cabinet of the London gentleman and adventurer Walter Cope at the end of the sixteenth century as including:

> an African charm made of teeth, a felt cloak from Arabia, and shoes from many strange lands. An Indian stone axe, "like a thunderbolt." A Stringed instrument with but one string. The twisted horn of a bull seal. An embalmed child or *Mumia*. The bauble and bells of Henry VIII's fool. A unicorn's tail. Inscribed paper made of bark, and an artful Chinese box. A flying rhinoceros (unremarked), a remora (explicated at some length), and flies of a kind that "glow at night in Virginia instead of lights, since there is often no day there for over a month." There are the Queen of England's seal, a number of crowns made of claws, a Madonna made of Indian feathers, an Indian charm made of monkey teeth. A mirror, which "both reflects and multiplies objects," A sea-halcyon's nest. A sea mouse (*mus marinus*), reed pipes like those played by Pan, a long narrow Indian canoe, with oars and siding planks, hanging from the ceiling.
>
> (Mullaney 1983, p. 40)

As Schnapper (1986) notes, there was no time-lag between the construction of cabinets by sovereigns and by the bourgeoisie. Besides individual collections, apothecaries and medical men sometimes developed cabinets to attract a curious public (George 1985). Romeo describes one such apothecary collection in *Romeo and Juliet*:

> I do remember an apothecary,
> And hereabouts he dwells, which late I noted . . .
> And in his needy shop a tortoise hung,
> An alligator stuff'd, and other skins
> Of ill-fitted fishes; and about his shelves
> A beggarly account of empty boxes,

Green earthen pots, bladders, and musty seeds,
Remnants of packthread, and old cakes of roses,
Were thinly scatter'd to make up a show.

(Act V, Scene 1)

Like the *trompe-l'oeil* paintings popular in the same period, the cabinets of curiosities emphasized the marvel and wonder of objects. Renaissance humanists, who prompted the initial interest in cabinets of curiosities, also began to pursue fantasy in gardens, architecture, art, and literature (Kaufmann 1993). It was an age of wonder. Were an image to be selected to illustrate Stevenson's short poem which opened Chapter One, it would be difficult to find anything more appropriate than one of the *trompe-l'oeil* paintings or one of the etchings, engravings, or woodcuts depicting the marvels of the wonder cabinet. They are all concerned with "wonderful things." What is more, the cabinets sometimes sought to surprise the viewer even more by arranging the objects in such a way as to heighten the contrasts between them:

> Early collectors arranged their objects so as to create surprising or striking contrasts. Thus, in this room [the reconstructed *Wunderkammer* of the catalogue quoted], very large items are juxtaposed with the very small – an ostrich egg and the egg of a hummingbird is one instance, a "giant's" (dinosaur's) bone and the bone of a bat is another.
>
> (Kenseth 1991b, p. 249)

Similarly in the masquerades that soon became popular in France and England, there was an attempt to produce surprise through wearing costumes that contrasted as sharply as possible with the wearer's normal identity:

> Dukes did not disguise themselves as marquises, or footmen as apprentices. At the moment of unmasking (if and when it came), one's disguise, seen in relation to one's real identity was to excite the onlooker by its absolute impropriety. The conceptual gap separating true and false was ideally an abyss.
>
> (Castle 1986, p. 75)

Further, improbable pairings among masked couples were highly regarded in the masquerades: a "nun" and a "heathen god," a "lion" and a "Shepherdess," or "Devil" and a "Quaker." As with the *Wunderkammern*, the intent in such surprises was to produce a pleasurable state of amusement and delight through the exaggerated contrast. Zoos, botanical gardens, extravagant fountains of dancing waters, exotic pets, "monsters," dwarfs, and midgets were other sources of delight exploited in sixteenth- and seventeenth-century Europe (George 1985; Hunt 1985; Tuan 1984; see also Connell 1974; Davies 1991; Foucault 1988). These fascinations anticipate the world's fairs of a subsequent era. There are also conspicuous collections (Mukerji 1993). In each case, the main sources of pleasure were the wonder produced by the Other in contrast to the ascendent European self.

This sense of marvelous contrast and broad eclecticism was greatest in the earlier *Wunderkammern*. While novelty was the impetus to early Renaissance collecting and the stimulation of marvel was its goal, collecting can also be a method of systematically assembling, ordering, and symbolically controlling the chaos that novelty threatens to create. The exhilarating sense of discovery and encyclopedic knowledge gave way first to greater classification and specialization in these cabinets. While Mullaney (1983) maintains that "No system determines the organization of objects on display or separates one variety of the marvelous from another" (p. 42), this was not true of even the earliest cabinets. Eye-pleasing symmetry of display and distinctions between broad categories of collectibles were present from the start (Hodgen 1964; Hooper-Greenhill 1992; Laurencich-Minelli 1985; Olmi 1985). The earliest and most basic classification was in assembling both *naturalia*, such as minerals, stuffed animals, plants, ethnographic artifacts, and fossils, and *artificialia*, with a special fondness for paintings, weapons, scientific instruments, and mechanical marvels such as clocks and automata. Religious objects and relics were often a third type of marvelous object included in the cabinets. Similarly, paintings of marvels as in Hans Holbein's *The Ambassadors* (1533) often acted as *memento mori* or vanity paintings by including emblems of life's brevity such as the elongated skull in the foreground of this painting (Berger *et al.* 1972). The religious hold on life did not immediately disappear with the turn to secular marvels. Later collections of *naturalia* and *artificialia* came to be displayed separately in rooms or showcases of their own. Eventually classifications became more detailed and the more specialized cabinets emerged. Ethnographic collections, art collections, natural history collections, geological collections, and others also became separate specialties, paralleling the disciplinary divisions of the arts and sciences. The full impact of this new classification of the world came in the late seventeenth and eighteenth centuries which is when Foucault (1970) places the shift from attempting to view the world as an interrelated whole to attempting to view the world in terms of classifications and discriminations. This new world view he labels the Classical episteme:

> The Classical age gives history a quite different meaning: that of undertaking a meticulous examination of things themselves for the first time, and then transcribing what it has gathered in smooth, neutralized, and faithful words. It is understandable that the first form of history constituted in this period of "purification" should have been the history of nature. For its construction requires only words applied without intermediary, to things themselves. The documents of this

new history are not other words, texts or records, but unencumbered spaces in which things are juxtaposed: herbariums, collections, gardens; the locus of this history is a non-temporal rectangle in which, stripped of all commentary, of all enveloping language, creatures present themselves one beside another, their surfaces volatile, grouped according to their common features, and thus already virtually analyzed, and bearers of nothing but their own individual names. It is often said that the establishment of botanical gardens and zoological collections expressed a new curiosity about exotic plants and animals. In fact, these had already claimed men's attention for a long while. What had changed was the space in which it was possible to see them and from which it was possible to describe them. To the Renaissance, the strangeness of animals was a spectacle: it was featured in fairs, in tournaments, in fictitious or real combats, in reconstitutions of legends in which the bestiary displayed its ageless fables. The natural history room and the garden, as created in the Classical period, replace the circular procession of the "show" with the arrangement of things in a "table". What came surreptitiously into being between the age of the theater and that of the catalogue was not the desire for knowledge, but a new way of connecting things both to the eye and to discourse. A new way of making history.

(Foucault 1970, p. 131)

Thus the demise of interest in the encyclopedic collecting in *Wunderkammern* at the end of the seventeenth century is related to a new way of viewing the world. There is no place for marvels in the Classical episteme.

The tremendous popularity of *Wunderkammern* and related cabinets during the sixteenth and seventeenth centuries does not mean that all collectors subscribed to the principles of encyclopedic collecting of the entire world, whether *naturalia*, *artificialia*, or supernatural. The cabinets were largely a Protestant Reformation phenomena, emphasizing as they did the secular wonders of the world, albeit initially tempered with reminders of religious miracles as well. In the Roman Catholic world the opposite emphasis predominated. Olmi (1985) notes that in Rome encyclopedic collections were in the minority. Of 150 Roman collections inventoried in 1664, over 90 percent excluded *naturalia*, preferring to restrict themselves to such *objets d'art* as paintings, antiques, medals, and cameos. Other collectors who could not afford such artwork, restricted their collections to such objects as peacock feathers, insects, and pressed flowers and plants (Kaufmann 1993). Religious pilgrims satisfied the collecting fervor of the times with souvenir pilgrimage badges, rubbings, and mementos of the pilgrimage sites including dirt, holy water, holy oils, stones, plants, and small pieces of shrines. As with the miraculous relics present in many *Wunderkammern*, contagious magic had not entirely disappeared, even though by the seventeenth century it was on the wane as science came to the fore through the phenomenon Max Weber called *die Entzauberung der Welt* or the disenchantment of the world (Berman 1981, p. 57). The intense desire and passion that prompted collections gave way to a more distanced cognitive perspective. As one critic, Bernard Lamy, noted in 1684, "When reason is not in control, and when one is carried away by curiosity, in other words a mad desire for knowledge, it is impossible to study in an orderly fashion" (quoted in Pomian 1990, p. 63).

The fashion for *Wunderkammern* declined with the rise of Cartesian science and the divorce of science from art. The cabinets were part of a liminal period (Turner 1969), betwixt and between the former control of passion by religion and its subsequent control by science (Pomian 1990, p. 77) as well as exploitation by commerce. However, the human fascination with marvel and fantasy and with marvelous and fantastic objects has not disappeared. Kenseth concludes:

> By the end of the seventeenth century cabinets of curiosities and *Kunst- und Wunderkammern* had lost much of their attractiveness, but they never fell out of favor completely. They continued far into the eighteenth century, especially in the Nordic countries and Russia, and had a revival as places of study in the early college and university museums of America. Today, however the encyclopedic museum is a rarity, a relic of the past reflecting a world view and an approach to learning that no longer exist. But this is not to say that the collecting of *mervaviglie* [marvels] therefore has vanished. People the world over still collect exceptional things. They marvel at these possessions, learn from them, and like the collectors of the past, display them with pride.
>
> (Kenseth 1991c, p. 98)

As continues to happen with collections and collecting, fads and fashions may shape the content of collections and the rules governing what constitutes accepted collecting practice. But the same acquisitive and possessive motivations and the same feelings of delight with objects that are, for the collector and others of like mind, fantastic, remain. Not only as collectors, but as consumers we continue to delight in the miniature and the gigantic, the fantastic, and the spectacular. It is not so true that magic disappeared with *die Entzauberung der Welt*, as it is that the locus of this magic changed, even if our theories fail to recognize it:

> Existing theory in economics, economic psychology, and social psychology blinds us to the mystery, beauty, and power of our possessions. In order to understand what our possessions mean, it is necessary to recognize, reestablish, and reclaim this magic. We more often than not wear magic clothes, jewels, and perfumes. We drive magic

cars. We reside in magic places and make pilgrimages to even more magical places. We eat magic foods, own magic pets, and envelop ourselves in the magic of films, television, and books. We court magic in a plethora of material loci that cumulatively compel us to conclude that the rational possessor is a myth that can no longer be sustained. It fails because it denies the inescapable and essential mysteriousness of our existence.

(Belk 1991a, pp. 17–18)

The continued popularity of collecting an increasingly varied array of things since the *Wunderkammern* offers strong support for this thesis.

EIGHTEENTH AND NINETEENTH CENTURIES: COLLECTING MANIA

The Netherlands

While the *Wunderkammern* represent an expansion of collecting from nobility to the bourgeoisie, the number of owners of cabinets was certainly no more than a few thousand. Other collectors of less attention-getting materials were more numerous, but still limited. When Belgian engraver and collector Hubert Goltzius toured Belgium, Holland, Germany, Austria, Switzerland, Italy, and France seeking other collectors of antiquities, he found 968 such collectors between 1584 and 1586 (Pomian 1990, p. 35). They included royalty, clergy, doctors, lawyers, scholars, poets, officers, and artists. Merchants were not mentioned, but were prominent collectors of art in seventeenth-century Netherlands (Alpers 1983). This was the "Golden Age" of the Netherlands. Still largely excluded from collecting were the middle classes which emerged with the growth of the European economy and the spread of education (Pomian 1990, p. 41). An exception to the lack of middle-class collectors was also found in the Netherlands where collecting tulip bulbs in the early seventeenth century affected a broad range of people. Whether it is called a case of "the collecting bug" (Muensterberger 1994), "tulipomania" (Mackay 1932; Posthumous 1929), or "an addiction" (Schama 1987), the passion for possessing rare tulip varieties brought from Turkey affected everyone from shopkeepers to aristocrats. Prices escalated to fantastic heights and fortunes were made and lost in tulips. One farmer traded for a single bulb: "two *last* of wheat and four of rye, four fat oxen, eight pigs, a dozen sheep, two oxheads of wine, four tons of butter, a thousand pounds of cheese, a bed, some clothing, and a silver beaker" (Schama 1987, p. 358). In 1637 the state intervened to control prices and the craze subsided, but the several years of intense collecting of this humble consumer good demonstrates that avid collecting is a shared passion and that it transcends utilitarian concerns.

Another Dutch collecting passion that reached the middle-class masses in the seventeenth century was the collecting of engravings, etchings, and even oil paintings (Mukerji 1983). Foreign travelers were surprised by this and the Englishman John Evelyn commented in 1641 that "pictures are very common here, there being scarce an ordinary tradesman whose house is not decorated with them" (quoted in Schama 1987, p. 318). Books were another broadly collected consumer good in the late-seventeenth-century Netherlands (Mukerji 1983). As Muensterberger observes, these trends were very much a part of the consumer culture developing among the Dutch at this time:

> There is little question that the material success achieved by the Dutch during this dynamic period had placed an undue emphasis on both possessions and possessiveness. After years of deprivation and chronic anxiety, a new mood had arisen out of the echoes of the past and the empirical evidence of plenty.
>
> (Muensterberger 1994, p. 223)

It is no accident that during the Netherlands' Golden Age, the Dutch economy, art scene, consumerism, and collecting all escalated together. Rembrandt, for example, was not only a celebrated artist in seventeenth-century Holland, but also an avid collector (Muensterberger 1994) and a man caught up in the "notorious living" of indulgent consumption (Schama 1987). Since the Netherlands was the economic center of Europe in the seventeenth century, it was the first country to experience socially broadening collecting trends that affected other European countries more slowly.

France

The Netherlands' dominance of the economic as well as fine-art worlds is symbolized by Amsterdam's remaining the main auction center of Europe until the early eighteenth century when the Parisian auction houses of Hôtel Bullion and Hôtel d'Alligre and the townhouse of the artist–dealer Lebrun began to dominate. This dominance was lost for half a century when French economic conditions and the French Revolution caused the art-auction scene to shift to England with the opening of Sotheby's, Christie's, and Phillips (Bazin 1967). By the mid-nineteenth century France again became the center of the art world with the opening of Hôtel Drouot (Learmount 1985; Pomian 1990). Tellingly, the location of the art dealers in Paris was adjacent to the Bourse, the stockmarket/banking district, near glamorous cafés, theaters, entertainments, and the shopping arcades (Green 1989). This is the same area in which the Bon Marché opened in 1852. The link between economic conditions and collecting has several threads. A growing economy puts money in the hands of consumers, fuels consumption and consumer desire, stimulates prices of collectibles, and provides money for speculation in the collectibles market. A booming art market in the eighteenth century also meant a market that attracted forgers, unscrupulous dealers, and disreputable auction houses that colluded and conspired to raise prices. All of these features were found in eighteenth- and early-nineteenth-century France (Bazin 1967). Since collecting is an extreme and passionate form of acquisitiveness, a growing interest in collecting offers temptations to those who would take advantage of such an emotional condition. At the same time, collector "treasure" stories of fantastic buys and finds combine with the competitive fervor of the auction to stimulate pride, desire, and greed. Nor were some avaricious collectors above theft to acquire a treasure they coveted. Such greed is depicted in Balzac's *Cousin Pons*, in which Pons's collection of antiques is avidly coveted by his otherwise disdainful nouveauriche cousin Madame Camusot, the concierge Madame Cibot, and the lawyer Fraisier. Pons himself is a sadly heroic character having sacrificed his life and savings for the sake of the collection which is the story's heroine. Like Balzac's *Le Curé de Tours*, the antiques and *objets de vertu* take on an anthropomorphic life and significance to Pons that is quite like the romantic affections of a lover for his beloved (Tintner 1972). Balzac himself was an avid collector and there is thought to be much of him in Pons (Muensterberger 1994). His own obsession as well as the collecting spirit of early-nineteenth-century Paris make Balzac's stories a telling mix of consumption, collecting, and what Freud would later characterize as sublimated sexual desire focused upon material objects.

Eighteenth-century France also provides examples of the changing fads and fashions of collecting. From an analysis of 723 eighteenth-century French collections (other than book collections) Pomian (1990) found that during the first two decades of the century the rage was for collecting ancient medals with little interest in natural-history materials. But during the last half of the century these preferences had completely changed and collections of shells, minerals, plants, and anatomical specimens were paramount. Even though the century saw a democratization of collecting in which a growing proportion of collectors was middle-class, it was instead the elite of scholars, lawyers, doctors, clerics, and antiquarians who first embraced natural-history collectibles. Pomian (1990) demonstrates that this development was a reaction to the growth of the Enlightenment ideal of an erudite study of collectibles to advance science. While there were historic issues that might be studied with medals, numismatists found themselves unable to synthesize the growing accumulation of medals and the facts surrounding them into anything like a meaningful whole – a problem also faced by Flaubert's Bouvard and Pécuchet. Natural-history material, on the other hand, became more socially acceptable as somehow involving important scientific issues of the day. Similarly, at the beginning of the nineteenth century German Old Masters were not yet acknowledged as art and Baroque paintings were just beginning to be accepted by collectors (Grasskamp 1983).

And the insistence in eighteenth-century Paris for small-size paintings resulted in a buyer's market for Flemish and Italian paintings, which quickly left the country (von Holst 1967, p. 190). Nationalism also affected preferences for collecting art of the collector's home country during this period in France and England (Haskell 1976). Such shifts in popular collecting domains are telling illustrations of the fact that, while the cycles may be longer, collecting is every bit as susceptible to fashion change as clothing.

The value of potentially collectible objects thus was, and remains, determined by social valuation and not by any intrinsic properties of the objects themselves. Rarity and scarcity are other non-intrinsic properties that affect the social valuation and collectibility of objects. Crabbe (1990) suggests that these properties pertain only to certain forms of art, noting that "If 'Mona Lisa' was a famous novel then few would argue that it was better to read the original manuscript in a museum than a printed reproduction" (p. 208). Yet book collectors would insist that it **is** infinitely better to have a first edition, or better still the original manuscript, than a paperback copy. Consider the fork. Originally forks were luxury objects crafted with gold and precious stones. But Rheims notes,

> Snobbery, elegance and finally function assured their widespread use with the result that, from being a luxury article only to be found in a few royal palaces in the sixteenth century, in the eighteenth century every bourgeois table had forks, and in the nineteenth century forks were a humdrum detail of life, sold by every ironmonger.
>
> (Rheims 1961, p. 63)

As will be seen, however, industrial mass production does not in itself destroy collectibility.

The eighteenth century has been called the age of the dilettante in Europe (Rigby and Rigby 1944; Taylor 1948). The label is, in contemporary use (Simpson and Weiner 1989), an indictment of the pursuit of collecting as an amusing and fashionable hobby pursued without either the dedication or the knowledge of collectors in the less democratic collecting era preceding the rise of consumer culture. More to the point, it was a century of increasingly specialized and nuanced categories of collecting as speculation became an alternative motive for acquiring collectibles and as the range of collectibles grew more extensive and the number of collectors multiplied. The category of connoisseurship stood at the other end of the continuum from dilettantism. While Pons was portrayed by Balzac as a connoisseur of moderate means but considerable discrimination, later in the nineteenth century Flaubert portrayed Bouvard and Pécuchet as his opposite – men of some means who were utterly lacking in discrimination. Like Pons, Bouvard and Pécuchet begin as petit-bourgeois clerks. But when Bouvard inherits a small fortune, the two friends retire to educate themselves through instructional books, collecting, and an eventual reversion to a clerk-like inclination to record and classify. Products of the Age of Enlightenment, they seek to understand the world through passionless reason. They seek wisdom through their bumbling attempts to collect antiques, geological specimens, anthropological specimens, ceramics, books, and documents for their personal museum as well as for their encyclopedic book project. Finding contradictions in the sources they consult they are reduced to a state of confusion:

> They had no longer, on the men and deeds of the epoch, a single decided idea. To judge it impartially, it would be necessary to read all the histories, all the memoirs, all the newspapers and all the documents in manuscript, since from the least omission an error may ensue which will lead on to others *ad infinitum*. They renounced the undertaking. But the taste for history had come to them, the need for truth on its own account. Perhaps it is easier to find in bygone epochs? Authors, being far from the events, should speak of them without passion.
>
> (Flaubert 1954b, pp. 138–139)

Flaubert uses Bouvard and Pécuchet to mock the pretensions of the era. The passionless objective accumulation of facts is shown as foolishness. A related pretension that their failures exemplify is the inability of mere taxonomy and classification to produce coherent meaning. As Donato summarizes their plight:

> The set of objects the Museum displays is sustained only by the fiction that they somehow constitute a coherent representational universe. The fiction is that a repeated metonymic displacement of fragments for totality, object to label, series of objects to series of labels, can still produce a representation which is somehow adequate to a nonlinguistic universe. Such a fiction is the result of an uncritical belief in the notion that ordering and classifying, that is to say, the spatial juxtaposition of fragments, can produce a representational understanding of the world. Should the fiction disappear, there is nothing left of the *Museum* but "bric-a-brac," a heap of meaningless and valueless fragments of objects which are incapable of substituting themselves either metonymically for the original objects or metaphorically for their representations.
>
> (Donato 1979, p. 223)

This fiction, a critical part of Michel Foucault's (1970) Classical episteme, remains an important part of collecting today as do further distinctions between, and sometimes transformations of, art versus craft, or artifact versus curio.

The first nineteenth-century collectors of French Impressionist art were a diverse group including financiers, department-store owners, bankers, singers, doctors, a count, a customs inspector, painters, industrialists, small art dealers, and the proprietor of a pastry shop and restaurant (Moulin 1987). While nineteenth-century France saw a great democratic expansion of collecting, it also saw a surge in elitist collecting by dandies. Beau Brummell, for example, had a fine collection of snuffboxes; Comte d'Orsay was a passionate collector of *objets d'art*, and brothers Jules and Edmund de Goncourt helped set the fashions for antiquities, Japanese art, and eighteenth-century French art (Williams 1982, pp. 123–125). Although the dandies were a part of nineteenth-century romanticism, Brookner (1971) calls the Goncourts' activities a "sick Romanticism" and contrasts them with Zola's "healthy Romanticism." This judgment is based upon their non-productive reliance on their inheritances, their elitist class biases, and their romantic belief that the past is superior to the present. However, unlike the failed mechanistic approach to romantic collecting of Bouvard and Pécuchet, the Goncourts' collecting was passionate. Edmond explained:

> Yes, this passion which has become universal, this solitary pleasure in which almost an entire nation indulges, owes its wide following to an emotional emptiness and ennui; but also it must be recognized, to the dreariness of the present day, to the uncertainty of tomorrow, to the labours of giving birth to a premature new society, and to worries and anxieties which, as on the brink of a deluge, drive desire and envy to seek immediate satisfaction in everything charming, appetizing and seductive: to forget the present moment in aesthetic satiety. These are the causes ... together with what is undeniably a completely new emotion, namely the nearly human affection for objects, which at the present day make collectors of practically everyone and of me, in particular, the most passionate of all collectors.
>
> (translated by Brookner 1971, pp. 142–143)

While romanticism needed no defense, the indulgence of a private accumulation of collectibles did and continues to require justification. In the preface to the catalogue for an 1880 show of a portion of the Goncourts' art collections, Edmund offered a further defense by referring to the period's mania for bibelots as a disease which he labeled "bricobracomania" (Saisselin 1984, p. xiv). For if collecting is a disease, the collector is a victim rather than a villain (this defense remains a common one among contemporary collectors). Nevertheless criticisms of the indulgence of collecting superficial luxuries continued. As one critic charged:

> The present rage for collecting, the piling up, in dwellings, of aimless bric-à-brac, which does not become any more useful or beautiful by being fondly called *bibelots*, appear to us in a completely new light when we know that Magnan [a French doctor] has established the existence of an irresistible desire among the degenerate to accumulate

useless trifles. It is so firmly imprinted and so peculiar that Magnan declares it to be a stigma of degeneration, and has invented for it the name "oniomania," or "buying craze." . . . He is simply unable to pass by any lumber without feeling an impulse to acquire it

(Nordau 1896, p. 27)

The criticism here is not one centering on elitism, lack of productivity, or misplaced nostalgia. It is instead clearly directed at consumerism. Acquisitiveness, possessiveness, and indulgent lack of restraint were the charges. The use of the term bric-a-brac rather than *objet d'art* or a similar honorific makes it apparent that the objects of such collector consumerism are insignificant trifles and thus delegitimizes the collector's pursuit as one of indulgent pleasure rather than scientific or artistic merit. For bric-a-brac is stuff found in the new department stores rather than galleries and museums. Thus there was a class distinction implied in these discriminations: anyone could buy bric-a-brac; not everyone could discern and acquire *objets d'art*. The latter objects were those sought by the bourgeois as "marker goods" (Douglas and Isherwood 1979) with which to make status claims. There was also, once again, a sexist bias implied in these distinctions, as Saisselin explains:

By 1880 in France women were perceived as mere buyers of bibelots, which they bought as they did clothing, in their daily bargain hunting. Men of course collected too, but their collecting was perceived as serious and creative. Women were consumers of objects; men were collectors. Women bought to decorate and for sheer joy of buying, but men had a vision for their collections, a view of the collection as an ensemble, with a philosophy behind it. Or so the argument went. But by the 1890s the distinction between feminine accumulation and real collecting tended, in the bourgeois interior and even the American millionaire "home," to be blurred, and the bibelot seemed to have triumphed, along with a certain view of what constituted "Art."

(Saisselin 1984, p. 68)

There was one further distinction made concerning collectors and that was between the passionate collector like Cousin Pons or the Goncourts and the speculative collector whose passion was for financial gain rather than for the objects themselves (Green 1989). Both the growth in the number of collectors and the growth in wealth led to rising prices for art objects throughout the eighteenth and nineteenth centuries (Bazin 1967), attracting an increasing number of speculative buyers. The issue here is one of speculative capitalism and commoditization of art versus a love of art and other objects for their own sakes. Such speculation is a counterforce to the romanticism of the bohemians and dandies (Campbell 1987). It is closer to the dealer side of marketplace exchanges than to the consumer side. While motives may sometimes be mixed, widespread speculation in collecting commoditizes the market in a way that other collectors greatly disdain.

England

The eighteenth and nineteenth centuries were also a period of great growth in English collecting. However, one collection of the seventeenth century which deserves further comment is that of the Tradescants. The rage for marvels died later in England than on the continent (Breckenridge 1989) and one remnant of this trend was the "Ark" of John Tradescant and his son, also John. In addition to natural-history objects, weapons, medals, garments, books, household utensils and "endless miniature objects," their collection included such curiosities as a piece of stone from John the Baptist's tomb, "Pohatan, King of Virginia's habit all embroidered with shells or Roanoke," carved plum stones, "a little Box with 12 Apostles in it," sculptures by Hans Holbein, "Jupiter, Io and Mercury wrought in Tent-stitch," a desk made of a single piece of wood, and "Halfe a Hasle-nut with 70 pieces of houshold-stuffe in it" (Rigby and Rigby 1944, pp. 233–235). There was also "A bracelet made out of the thighs of Indian flies, a cherry stone carved with the likeness of 88 emperors' faces on one side and St. George and the Dragon on the other; blood that rained on the Isle of Wight; and a coat made out of the entrails of fishes" (Lambton 1987, p. 10). After running the Ark as a tourist attraction, in the years following the younger John's death in 1662 the collection became the Ashmolean Museum at Oxford, generally acknowledged as the first museum in the modern world. Similarly, Dr. Hans Sloane's less marvel-laden collection became the foundation for the British Museum in 1753. During the eighteenth century collecting was so popular in England that how-to-do-it guides were published for amateurs, still clinging to the *artificialia* and *naturalia* distinctions of the *Wunderkammern* (Bazin 1967, p. 115). Near the middle of the eighteenth century Learmount's (1985) analysis of auction catalogues shows that the Great Exhibition of 1851 caused a rage for both natural-history specimens and the sale of live animals including at least one tiger. The fascination with marvels died a slow death and as late as the start of the nineteenth century an auction of the estate of one collector included:

> ARTICLES, comprising Minerals, Shells, and Insects; several Mathematical Instruments, a Cabinet, containing about 400 Roman, Greek, and English, Silver and Copper Coins; old China; a curious carved Ivory Cup and Cover; Mahogany Cabinet, with sliding glass drawers, filled with Insects, &c. from China, many of them rare, an Indian Gun, inlaid with Gold &c.
>
> (Learmount 1985, p. 58)

Throughout the eighteenth century the English aristocratic, professional, and merchant classes steadily moved artworks from the continent to

England (von Holst 1967). While the collecting fad in England was a generation behind that of France, it was equally enthusiastic and widespread (Taylor 1948). When the royal collections of France were dismantled in the wake of the French Revolution, British collectors were quick to expatriate the treasures of Versailles to England. The sale of 17,182 treasures from Versailles in 1793 is labeled a "wholly disastrous mistake" by Rheims (1961, p. 113), a judgment concurred in by others. However, the acquisition of the Parthenon Marbles by Lord Elgin from the Ottomans early in the eighteenth century proved a more controversial expatriation, still strongly contested by Greece. They were controversial from the start. After acquiring the Marbles, Elgin was imprisoned by the French for three years and returned to England in 1806, fully expecting a grateful England to reimburse him for his expenses in acquiring 250 feet of the Parthenon frieze and transporting it to London. Instead the respected Dilettanti Society (still an honorable term at the time) expressed moral misgivings about such vandalism as well as doubts that the marbles were authentic (Holt 1979). Their authenticity was questioned because they looked too perfect and were thought to be casts of human figures. But finally in 1816 they were judged authentic and purchased by Parliament. The purchase was effective in stoking the British passion for collecting antiquities.

Much a part of earlier British collecting was the ideal of the English gentleman's country house. Since the Middle Ages this ideal involved being able to claim an established lineage documented with established paintings, heirlooms, manor house, and possessions. Wainwright (1989) shows that most collectors added to the collections of their ancestors installed at their country seat. But as McCracken (1988) discerns, the "patina" system of status with its "five generation rule" for deriving status from such a house and collected treasures was replaced during the eighteenth and nineteenth centuries by a wholly new system of status in which novelty and fashion supplanted this conservative principle. "Novelty became an irresistible drug" (McKendrick *et al.* 1982, p. 10). In the longing for novelty it is evident once again that the fascination with the curious marvel did not die with the *Wunderkammer*. It was only the organizing principles of collecting that changed. As Susan Stewart (1984) specifies, a dramatic change from normal scale to miniaturization or giganticism is one sure way to achieve novelty and have something transcend the realm of the ordinary and become collectible. Another sure novelty is something totally different from the ordinary: the "freak" of nature for example (Bogdan 1988; Fiedler 1978). Peter the Great kept the bones of his footman Bourgeois who had been over 7 feet tall, kept a hermaphrodite for a time, and treasured Foma who had only two digits per hand and foot, and who after his death was stuffed and exhibited by Peter (Purcell and Gould 1992). Each of these sources of novelty was represented in eighteenth-century English collections, and each is also reflected in Swift's satire, *Gulliver's Travels* (1729). When Gulliver returns from the miniature land of Lilliput he brings with him miniature sheep and cattle which he subsequently raises and exhibits for profit to "many Persons of Quality, and others" (Swift 1980, p. 109). Similarly when he returns from Brobdingnag, land of the giants, he astounds his rescuer with a collection including a comb made from the Brobdingnagian king's beard hair, a collection of pins and needles ranging from a foot to half a yard in length, giant wasp stingers, a gold ring large enough to fit over his head (from the queen of Brobdingnag), and a tooth a foot long and 4 inches in diameter. As Smith (1990) points out, such objects provide an apt satire on the Royal Society's collection of curiosities in its Gresham College repositories at the time (see Hunter 1985). As the sole representative of his size in these lands, Gulliver is himself a freak of outlandish proportions and is greatly admired as a novelty. Through his status as a caged amusement in Brobdingnag and through later inversions of human dominance over animals, Swift challenges whether collecting animals for our entertainment is quite so amusing when the keeper becomes the kept (see also Ritvo 1987; Tuan 1984). The rise of zoos as well as African game trophy-hunting, decorative status-enhancing pet-keeping, and animal entertainments such as bear-bating, bull-bating, and dog fights in nineteenth-century England partake of the same novelty-seeking and colonialist dominion as does British collecting during this era. Even the mental hospital of Bedlam was opened up for tours for public amusement (Ellenberger 1974). In light of such practices as well as the occasional inclusion of human beings in collections (Boesky 1991), the later exhibition of native villages in European and American world's fairs is less of a departure than it might otherwise seem.

Another eighteenth-century English literary work, Pope's "The Rape of the Lock", has Belinda's maid at her dressing table reveal some of the luxury objects found attractive by English collectors of the period:

> Unnember'd treasures ope at once, and here
> The various offerings of the world appear;
> From each she nicely culls with curious toil,
> And decks the goddess with the glitt'ring spoil.
> This casket India's glowing gems unlocks,
> And all Arabia breathes from younder box.
> The tortoise here and elephant untie,
> Transform'd to combs, the speckled and the white.
> Here flies of pins extend their shining rows,
> Puffs, powders, patches, Bibles, billet-doux.
>
> (Canto I, lines 129–138)

As Landa (1980) observes, Pope's contemporaries would have recognized that the gems from India, perfume from Arabia, and ivory from Africa were an appeal to the reader's geographical imagination and the romantic image of England as the mercantile center of the world. In England the mercantile period began in 1688 when the Stuarts were deposed and the English economy became the focus of national attentions (Bunn 1980). For England and other colonial European powers the mercantile era ended in 1763 with the peace conference in Paris after the Seven Years' War. After that the colonies were no longer viewed primarily as suppliers of raw materials, but as consumers of exported goods. The mercantile period between these years was one of exploitative and protectionist policies on the part of England against which Swift's satire was also directed. But while Swift criticized the anti-mercantile fashion for foreign luxuries, Pope celebrated it, making Belinda his heroine. The mercantile era was also a period in which exotic imports fueled the taste for collections of objects which, as in France, were disparaged as bric-a-brac (Bunn 1980). Soft porcelain Chinaware, curios, Greek and Roman statues, coins, books, paintings, prints, furniture, and other imported luxuries were the stuff of which period collections were made. Even love poets, Boesky (1991) observes, were prone to make their poems a collection, "stuffing it with *stuff* – compasses, magnets, coins, maps, and pictures" (p. 313). Paralleling the bricoleur as the prototypical French consumer of the time (Lévi-Strauss 1966), the English collector of the day was eclectic. But as Bunn (1980) distinguishes, the bricoleur accumulates potentially useful things, whereas the collector acquires things without use; "bric-a-brac is excess, caused by aesthetic distance" (p. 313). In this charge, the familiar French charge of dilettantism is plainly heard. An example is found in the diary of bibliophile Samuel Pepys who agonized repeatedly at booksellers over the color of book bindings and decided to classify his library according to the size of each volume (Boesky 1991). Rigby and Rigby (1944) add to this portrait: "Although he bought paintings, miniatures, engravings and objects of *virtu* as well as books, in no sense of the word could Pepys have been called a connoisseur" (p. 239).

If Pepys was no connoisseur, it is worth considering what does constitute connoisseurship. Since the Enlightenment, being a connoisseur has meant specialized knowledge about an area of collecting and the corresponding abilities to classify collectibles according to acceptable taxonomies, to possess and exercise taste and judgment, and to assess authenticity and value. In other words, the amateur collector is a passionate subjective consumer, while the connoisseur is a rational objective expert. This is not to say that these categories never intermingle, but they are sufficiently distinct that Danet and Katriel (1989) separate collectors into the taxonomic "type A" collector and the aesthetic "type B" collector. As Herrmann (1972) also stipulates, the passionate amateur type B collector is self indulgent and acquisition and ownership are driving concerns. It is in this respect that the non-connoisseur collector is a perfect exemplar of consumer culture.

By the Victorian period in England, the passionate amateur came from the broad ranks of society and included collectors of postage stamps, match-boxes, Staffordshire figures, postcards, biscuit tins, "railroadiana," military medals, sports memorabilia, thimbles, coins, fossils, and samplers (Briggs 1989). The emphasis of the day was on plentitude and abundance in all things, as Praz observes:

> It seems as if the pleasure of inventorying and mustering a universal-ity of things is behind both the accumulation of furnishings . . . and the cumulative representation of a whole family in painting, as well as the minute – and often superfluous and cumbersome – descriptions of milieux in novels.
>
> (Praz 1971, p. 23)

Briggs (1989) traces the greatly expanded agenda of collectibles in Victorian England and concludes that "The term 'art' was interpreted in radically dif-ferent ways even by big dealers and . . . even small collectors of 'trivial objects' could make large claims" (p. 44). While coins had been collected for some time, the number of manufactured objects in Victorian collections suggests a legitimization of mass-produced objects as collectibles. Far from the encyclopedic collections of the *Wunderkammern*, Victorian collections were highly specialized. For instance, with the production of postage stamps by a number of countries beginning in the 1840s and 1850s, collectors began to specialize not only in stamps, but in stamps from certain areas and periods (Gelber 1992). The self-generated Victorian labels of *timbromanie* or stamp mania attest to its popularity (Briggs 1989). Stamps also became a prototypical area for type A collecting, since the taxonomic categories and possible acquisitions are fixed, if growing, and readily classified by area, period, type, face value, cancelation type, and so forth. The traits or appear-ance of orderliness, scientific precision, and completeness are readily pursued with such a collection. As Breckenridge (1989) observes, following the Great Exhibition, British collecting and British culture both became internationalized and institutionalized. Collecting, especially of the classi-fying sort epitomized by stamp collecting, offered a means to seem to gain control of the world and of the past. Kendrick (1987) finds that the taxonomic inclination even struck collectors of pornography in Victorian England. While theirs was a private and publicly forbidden arena of col-lecting, their habits were otherwise indistinguishable from those of other bibliophiles of the day.

America

In the eighteenth and nineteenth centuries then, English collecting became more diverse, more specialized, more popular, and more taxonomic. These same tendencies occurred in America, but at a later date and with some notable variations. Early Americans may have had collections of Indian arrowheads and hunting trophies, but such imported luxuries as books were too expensive for most people to collect, even if they had the time to devote to such an indulgence (Rigby and Rigby 1944). Instead the Colonies were more a source of exotic materials for European cabinets. By the late seventeenth century one notable exception was Cotton Mather (1663–1728) whose book collection was sufficient to justify several visits by the London bookseller John Dunton. The collection was continued by Cotton Mather's son Samuel and grew to an unprecedented seven or eight thousand books plus additional manuscripts by the eighteenth century (Rigby and Rigby 1944). Thomas Jefferson was another famous early American book collector and in 1814, when the Library of Congress burned, he sold his collection to the government as a replacement. Statesmen, clergymen, doctors, lawyers, writers, architects, and artists were prominent among American collectors of the eighteenth and early to mid-nineteenth centuries. Besides Mather, another clergyman collector was the Reverend William Bentley (1759–1819), who collected portraits, prints, books, manuscripts, furniture, decorative arts, coins, and specimens from natural history, ethnology, and archeology (Stillinger 1980). The most significant artist collector, Charles Wilson Peale (1741–1827), was at least as diverse in his collecting activity. His personal collection began with portraits of famous Americans he had painted and installed in a small personal museum opened in his Philadelphia home in 1784. In 1785 he began collecting natural-history specimens and in 1801 he helped uncover a complete mastodon skeleton (Rigby and Rigby 1944). The following year he opened Peale's Museum in Philadelphia on the second floor of Independence Hall and included besides the mastodon and famous Americans, fossils, seashells, wax figures of North American Indians in appropriate costume and weaponry, and models of the latest machines (Bazin 1967). By 1822, when he painted *The Artist in His Museum*, showing him in the Long Room of his museum, he had collected and displayed in appropriate taxonomic order various pre-served predators, birds, minerals, insects, fossils, and in the highest places of honor, portraits and busts of heroes of the American Revolution. But Peale received no state funding and knew that he must attract the public to support the museum. To that end, he set out to show the wonders of divine creation, assembling and displaying a number of curiosities including a cow with 5 legs, 6 feet, and 2 tails, a petrified nest, a devilfish, *trompe-l'oeil* paint-ings, a speaking tube installed in a lion's head, tattooed human heads, monkeys dressed as various artisans, and "experiments in light, sound, and clockwork motion, offering his visitors views of nature, technology, naval battle, and scenes from Milton's *Paradise Lost*" (Kulik 1989, p. 5). When Peale died in 1827, the museum, which had become a joint-stock company, turned to live animal shows, dwarves, "giants," and Siamese twins to gen-erate profits. By mid-century when the Smithsonian Institution was estab-lished, Phineas T. Barnum had purchased Peale's collections and moved them to his own American Museum in New York. Peale's educational vision for the collections was soon lost as Barnum stressed elements of the carnival, circus, zoo, and sideshow in his museum,

> including three serpents fed noonday meals before the public, two whales that swam in a tank of salt water, a white elephant, hippos, bears, wolves, a herd of American buffalo, waxwork figures, midgets, dwarfs, giants, bearded ladies, fat boys, rope dancers, jugglers, performing American Indians, a tattooed man, gypsy girls, albinos, and a group of "industrious fleas."
>
> (Ames 1986, p. 14)

If Barnum gave the public freaks and oddities, James Herring gave them gambling in his art lottery. His New York gallery charged $5 for a print and a chance at winning paintings by American artists in an annual draw. This venture became the Apollo Association in 1838 and the American Art Union in 1844, when it distributed 92 paintings in its lottery (Lynes 1955). Four years later the number of paintings distributed had grown to more than 450 per year. It was both the speculative and the egalitarian nature of the art lottery that accounted for its popularity. The lottery concept faltered on legal shoals in 1853, but it was influential in awakening fledgling American tastes for art (Rigby and Rigby 1944). As a result of the Art Union, a few committed collectors, and the emergence of dealers, galleries, and auction houses, for a time there emerged a fashionable American interest in buying art: "It became a fad to buy pictures – good pictures, bad pictures, new pictures or old ones (so long as they weren't 'primitives'), American pictures or European ones" (Lynes 1955, p. 44). Still, this interest was limited to the relatively affluent. It was not until after the American Civil War that a substantial number of Americans collected (Grampp 1989). After the Civil War and before the depression of the early 1870s there was a boom of interest in artwork by the American masses, this time fueled by the cheap prints of Currier and Ives. Echoing the Dutch fascination with prints during the Netherlands' Golden Age, these prints were found in a vast number of American homes. Prices were mostly in the 15 to 25 cent range, and popular subjects, deprecated by more affluent collectors as sentimental kitsch, included idyllic country scenes, the American Indian as noble savage, kittens and puppies, scenes of domestic bliss, patriotic motifs, children playing, dramatic boxing or big-game hunting-scenes, and panoramic landscapes (Lynes 1955, p. 69).

At the higher end of the social-class spectrum, the 1876 Centennial Exhibition in Philadelphia helped make American antiques a status symbol for certain nouveaux riches with aspirations to upper-class status (Stillinger 1980). But for the most visible art-collecting tycoons of the latter half of the nineteenth century it was not American antiques and art that captured the imagination. Rigby and Rigby explain:

It is obvious that mimicry of the old European aristocracy was largely responsible for the fact that extensive collecting now became fashionable also among American merchant princes. . . . Certainly some form of personal ambition was most often responsible for the apparently incongruous phenomenon of men turning from the collecting of mines, of railroads, of corporations, to the gathering of books and paintings, of porcelains and tapestries and French furniture; for though money became, at this time, power in the truest sense, even so it could not satisfy all a man's desires, nor achieve for him the complete and unqualified recognition of many of his fellows . . . most of these wealthy collectors were tarred with the same black spirit of ruthless acquisitiveness, with that fierce will-to-power, which were characteristics of the new industrial age in which they lived; and by Europeans even the best of them were accused of being "people of enormous wealth and little taste who accumulate masterpieces of art without appreciating them."

(Rigby and Rigby 1944, pp. 280–281)

These acquisitive American robber barons are portrayed in Dreiser's trilogy about Frank Algernon Cowperwood, *The Financier*, *The Titan*, and *The Stoic* and in the Henry James novels *The American, Roderick Hudson, The Golden Bowl*, and *The Outcry*. As a recent American expatriate James may have made himself the model for Christopher Newman in *The American* (Tintner 1986), but it is likely that J. P. Morgan was the model for Rowland Mallet in *Roderick Hudson* (Harris 1987), as well as for Adam Verver in *The Golden Bowl* and Breckenridge Bender in *The Outcry* (Auchincloss 1990). The last novel is, as the title suggests, an outcry against the plunder of European art treasures by such upstarts as the Morgans, Rothschilds, and Vanderbilts. But as Chamberlin (1983) and Saisselin (1984) remind us, the conspicuous consumption of the turn-of-the-century robber barons is not the first instance of rampant consumerism or expropriation of art treasures.

J. Pierpont Morgan began his banking career as a boy collecting stamps, coins, and autographs, and, prophetically, pieces of stained glass he found fallen from European cathedrals (Sinclair 1981). As with Sigmund Freud (Belk *et al.* 1991), Jean de Berry (Muensterberger 1994), and a number of other prominent collectors, it was not until his banker father's death that J. P. Morgan's collecting activity began in earnest (Auchincloss 1989). While he neglected American artists, perhaps because he wanted to bring to the country what did not already exist, he collected promiscuously and avariciously from the best of foreign collections, often buying entire collections intact. Provenance was important and he acquired Leonardo da Vinci's notebooks, Catherine the Great's snuff box, Shakespeare first folios, a letter from George Washington, and Napoleon's watch (Chernow 1990). The decorative arts were his major focus and paintings only accounted for

5 percent of his collection. In this respect he was like the Medici. However, unlike the Medici he did not commission works of art and instead regarded his acquisition of largely European treasures as a "shopping" expedition (Saarinen 1958). Besides neglecting American art he also neglected the impressionists and anyone who came after them. He was widely regarded as collecting old masters and young mistresses, as his extra-marital affairs were widely known, if seldom publicized. Much of his acquisition was done through the Duveens who also sold art to a number of other wealthy American industrialists. When he died his collection was conservatively valued at $60 million, making it the most costly collection ever assembled. Like Cowperwood in Dreiser's trilogy, Morgan was not the vulgar and unknowledgable philistine that the robber barons were widely thought to be (Josephson 1934). Both were more complex characters with a love and growing knowledge of art. But like Cowperwood's, it seems clear that Morgan's devotion to art and his involvement with the Metropolitan Museum of Art, of which he eventually became director and to which approximately half of his collection went, arose from a need to "launder" money acquired from the still "dirty" business of banking and investment. No mere conspicuous consumption (Veblen 1899), art has the power to redeem and sacralize money (Belk and Wallendorf 1990). The contagious magic of acknowledged masterpieces and collectibles with special prove-nance, the collector hopes, will ennoble even the most ill-gotten gains. And when the collector is also a benefactor adding to the sparse collections of a young nation, a robber baron can perhaps come to be seen as a captain of industry and patron of the arts. Americans, priding themselves on being a non-aristocratic and supposedly egalitarian society, have long had a love–hate relationship with their rich (Belk 1993a). But in the case of Morgan, his art collecting was regarded as more redeeming than such lux-uries as his yacht and automobiles and some national pride was evident when he outbid royalty to bring artwork to America (Harris 1987).

TWENTIETH-CENTURY COLLECTING

If Morgan's collecting was and is viewed with some pride, the art collect-ing of William Randolf Hearst during the twentieth century is not. Hearst too started from relative wealth and began his collecting in childhood – in Hearst's case not only with stamps and coins, but also beer steins, porce-lain, pictures of actors and actresses, and German comic pictures (Rigby and Rigby 1944). During the twenty-nine years in which Hearst was build-ing his San Simeon, California, mansion, "La Cuesta Encantada", at a cost of $35 million, he spent another $50 million on art from the palaces, monas-teries, and collections of Europe (Folsom 1963). Paralleling some early royal collectors and the development of institutional zoos, Hearst also maintained a private zoo on his large coastal estate. Besides intending no public legacy from his monumental art acquisitions, Heart's chief sin was seen as a vulgar lack of taste:

> With raw insensitivity, exquisite Greek vases, handsome Hispano-Moresque plates, tapestries of unsurpassed quality were joined with fourth-rate paintings of Madonnas, a stuffed owl, a crudely restored façade of a Roman temple and academic sculptures of cast marble as unpleasantly white as a pair of store-bought dentures. On the façade, the teakwood gable of an Oriental pagoda was clutched between pseudo-Spanish–Italian towers. A fourteenth-century confessional served as the elevator, disgorging the castle's owner to a secret door cut into a choir stall.
>
> (Saarinen 1958, p. 75)

According to one of the guides I interviewed at the present-day estate, Hearst used to delight in presenting improbable seating arrangements for his invited dinner guests, such as seating Mae West next to a church official. This seems to partake of the same sense of shock sought in *Wunderkammern* and eighteenth-century European masquerades. The sense of violation of the sacred with the profane was expressed even more sharply by Dorothy Parker, with reference to Hearst's none too secret mistress, Marion Davies:

> Upon my honor, I saw a Madonna
> Hanging within a niche,
> Above the door of the private whore
> Of the world's worst son of a bitch.
>
> (quoted in Alsop 1982, p. 94)

And profaning American morals and the canons of the art world do not exhaust this list of Hearst's sins against "good" collecting:

> Supreme example of what Lewis Mumford calls the modern "department-store collector," this man succumbed to every one of the pitfalls which may so easily engulf the wealthy would-be connoisseur – personal ambition, lack of discrimination, ostentation, and emphasis on the symbolic values of mere size and quantity. Moneyed American collectors have often, in one way or another, given evidence of one or more of these faults, but the concentration Hearst represents is the nux vomica of bad collecting on the grand scale.
>
> (Rigby and Rigby 1944, p. 286)

Nevertheless, the continued ambivalence of Americans toward the shrines of their most financially successful historical figures is expressed in the fact that the remains of the collection at "La Cuesta Encantada" are California's second most popular tourist attraction after Disneyland. And the love–hate regard for wealthy collectors continues in public attentions to more recent residues of collecting lives, such as those of J. Paul Getty, Andy Warhol, and Malcolm Forbes.

If Hearst is reviled as a collector, consider then what makes a good collector. In 1954 an unknown Parisian dentist, Maurice Girardin, died leaving the city the major part of his magnificent art collection (Cabanne 1963). The collection included numerous works by Rouault, Dufy, Modigliani, Braque, Utrillo, Matisse, and Picasso, and 380 of these canvasses were immediately displayed in the Petit Palais. The collection had cost Girardin no more than a million francs to acquire, but it was estimated that it would require more than 800 million old francs to replace it four years after his death (Rheims 1961). So it appears that Dr. Girardin had acumen, taste, and modesty, all traits evaluated positively by the public whether they pertain to collectors or to consumers in general. Further, he had dedication and passion, and was willing to sacrifice everything to the pursuit of his collection (Cabanne 1963). In leaving his collection to the city, his ultimate generosity is also without question. Inasmuch as these are characteristics revered in heroes generally, it is possible to see Girardin posthumously as a martyr to the worthy cause of art for the French people. While he came from a well-to-do family, Maurice's means were modest. He nevertheless befriended artists he admired, especially Rouault. Nor did he rely on intermediaries and advisors to make his selections and discoveries. He stood behind the artists whose work he admired or ʼon whom he took pity and opened a gallery to help start their careers and sell their works. These too are well-respected traits in collectors (Materer 1988). Cabanne (1963) uses words like "apostle" (for art) in describing Girardin and notes that he launched the art career of the hermit and "chronic and pathetic invalid" Maria Blanchard. The gallery was a financial failure due to the doctor's poor business practices and because he bought a number of the works himself; it eventually closed. And one further admired collector trait was that

> Dr Girardin never speculated. The idea did not so much as cross his mind; when he sold pictures from his collection, he always did so in order to buy works of uncertain value by young artists who were unknown or difficult to understand, such as Rouault and Gromaire, or Buffet who was also in this state when the doctor discovered him.
>
> (Cabanne 1963, p. 211)

Speculation and profit-making were, on the other hand, the sole intent of members of the Bearskin Club whose members contributed 250 francs a year for each share of art purchases selected by the Club's buying committee. While they had "losers," they also had a Bonnard, ten Matisses, and a dozen Picassos in their first sale in 1914 at the Hôtel Drouot (Moulin 1987). The sale raised more than 100,000 francs and the club became the model for a number of art-investment clubs that followed. Unlike the Art

Union whose purpose was to get art into the hands of lucky lottery winners, the Bearskin Club members saw art as a promising commodity. While art had been used for investment purposes previously and art dealers are ostensibly in business for profits, their lack of personal connection to or even personal examination of the art work would cause many to deny the label of collectors to members of the Bearskin Club. A similar criticism was made of U.S. collectors in the New York art scene in the 1960s and 1970s who "approached art with the dispassion of a stockbroker . . . ignored the visual appeal of a work, often selected over the telephone. He was concerned only with the name of the artist who created the work, and his short-term or long-term growth potential in the market" (Naifeh 1976, p. 31).

While tastes and fashions in what is collectible continue to change, the sheer range of what is considered to be collectible has greatly expanded in the twentieth century. Within the scope of fine art, an increasing range of art from American (Berlo 1992), Canadian (Cole 1985), Pacific (Thomas 1991), African (Torgovnick 1990), and Australian (Sutton 1988) aboriginals has come to be considered collectible. Outside of the domain of "fine art," the range of articles considered collectible by different subsets of society also continues to expand and proliferate. Mass production, growing world affluence, and the spread of consumer culture have made it possible for collecting to become a truly mass phenomenon. This is seen routinely in feature-section newspaper accounts of so-and-so's unique collection of such and such. Two of several recent books depicting interesting private collections in the U.S. and Great Britain include collections of: pencils, Winston Churchill memorabilia, maps of Transylvania, farm machinery, canning jars, police batons, Hawaiian shirts, Uncle Scrooge comic books, toy soldiers, sewing machines, dolls, photographs of midgets, advertising posters, automobile license plates, beer cans, lawnmowers, matchbooks, Snoopy merchandise, cigar bands, radios, and anvils (Johnston and Beddow 1986; Land-Weber 1980). Besides the sanction and encouragement given to such collections in newspaper features and books, a number of recent shows of such collections at museums in Europe and North America have provided further acknowledgment and attention (e.g., Belk 1989; Franco 1980; Grasskamp 1983; Hooper-Greenhill 1992; Jones 1992; New Yorker 1992; Pearce 1992). Even China has recently had an exhibition of citizens' formerly secret collections, including collections of cameras, watches and clocks, matchboxes, cigarette packages, and other pre-Communist packaging (Liming 1993). Increasingly collectors of objects outside of the sphere of fine arts are also opening museums to display their personal collections (Hughes 1987; Sobol and Sobol 1991). It is not the case that such things have suddenly become art objects, but in terms of Clifford's (1990) Greimassian semiotic square based on the oppositions of masterpiece/ artifact and authentic/inauthentic, they have moved from being considered inauthentic artifacts to authentic artifacts. That some of these things are not only commercially produced commodities, but advertisements for other commodities is not entirely new. Bon Marché passed out advertising cards to children in the 1890s that became collectors' items (Miller 1981, pp. 174–175) and during the 1880s and 1890s collecting advertising trade cards was popular in America (Strasser 1989, pp. 164–165).

At the start of the twentieth century while robber barons like J. P. Morgan were assembling their collections of European paintings and decorative arts, American children were avid collectors of more humble objects. Burk (1900) surveyed American grade-school children and found that each child averaged three to four active collections, with the peak years of collecting interest between ages 8 and 11. A study by G. Stanley Hall (1907) based on over 1,200 grade-school children in California found similar results and listed more than 300 items collected. The most popular objects collected were, for boys, cigar bands, stamps, birds' eggs, marbles, seashells, buttons, rocks, and advertising cards. Girls were most likely to collect stamps, seashells, advertising cards, cigar bands, buttons, marbles, pieces of cloth, paper dolls, and other dolls. In a 1927 study Lehman and Witty found a lower frequency of collecting and pronounced that the collecting fad was declining. However, a 1929 study using different questions reported an even higher incidence of collecting than that found by Burk at the turn of the century (Whitley 1929). Additional studies after the start of the Great Depression found interest in collections continuing to increase and peaking at a somewhat older age (Witty and Lehman 1930, 1931). A survey by Durost (1932) found that boys' collecting peaked at age 10 with an average of 12.7 collections, while girls' collecting peaked a year later and averaged 12.1 collections at the time. A recent study in Israel found that over the first six grades 93 percent of children reported collecting something, with the figure dropping below 50 percent in grade eight (Danet and Katriel 1988). The teenage years thus appear to be the period during which faddish collectors drop their collecting activity, while those with long-term collecting interests continue (Katriel 1988/89). In England Newson and Newson (1968) found that even at age 4, some 80 percent of boys and 66 percent of girls collected something. A 1988 study on the American East Coast found that children's collecting activity was highest between the ages 9 and 10 with an average of three active collections (McGreevy 1990). The study reports that a higher (but unspecified) proportion of children collect nothing than was the case in the turn-of-the-century studies and that, compared to the earlier studies, a much greater proportion of the objects collected were now bought rather than found. Rocks, stamps, marbles, dolls, seashells, and picture cards (now of baseball players) were still collected, as well as miniature vehicles, coins, foreign currency, He-man figures, GI Joe, books, posters, stickers, and stuffed animals. Danet and Katriel (1988) report a somewhat different set of manufactured objects collected by children in Israel, including collector cards of rabbis.

Estimates of the incidence of adult collecting vary. One study estimated that one of every three Americans has at least one active collection (O'Brien 1981). Another American study found that over 60 percent of households reported at least one collection with an average of 2.6 collections per household (Schiffer *et al.* 1981). Nearly 10 percent of American men report collecting coins and about 4 percent of both men and women currently collect stamps (Crispell 1988). It appears that the number of active collectors was even greater during the Great Depression (Gelber 1991). A new kind of ethos that has been ascendent throughout the twentieth century was codified in the 1930s: the hobby as "serious leisure" (Stebbins 1979, 1982). Three factors since the Industrial Revolution have supported a gradual legitimization of hobbies: fewer work hours, greater alienation from work activities, and increased affluence (Ackerman 1990; Gelber 1991; McKibbin 1983). We may have lost contact with the product of our labor in the workplace, but in collecting we are in total control of our time and totally in possession of the collection we create. Because hobbies are often seen as being closer to work than leisure, they provide a guilt-free activity that supports the work ethic and offers more self-control and reward than a corporate or factory career. In Gelber's assessment, hobbies offer "the promise not of eternal leisure but of eternal work" (1991, p. 743). In Menninger's (1942) depiction, collecting is a "constructive leisure time activity." This became especially important during the Depression when many jobs were lost and those that remained were often tenuous. Exhibits of ordinary collectors became common in the United States at this time, and dignity was further enhanced by playing up the generally false potential for profits through collecting (Gelber 1991). Youth organizations like the Boy Scouts, Girl Scouts, and Campfire Girls have also systematically encouraged collecting during the twentieth century (Aristides 1988; Gelber 1991; Mechling 1989). Adults have seen collecting as an activity that inculcates desirable habits in children. We have accordingly encouraged and nurtured such activity.

Gelber (1992) offers an explanation for this social sanction for collecting. While the central premise of this chapter is that collecting arose with consumer culture and that the objects that comprise collections are luxury consumer goods, collecting is an act of production as well as consumption. Collectors create, combine, classify, and curate the objects they acquire in such away that a new product, the collection, emerges. In the process they also produce meanings. More precisely, they participate in the process of socially reconstructing shared meanings for the objects they collect. Moreover, in the process of collecting collectors rehearse and imitate the market-based economy in which we are increasingly embedded. These processes are articulated more clearly in certain collecting arenas, with stamp collecting being a prime example, as Gelber effectively demonstrates. Arising as it did in the latter half of the nineteenth century, Gelber sees stamp collecting as "recapitulating many of the fundamental structures and relations of Gilded Age capitalism" (1992, p. 743). Among these structures and relations are competition, commodity trading, and buying, accumulating, and later selling at an anticipated profit. While recognizing that not all stamp collectors pursue their hobby from this perspective, Gelber outlines three models employed by those who do. The first is the merchant model, which he characterizes as dominant in the nineteenth century, especially among children. Operating from this model, collectors act as small-scale merchants constantly buying, selling, and trading their stamps and seeking to add to their own collections and make a little on each transaction; they act as stock-exchange brokers in the stamp market. Still there is much love of the stamps themselves among such merchants. A second model, the investor, views stamps as more of a life insurance or annuity policy, constantly increasing in value and eventually to be cashed in, typically in old age. In the mean time, the collector can enjoy the leisure activity of collecting. The third model Gelber outlines is that of the speculator who buys low and sells high simply to make a profit. Unlike the other collector groups, the speculator has little interest in completing a collection and is much like the members of the Bearskin Club or those buyers in the 1960s and 1970s New York art market who needed never see the works they had acquired. As one of the latter "collectors" said, "You wouldn't go to see a stock certificate" (Naifeh 1976, p. 31).

Not only has there been commoditization of stamp collecting from within stamp-collector ranks, there has also been commoditization from without. Gelber (1992) notes that starting in the 1860s a number of open-air stamp markets opened in European countries and were referred to as bourses, after the French stock market. A number of these open-air stamp markets still continue. The number of stamp dealers in Europe was estimated as 2,000 in 1864 (Briggs 1989), so the number of collectors of stamps is likely to have been in the hundreds of thousands. A similar commoditization took place in model-airplane collecting as kits became commercially produced and dealers replaced amateurs (Butsch 1984). However, until the 1890s post offices refused to cooperate with stamp collectors and those in the United States and Canada even made it illegal to buy and sell uncanceled stamps at more than their face value (Gelber 1992). Now of course governments have come full swing, marketing numerous stamps they hope will never be used as well as continually offering new albums, commemorative stamps, and first-day covers solely to attract collectors. An unsuccessful experiment in marketing colorful stamps for Central and South American nations was attempted by N. F. Seebeck in 1893, but in 1894 the republic of San Marino profitably began to market stamps intended for collectors rather than postage (Bryant 1989). In 1994 the U.S. government planned over 100 special stamps, including issues commemorating sports heroes, TV news commentator Edward R. Murrow, black educator Allison Davis, silent-screen stars, Buffalo Soldiers, World Cup soccer, World War II, Norman Rockwell, and Elvis Presley (U.S. Postal Service 1993). Bryant (1989) estimates that 40 percent of U.S. stamps currently sold are bought by collectors and dealers and never circulate. With post offices reinforcing the educational and investment potential of stamp collecting it is increasingly easy for collectors to believe they are participating in a productive activity rather than a leisure consumption activity. Like the loss of work during the Depression, retirement often leads to an increase in collecting activity, allowing a sense of continued work in retirement (Christ 1965; Unruh 1983). There are, however, certain problems with Gelber's stamp-collector types if they are applied to stamp collectors as a whole. One problem is that the more mercenary collectors of the speculator variety, in particular, may not be regarded as true collectors by other stamp collectors. During several days spent interviewing stamp collectors at the Collector's Club in New York City, I found these collectors more often labeled "dealers" by other members, even though most had no fixed retail location. A second problem is that despite the market metaphor, most stamp collections, especially of the sorts of stamps promoted by the U.S. postal service, fail to recover their costs once they are sold, much less make a profit. And a third problem is that for a number of stamp collectors the actions of buying and socializing with other collectors may be more important than the economic aspects of their collections (Christ 1965). Consistent with this, rather than *caveat emptor* and taking advantage of fledgling collectors, among child collectors of popular thematic cards in Israel, there tend to be sharing coalitions and protection of naïve collectors (Katriel 1988/89). Inasmuch as friendship plays an important role in business relations (Granovetter 1985; Silver 1993), it would be surprising if it were not also a part of collector relations. But despite its problems, Gelber's (1992) observation that stamp collecting is a model of production and business is an important one. In the next chapter more will be made of the pervasive investment and market metaphor found in many areas of collecting.

Not only may some collectors adopt a business vocabulary in pursuing and describing their collecting activity, many twentieth-century businesses have found that adopting a collecting vocabulary and product line is profitable. A conservative estimate of the annual sales volume of new baseball cards (which began as cards included with cigarettes in the 1880s) in the American market is $500 million (Rogoli 1991). The sale of Elvis Presley records and collectibles is greater today than when he died (Gregory and Gregory 1980). Members of the Coca-Cola Collectors Club International meet annually to buy, sell, and trade Coke collectibles (Pendergrast 1993), while the Coca-Cola Company caters to them with stores on 5th Avenue in New York, in the Atlanta airport, and in the company's museum in downtown Atlanta. A fairly recent entrant into the business of marketing to collectors is the instant collectibles company (Roberts 1990). The

February 20, 1994 issue of the U.S. national newspaper supplement *Parade* contained seven full-page advertisements for these firms:

1 Franklin Mint offered a 1:24 scale model of the 1955 Ford Fairlane Crown Victoria. It is "assembled by hand from 177 separate parts" and "is *hand painted, hand polished, hand finished* and handsomely priced at just $120, payable in monthly installments." Since middle-aged men often long for the dream cars of their youth (Belk *et al.* 1991), the choice of year is well timed.

2 The Hamilton Collection advertised a plate depicting the Denver & Rio Grand's "High Line" steam locomotive as it passes beside a river gorge on its way from Durango to Silverton Colorado. The plate, "Above the Canyon" is a "limited-edition by Ted Xaras," "limited to a total of 14 firing days," and limited to "one plate per collector." The reader must respond by April 4, 1994 and "on acceptance" will be billed $29.50 for the 8¼ inch diameter plate.

3 Lenox Collections presented "the Enchanted Swans" of "Lenox Full-Lead Crystal," "a remarkable value at $39." They are "individually crafted" and "not currently available through art galleries or even fine collectible stores." "So to acquire this imported Lenox® work of crystal art, be sure to return the Reservation Form promptly."

4 The Bradford Exchange offered a snowy northern scene plate, "'Two By the Night, Two By the Light' In full color on fine porcelain." The firm, which also runs a service buying and selling plates (Berman and Sullivan 1992), provides a number which "certifies that your plate is officially listed for trading on The Bradford Exchange." It lists the following advantages of the Bradford Exchange:

- A hand-numbered limited-edition plate with a correspondingly hand-numbered Certificate of Authenticity
- A complete plate story introducing you to the artist and detailing the significance of this recommendation
- The potential for appreciation – like 1989's "The Jaguar," which last traded on The Bradford Exchange at $84.00 281% of its $29.90 issue price
- The BRADEX® number fired on the back of your plate means it is listed for trading on The Bradford Exchange

Finally, it notes that "Some exceptional plates appreciate in value; some plates go down, and many remain at or near issue price. But the edition of this plate is strictly limited to a maximum of 95 firing days, and demand is expected to be strong. So if you wish to obtain this plate at the $29.90 issue price, the time to act is now."

5 Timeless Creations, The Collectibles/Specialty Doll Division of Matel, Inc. advertised "Royal Splendor Barbie" from "The Presidential Porcelain Barbie Collection." The design of the embroidery on the doll's gown "was created by master artist Francois Lesage – the most renowned high fashion embroiderer in the world. Founded in 1924, the House of Lesage creates 90 percent of the beading and embroidery that decorates French high fashion." It features "Handsewn sequins and beads" and "genuine Swarovski® crystal earrings," is "In every way, a work of art," and "can only be purchased by direct subscription for a first issue price of $189."

6 The Danbury Mint promoted the "Fantasy of the Crystal Chess Set" featuring "the power of the crystal" through "A sparkling crystal [which] adorns each playing piece!" The pieces themselves are "Remarkably detailed pewter sculptures; magnificent chessboard included at no extra charge!" when the purchaser buys all 32 pieces at $19.95 each plus shipping and handling. On the "reservation application" is a space for the "Name to print on Certificate of Registration."

7 The final such ad in this week's supplement was for the Franklin Mint's "Limited Edition Collector Plate," "The Pause That Refreshes" authorized by the Coca-Cola Company and showing one of Haddon Sundblom's illustrations done for Coca-Cola Christmas season advertising. "In the tradition of the most prized collectibles, this imported heirloom collector plate is crafted of fine porcelain and lavished with breathtaking color. And it is hand-numbered and bordered in *24 karat gold*." At "just $29.95, this Limited Edition will be *closed forever* after just 45 firing days" and is "Available *exclusively* from The Franklin Mint."

Prior to a recent law suit settled out of court, Bradford Exchange's advertising alluded to the potential for appreciation in more seductive terms, even though only 18 percent of its plates traded at above their original selling price after its 30 percent commission charges, and declines outnumbered advances in plate prices by 475 to 269 (Berman and Sullivan 1992). An analysis of themes on the seventy plates in a 1993 copyright Bradford Exchange catalog suggests a strong parallel with the sentimental themes of Currier and Ives a century ago (Lynes 1955). There are an abundance of kittens, puppies, flowers, birds, angels, exotic jungle animals, horses, nostalgically rendered cottages, heroic baseball greats, cherubic children, cheery Charles Wysocki early American rural scenes, Disney cartoons, American heroic presidents Lincoln and Kennedy, Egyptiana, and Elvis Presley plates. As the advertisements suggest and as Roberts (1990) also reports, these mass-produced pieces are typically tiny miniatures, lovingly crafted by famous artisans in time-honored ways that reek of authenticity and promise to lend any would-be collector's home a touch of enviable class. They are produced in limited editions of perhaps 25,000 pieces and the reader will become a serious connoisseur by simply completing a reservation application.

It is all too easy to strike an elitist pose and adopt an attitude of ridicule toward those who would respond to such offerings (Beckham and Brooks 1989), and each social stratum will find its own example of inferior taste, as with the criticism of three art gallery chains "whose shares trade over the counter, use mass merchandising to sell 'signed limited edition' prints and sculptures, usually produced in lots of 300–500" (Schiff 1989). The latter indictment goes on to complain that:

> Each work is described as "fine art" – a term that many critics would call a misnomer. And these art objects carry very lofty retail margins. Simply put, the name of the game is selling class to the masses – at least the masses of 30- to 50-year-olds with enough discretionary income to shell out several thousand dollars for objects produced in bulk and which may satisfy some buyers' psychological need to show that they have "arrived."
>
> (Schiff 1989, p. 14)

Still something is going on here that deserves further consideration. Is this any more than the usual elitist criticism of the popular art of a lower social class as kitsch (e.g., Dorfles 1969), or the broader criticism of consumerism and the market in general (Belk 1983)? Yes. The issue is that of what shall constitute and be the fate of "the work of art in the age of mechanical reproduction," to use Walter Benjamin's (1968a) famous and apt delineation of the issue. It is not just that these objects are for sale that is new. As Carpenter (1983) points out, "Michelangelo worked for money without loss of integrity. Yet he never mass-produced debased Christian altar pieces, suitably modified to meet Arab taste, to peddle on the wharfs of Venice" (n.p.n). Commercially, the fact that we are dealing with collectibles is also relevant. Because collectors require constant serial additions to their collections, the sale of durable goods (collectibles) is very much like that of non-durable goods requiring repeated replenishment (Hansen 1966). Coupled with implicit promises of investment potential and snob appeal, it is easy to see why firms like those in the advertisements quoted above are doing well. The Bradford Exchange is estimated to have sales of $250 million and a pretax income of $20 million (Berman and Sullivan 1992). Even more profitable is the more upscale limited-edition print firm of Martin Lawrence which is estimated to have earned an after-tax profit of 17 percent, or over $8 million, on sales of about $48 million in 1989 (Schiff 1989).

Benjamin's concern was that with the advent of lithography, photography, film, and other mass-reproduction techniques, art is threatened with a loss of authenticity and aura; it becomes a mere commodity. Aura is a ritualistically instilled magical power that Benjamin argued inhered only in the original. He thus recognized that authenticity is socially constructed and transcends "mere genuineness." "This is particularly apparent," Benjamin says, "in the collector who always retains some traces of the fetishist and who by owning the work of art, shares in its ritual power" (1968a, p. 246). Stated in different terms, Klapp (1991) uses the metaphor of inflation to suggest that the more common a symbol is, the less powerful it becomes. As epitomized by Andy Warhol's silk-screen renderings of mass-produced brands, made in a studio appropriately named "the Factory," Pop artists' appropriations of mass media, mass advertising, mass production, mass brands, and mass taste to produce what the art world sanctions as art, seem to make a mockery of Benjamin's concern. In fact, Warhol print production was geared to demand, so that the most expensive of his prints today are also the most abundant; rarer ones are rarer because they were less well received. By locating power only in the unique (what Kubler (1962) called "prime objects"), Benjamin joined Adorno as a Marxist elitist attempting to defend high culture from the threatened encroachments of the masses. He failed to acknowledge the power and magic that can be generated by mass-produced images (Belk *et al.* 1989). As Warhol, Tom Wesselmann, Claes Oldenburg, James Rosenquist, Robert Rauchenberg, Roy Lichtenstein, and other Pop artists showed in the 1960s and 1970s (Danto 1992; Kunzle 1984; Mamiya 1992), as Kurt Schwitters, Aleksandr Rodchenko, Pablo Picasso, Georges Braque, and other Cubists hinted in the 1910s and 1920s (Varnedde and Gopnik 1990), and as Haim Steinbach, Sylvie Fleury, Jeff Koons, Louise Lawler, and other Neo-Conceptualist, Neo-Geoists, or Simulationists have shown in the 1980s and 1990s (Cotter 1988; Janus 1992; Joselit 1988; Lurie 1986; Smith 1988), there is considerable magical power in consumer goods, advertising, and brands. Tomlinson (1990) reverses Benjamin and calls this the aura of the commodity. Benjamin should have known better. He himself was an inveterate collector of a mass-produced commodity: books (see Benjamin 1968b). If such mass-produced objects as books, even rare editions, lack an aura by themselves, their ardent pursuit, passionate acquisition, and worshipful possession in a collection can provide one. As Benjamin (1968b) recognizes, "The period, the region, the craftsmanship, the former ownership – for a true collector the whole background of an item adds up to a magic encyclopedia whose quintessence is the fate of his object" (p. 60). Besides the aura-generating power of such contagious magic, "It is as if under certain conditions, the experience of possession could be transformed into the possession of experience" (Abbas 1988, p. 230). As Benjamin (1968a) unpacks his books and reflects on each hunt and each acquisition whose result he holds, he re-possesses his collecting experiences. But more than this is involved in investing ordinary objects with an aura through their collection. Kopytoff explains how collecting singularizes a former commodity and turns it into something absolutely unique and verging on the numinous:

There is clearly a yearning for singularization in complex societies. Much of it is satisfied individually, by private singularization, often on principles as mundane as the one that governs the fate of heirlooms and old slippers alike – the longevity of the relation assimilates them in some sense to the person and makes parting from them unthinkable. Sometimes the yearning assumes the proportions of a collective hunger, apparent in the widespread response to ever-new kinds of singularizations. Old beer cans, matchbooks, and comic books suddenly become worthy of being collected, moved from the sphere of the singularly worthless to that of the expensive singular. And there is a continuing appeal in stamp collecting – where one may note, the stamps are preferably canceled ones so there is no doubt about their worthlessness in the circle of commodities for which they were originally intended.

(Kopytoff 1986, p. 80)

A large part of what makes certain ordinary consumption objects extraordinary to collectors is that they have been selected and saved by the collector, not because of any inherent use value, but precisely for their non-use value. The delight of Benjamin and most other avid book collectors is not in reading these books, but rather in acquiring and possessing them (Brook 1980; Jackson 1989; Wright and Ray 1969). Thus, Abbas (1988) succinctly discerns, "the collector is engaged exactly in a struggle *against* universal commodification" (p. 220). The introduction of investment motivations in collecting is problematic in this regard. Kopytoff notes that this makes advertisements like those quoted above employ a curious line of logic: "The appeal to greed in their advertising is complex: buy this plate now while it is still a commodity, because later it will become a singular 'collectible' whose very singularity will make it into a higher-priced commodity" (p. 81). As Kopytoff (1986) also points out, areas of collecting activity must be socially sanctioned rather than absolutely idiosyncratic. This social specification of collecting-area boundaries and the collector's selection of this area of collecting then create the liminal border across which the empowered (priestly) collector brings special objects into the collection, and in so doing decommoditizes, singularizes, and sacralizes them (Belk *et al.* 1989). This is not to suggest that collecting-area subcultures do not have their own social definitions of authenticity and genuineness, especially – though not solely – in the West. But the phenomenon of singularizing objects through collecting them vividly shows how aura, which has never been inherent in the object, can in the twentieth century attach to mass-produced branded commodities as well as unique works of art.

Two further characteristics of mass-produced objects that make them suitable for collecting are their frequent seriality and abundance. Seriality provides a new type of collector goal, as Johnson (1986) suggests: "Only certain kinds of collectibles produced in identical multiples – stamps, coins, beer mats – lend themselves to a pattern of acquisition whereby collectors own an example of every type ever produced" (p. 73). Thus, the type A, ordering, collector produced by the Enlightenment is uniquely catered to in a mass-production economy. But with the principle of abundance, so too is the type B, aesthetic, collector. There is a romantic aesthetic delight in abundance that Walter Benjamin (1978) ascribed to Eduard Fuchs – an avid collector of caricatures, genre pictures, and pornography – thus: "he takes a Rabelaisian delight in quantities" (p. 243). This is the same delight evident in *Kunstkammern*, in the numerous paintings depicting such overstuffed cabinets, studiolos, and early galleries, and among the vast majority of collectors who delight in the sheer quantity of wonderful objects they have amassed. This delight in profusion was greatly facilitated by mass production and by the corresponding democratization of luxury consumption in general and collecting in particular.

Returning to what we might find objectionable about the "instant collectibles" for which advertisements were summarized above, there is one argument that is most likely to arise from a type B aesthetic collector, but which might also be heard from a type A taxonomic collector. This objection concerns the fact that such collectibles have been pre-selected for the buyer. Grasskamp captures the loss that this may entail:

> it is in any case no longer a case of genuine collecting, especially when the final state of the completed collection is already fixed in advance. The aura of dreariness which emanates from those empty stamp albums in which the appropriate space for every stamp is reserved with a clear pre-printed indication as to which stamp is to be stuck in where, is characteristic of many other areas of collecting in which collecting is degraded to the status of a species of time-tabled acquisition by the existence of products which are manufactured for the express purpose of becoming "collector's items." The art of collecting demands the element of surprise; the collector should not be allowed to know right from the outset what lies in store when he decides for instance to collect radios, even though it is clear that it is only radios he is going to collect. What those radios are going to look like, how and where the collector is going to ferret them out, how he is going to keep the price down – all these things are an intrinsic part of the ritual of collecting which all boils down to a matter of the *organization of coincidences*. The only objects which can be considered worth collecting are those which are not easy to find but which are likely to be discovered incidentally and unexpectedly; collecting along these lines is an effective life-insurance policy against boredom, it is a game of chance.
>
> (Grasskamp 1983, pp. 139–140)

Most people engaged in "genuine collecting" would no doubt agree with Grasskamp's diagnosis of what is missing with instant collectibles. His analysis also hints at some of the motives that seem to be involved in twentieth-century mass collecting. These motives are the subject to be explored more fully in the next chapter.

Grasskamp's analysis also emphasizes that collecting is an ordering, sense-making, modernistic pursuit. For the type B aesthetic collector, there is still a category that defines the collection's boundaries and the collection still has unity. Although·Nicholson's (1994) novel *Hunters & Gatherers* introduces the possibility of postmodern collections that lack unity, collecting remains firmly rooted in modernism. As we shall see, this seems essential for some of the pleasures sought through the activity of collecting.

SUMMARY: THE DEVELOPMENT OF COLLECTING AND CONSUMER CULTURE

We have seen in the development of collecting a strong coincidence with the development of consumer culture. This coincidence is not entirely due to factors on the supply side of the economy – those of producing more potentially collectible products, lowering their prices, and selling and advertising them in romantically appealing ways. It is also due to factors of demand as the materialistic consumption ethos of a consumer society emerged, as the increasing affluence of time and money made collecting possible for almost everyone, as alienation in the workplace made work-like hobbies an appealing source of dignity, and as the hope for transcendent magic shifted from religion to science to consumption. Museums played more of a role as both a cause and an effect of such changes than has been acknowledged in the treatment thus far, and this will be addressed in Chapter Four. In the final chapter I will also offer a critical assessment of the desirability and consequences of collecting for the individual and for society. Another important missing piece in understanding collecting is the individual phenomenology of collecting that is the subject of the next chapter. What collecting is and why we collect are the key questions that are addressed in Chapter Three.

INDIVIDUAL COLLECTORS

—— •◆• ——

COLLECTING AND OTHER TYPES OF CONSUMING

What does it mean to collect? What distinguishes collecting from other types of consuming? What constitutes a collection? In Chapters One and Two I have assumed that we all know what collecting is and in general that is true. However, we must now be more precise in specifying what collecting means and in distinguishing it from other activities with which it might be confused. Once we have done this we can begin to explore the phenomenon of collecting and the even more fundamental question of why we collect.

Collecting defined

I have maintained thus far that collecting is a special type of consuming. It is therefore appropriate to begin with an understanding of what constitutes consuming behavior. Many definitions exist, but most consumer researchers would agree that consuming involves individuals or groups acquiring, possessing, using, and disposing of valued things. One way to acquire things is to buy them, but we could also find them, make them, lease them, borrow them, steal them, or receive them as gifts. Possession may be relatively brief for some things like food and other non-durables and relatively long for other things like heirlooms, monuments (most often a group possession), houses, and other durables. Use may be active or passive and may be symbolic (e.g., signaling status) as well as physical. Disposition may also be active or passive and in the case of such non-durables as food may be simultaneous with use. Most consumer researchers would also consider both active and passive gathering of information about a possession or possible acquisition to be a part of consuming behavior. In the case of households, businesses, and other formal or informal organizations, different members may be involved in different stages of the consumption process; those who obtain information about a given item or acquire, use, or dispose of it need not be the same person. Besides tangible objects, certain services and experiences such as travel, banking, and medical care are also among the things we consume. As long as we value possessions, we are likely to be saddened if we are deprived of them involuntarily. When we no longer value these things we are likely to stop using them and be willing to dispose of them without compensation. In a consumer society, possessions may physically remain useful but be perceived as symbolically obsolete or inappropriate. It is sometimes said that we live in a disposable society where we have only fleeting attachments to things. But collecting involves strong attachments that challenge this view. After sufficient remove from use (i.e., original or intended use), obsolete items may appeal to collectors even more strongly because of their obsolescence (Thompson 1976). Thus collecting differs from most other forms of consumption in being relatively immune from fashion obsolescence.

In the collecting form of consumption, acquisition is a key process. Someone who possesses a collection is not necessarily a collector unless they continue to acquire additional things for the collection. The collection usually grows as a result, but because some collectors concentrate on upgrading rather than expanding their collections, quantitative growth is not inevitable. Collecting differs from most other types of consumption because it involves forming what is seen to be a set of things – the collection. In order for these things to be perceived as comprising a set there must be boundaries distinguishing what is and is not appropriate for inclusion in the collection. These boundaries can be either conceptual (as with the *artificialia* and *naturalia* objects of marvel in the *Wunderkammern*) or perceptual (as with a collection of postage stamps depicting fish). On the principle of "no two alike," despite sharing something in common with other objects in the collection, the items comprising the collection must not be identical (Danet and Katriel 1989; Nicholson 1994; Walls *et al.* 1975). Therefore, a set of indistinguishable 29-cent U.S. Elvis Presley postage stamps would not constitute a collection, while a set of **different** rock-singer postage stamps or a set of **different** stamps featuring Elvis Presley could be a collection if the person acquiring them perceives them as a set. Usually collecting is also an active process of personal selection of items, but if the boundaries of the collection are known to others, additions could also be acquired as gifts. The things collected are generally tangible objects, but could potentially be experiences, as with someone who collects travel destinations or sexual partners. Finally, the things comprising a collection are removed from ordinary use. This may either be the case from the start as with art objects which exist for their own aesthetic sake, or by virtue of being taken out of use as with postage stamps which will not be used to send mail or salt-and-pepper shakers which are no longer expected to dispense salt and pepper. There is also another sense in which collecting is non-utilitarian. Collecting is highly involving passionate consumption rather than an uninvolving form of consumption like buying canned peas (unless of course one is a collector of canned peas in which case such a purchase for the collection may matter a great deal). As a result collectors tend to feel attached to their collections in ways that may seem irrational if viewed in terms of the normal functions of the things collected.

Putting these elements together results in the following definition: **collecting is the process of actively, selectively, and passionately acquiring and possessing things removed from ordinary use and perceived as part of a set of non-identical objects or experiences**. This definition of collecting is essentially compatible with others by Alsop (1982, p. 70), Aristides (1988, p. 330), Belk *et al.* (1991, p. 180), Durost (1932, p. 10), Kron (1983, pp. 193–194), and Muensterberger (1994, p. 4). The definition also distinguishes collecting from other consumption activities and patterns. Objects of ordinary consumption, even when the objects are part of a set (as with spices in a kitchen or tools in a workshop), are primarily intended for use and therefore do not comprise a collection. The same is true of acquiring objects primarily for investment purposes with little regard to either their place in a set or feelings of possessiveness toward these objects. Investment may be a secondary purpose of collecting, but where it is the primary purpose the specific objects matter little. In this case the passion and resulting attachment involved in collecting are lacking.

When consumers hoard objects like fuel or toilet paper, these objects are generally identical and do not follow the principle of no two alike. These objects also tend to be acquired for ordinary use. A consumer who merely accumulates objects by failing to dispose of them may also regard the objects as usable and is unlikely to regard them as part of a set with specific boundaries. This is possessiveness without the selective acquisitiveness of collecting. Accumulating does not preclude a consumer from imposing or finding a unifying principle for items accumulated and then proceeding to add to the resulting collection according to this principle; by so doing an accumulation can become a collection. Collecting also differs from simple acquisitiveness in which the items acquired are neither regarded as a set nor retained and possessed as such. This is acquisitiveness without the unifying possessiveness of collecting. Although some (e.g., Humphrey 1979) maintain that there are animals that collect, such behavior seems better characterized as acquisitiveness, accumulation, or hoarding. As an anonymous writer in *The Times* of London on August 12, 1910 put it:

When a dog makes a store of bones, old and entirely fleshless, he is like the collector who keeps things because they are obsolete. A used postage stamp is to a man what a bone without flesh is to a dog: but the collector of postage stamps goes further than the dog, in that he prefers an old postage stamp to a new one, while no dog, however ardent a collector of bones without flesh, would not rather have a bone with flesh on it. There is more method in the human collector, however, since he always has before him the ideal of a complete collection, whereas no dog, probably ever dreamed of acquiring specimens of all the different kinds of bones that there are in the world.
(quoted in Johnston and Beddow 1986, pp. 13, 15)

Therefore, collecting is distinct from ordinary consumption, investment, hoarding, possessive accumulating, and acquisitive buying. Nevertheless, as what was earlier called the distilled essence of consumption, our analysis of individual collecting must begin with collecting as a form of consumption.

Collecting as consuming

While collecting, like some ordinary consumption, may be done as a family or among other coalitions, collecting is most often an individual pursuit. Witty and Lehman (1933) found that American children rarely collected in teams. Katriel (1988/89) found that coalitions of child collectors in Israel tended to break down sooner or later. The reason seems to be that collecting is usually a competitive activity. No matter how narrow or obscure the collecting area, it is usually not long before others begin to collect the same thing. The collector may seek out others as kindred spirits sharing a common passion, to learn from them, or to compare their collections to his or her own in order to see "How am I doing?" As with more general consumption, success in competition with others brings the collector heightened status (within his or her collecting sphere) and feelings of pride and accomplishment. As a form of achievement, the collector can also compete against a self-imposed standard of excellence (Jackson 1976; McClelland 1961). Whether it takes the form of competition with self or others, an achievement orientation has been found to have both positive and negative effects not only in work and sports but also in competitive consumption, including collecting (Neumann 1975; Spence 1985). Collecting takes place within a much narrower sphere than general consuming, and this may make status competition more manageable and enhance chances of success. However, rather than reducing competitive fervor, this narrowing is likely to enhance it. The passionate involvement of collectors makes it difficult to remain detached when we share an interest in a collectible object with other collectors. The first curator of applied arts at the Louvre, Edmond Bonnaffé, revised an old Latin proverb to convey this fervor: "*Man against man is like a wolf; woman against woman is worse; but worst of all is collector against collector*" (quoted in Rigby and Rigby 1944, p. 34). It is no accident that auctions are a popular means of selling collectibles, for nowhere else is this competitive spirit likely to be more of a public spectacle and lead "many collectors to abandon logical decision and self-restraint in favor of competition and, not inconceivably, exhibitionistic grandeur" (Muensterberger 1994, p. 247). The exhibitionistic pride of competitive acquisition is evident for instance in Evan Connell's (1974) *The Connoisseur* when the neophyte collector Muhlbach has just won the bidding for a Mexican jade mask being auctioned by a Mr. Piglett: "Then just for an instant while Piglett is jotting down his number Muhlbach becomes the most important person in the room. People turn around to contemplate him" (p. 103).

Muhlbach later learns that the mask he bought is not authentic, but for a brief moment he revels in the envy he imagines himself to be provoking among the bidders whom he believes he has bested. There is a special moment of pride because, unlike ordinary purchasing with fixed prices and large supplies, money alone is not enough to acquire collectibles in competition with others. Collectible objects are not only luxuries, they are almost by definition rare or difficult to assemble. The collector must be shrewder, quicker, more knowledgeable, more discerning, more diligent, or simply luckier than other collectors in order to be successful. Moreover the auction is a ritual that may turn commodities into sacred collectibles, as Smith explains:

> a record sale of a horse at Keeneland or a masterpiece at Sotheby's will nearly always be followed by applause. In fact, whenever an item sells for considerably more than its apparent economic value there is likely to be applause. A new "reality" has been created. Be it a high price for the footstool made for Rock Hudson by Elizabeth Taylor or a record price for an old duck decoy, the audience realizes that they have seen a mundane item transformed into a valuable social object.
>
> (Smith 1989, p. 129)

The profane object for sale has become part of a sacred collection where it is above price. Indeed, the collector's having just paid "too much" for it may demonstrate this as well as contribute to the sacralization.

Although the competition of collecting takes place within a more delimited realm than overall consumption, it is still a materialistic pursuit. Materialism has been defined as: "The importance a consumer attaches to worldly possessions. At the highest levels of materialism, such possessions assume a central place in a person's life and are believed to provide the greatest sources of satisfaction and dissatisfaction in life" (Belk 1985, p. 265). As specified in the earlier definition of collecting (p. 67), collectors are acquisitive, possessive, and passionately involved with the objects collected. These are the factors normally thought to comprise materialism (Belk 1985; Richins and Dawson 1992). As Danto (1981) observes with regard to art collecting: "the history of taste and the history of acquisitiveness run pretty much together, and men are pleased enough to claim ownership of the beauties of the world. Indeed, attempting to possess may be one form of aesthetic response, as laughter is of the sense of humor" (p. 93). The centrality of collected objects to the lives of some collectors is seen in Balzac's *Cousin Pons*, Connell's *The Connoisseur* (1974), and Chatwin's *Utz* (1989). Utz begins collecting ("rescuing" in his view) Meissen porcelain in communist Czechoslovakia after his grandmother has attempted to console him following the death of his father by giving him one of her Meissen figures that he had admired. He subsequently decides to devote his life to "saving" these objects and observes in a book he writes entitled *The Private Collector* that, "private ownership confers on the owner the right and the need to touch. As a young child will reach out to handle the thing it names, so the passionate collector, his eye in harmony with his hand, restores to the object the life-giving touch of its maker" (Chatwin 1989, p. 20). If there is an allusion to playing God here, perhaps it is apt. The collector as the creator of the collection assumes the role of possessor, controller, and sometimes savior of the objects collected. For while consumers can almost always control what they own and possess, collectors who possess an interrelated set of objects control a "little world." Just as the *Wunderkammer* was intended to order, grasp, and control the world, so too are many if not all collections. Clifford observes of children's collections that:

> a boy's accumulation of miniature cars, a girl's dolls, a summer-vacation "nature museum" (with labeled stones and shells, a hummingbird in a bottle), a treasured bowl filled with bright shavings of crayons. In these small rituals we observe the channelings of obsession, an exercise in how to make the world one's own, to gather things around oneself tastefully, appropriately.
>
> (Clifford 1990, p. 143)

Grasskamp (1983) too notes that "the model railway ... can count on arousing those cozy feelings which any miniature triggers off in the observer" (p. 144). Stewart's (1984) insightful analysis of the miniature suggests that it partakes of the diminutive world of childhood. A prime childhood example is the dollhouse which allows manipulation of time, space, and activity in this "homemade universe" (Stewart 1984, p. 163). By providing physical control of the objects in a collection, the "illusion of control" (Breckenridge 1989) of broader physical domains, people, and knowledge may occur. The collection may provide its owner with an omnipotent sense of mastery. This helps to explain why miniatures and toys are such popular collectibles. It also helps to explain why collectors often resent well-intended gifts of objects for the collection offered by friends and family (Belk *et al.* 1991, p. 200; Muensterberger 1994, p. 236). For in such gifts, the collector is deprived of the selective control normally exercised over the objects that enter the collection.

If collecting is consumption, it follows that one important form of acquisition (besides auctions) is shopping. Saarinen (1958) said of J. P. Morgan, "He collected because he enjoyed shopping" (p. 76), and Marquis (1991) notes that "For many collectors today, buying art is just a glorified form of shopping" (p. 200). With the commoditization of collecting markets (e.g., Butsch 1984; Gelber 1992), manufactured objects join art and objects of nature in the collector's treasure hunt. Thus may a bookstore resemble a *"fairy gold mine"* to the bibliophile (Jackson 1989, p. 469). Walter Benjamin (1968b) argues that "The purchasing done by a book collector has very little in common with that done in a bookshop by a student getting a textbook, a man of the world buying a present for his lady, or a businessman intending to while away his next train journey" (pp. 62–63).What he is saying is not that book collectors do not shop, but that those who purchase books for their normal use – to read them – shop far more casually and less passionately than the collector. Marquis (1991) describes how art collectors Eugene and Barbara Schwartz spend all of each Saturday combing thirty New York galleries for new acquisitions, hiring a car because they can't move fast enough in a cab and grabbing a quick sandwich for lunch between purchases. Although his collection was broader and more eclectic, Andy Warhol was a similar collector. Jed Johnson described his pattern:

> They say that the biggest pleasure a compulsive gambler has is gambling and winning, and that his *second* greatest pleasure is gambling and losing. In other words, the thrill isn't in the winning *or* in the losing – it's in the *action*. Andy's collecting was all about that same thing: more than anything, he was in it for the action. Before I realized this, I'd ask him why he bothered to buy twenty little things instead of one big one for the same price. The answer should have been obvious to me – one big thing would have required less shopping, less action. He shopped for two or three hours a day for as many years as I can remember. He started buying American Indian artifacts first because he lived around the corner from a store that had great things that were relatively cheap; he continued to buy them until he died. He bought Americana then, too, because he loved everything he saw at Serendipity, his old haunt from the fifties, on East 60th Street – the Tiffany lamps, the carousel horses, the Punches, and old trade signs that helped propel him toward Pop insights. After that he bought primitive portraits and country painted furniture, then high-style painted furniture. Then on to Federal furniture in 1974 after he bought a Georgian-style townhouse.
>
> (Johnson 1988, n.p.n.)

Similarly, Stuart Pivar recalled:

> Andy Warhol loved to buy art. We used to go shopping for it together for a few hours practically every day in the past couple of years. He bought many, many things. After discussion and planning by phone in the morning we would set out around 11 o'clock. I would usually pick him up or we would meet at a gallery. He often brought a stack of *Interviews*, which he gave away as we went along. There was a lot of ground to cover. It included Madison Avenue and Fifty-Seventh Street galleries, the antique shows as well as the auction exhibitions at Sotheby's, Christie's, Christie's East, Phillips, Doyle's, Manhattan Galleries, and even Lubin's. Every Sunday I used to pick up Andy at

Church and we spent the day at the flea markets at Twenty-Sixth Street and the one on Columbus Avenue.

(Pivar 1988, n.p.n.)

These excerpts are from the six-volume catalogue published by Sotheby's for the two-day sale of over 6,000 pieces Andy Warhol collected over three decades (Kaylan 1988). It is the collection of a Type B aesthetic collector who bought anything that struck his fancy in a number of collecting areas, despite advice from friends. He was an unapologetic bricoleur and his collection is one of trash among the treasures. As Kaylan concludes, his apparent intent was to make us re-examine both types of objects, and question which is trash and which is treasure. Of course Warhol played a large part in the Pop Art movement which paid either reverent or critical homage to consumer brands. Here too his effect has been to make us re-examine the nature of art and the nature of consumer commodities.

The sort of shopping that collectors do is as far as it can possibly be from being an odious task. It is instead a treasure-hunt, an adventure, a quest, and a delight. As Lehrer describes this quest:

> all our car trips down country lanes and "blue" highways are treasure hunts. . . . Envy us because every mail delivery has the potential for having the note about or Polaroid shot of an item we have been looking for desperately. . . . Envy the adventures we have while on The Hunt. . . . But mostly envy us for the Thrill of The Find.
>
> (Lehrer 1990, p. 58)

Often the concentration on finding treasures is intense. Sigmund Freud, a prolific collector of antiquities (see Belk *et al.* 1991), described in *The Psychopathology of Everyday Life* (1914) how he would misread even vaguely similar signs above shops in foreign cities as proclaiming "antiquities," and observed that "this displays the questing spirit of the collector" (pp. 119–120). Such a preoccupation with buying oneself things for the collection might well be considered a selfish indulgence. It is, but it is one that is generally condoned because it occurs within the socially constructed realm Stebbins (1982) labeled "serious leisure." Herrmann sees collectors who engage in such pursuits as saviors:

> Collecting is a form of self indulgence, but by and large it is a beneficial one. Probably the simplest differentiation between the dabbler and the genuine collector is that the latter has stilled once and for all any inhibition against spending money on the inanimate objects of his choice. Once this resolute state of mind has been reached and some money is available, progress is assured. The preservation of many of the world's greatest works of art in the face of deliberate destruction, contempt or neglect has been due to the collector's acquisitive urge,

the quest for beauty, the indulgence of taste and the desire for association and continuity with the past.

(Herrmann 1972, p. 22)

A related line of argument, also applied to defenses of wealth in general
(Belk 1983), is that collectors are stewards of treasures that are only
temporarily theirs. As Herrmann (1972) goes on to note, "Works of art are
permanent (or nearly so!): collectors come and go" (p. 22). Justifications
aside, the continual purchase of things for the collection is an acquisitive
self-indulgence that Mick and DeMoss (1990) have insightfully labeled
"self-gifts." On more than one occasion Sigmund Freud wrote of his collecting this way. For instance, he wrote to a colleague that "I got myself
an expensive present today, a lovely little dipylon vase – a real gem – to
fight my ill humor" (Dudar 1990). Despite the justifications, a number of
the collectors I have interviewed feel some guilt about these purchases and
some routinely hide purchases from their spouses and families. One collector, a man of 48, had accumulated an entire double garage full of metal
toy vehicles largely without his wife's knowledge. While this is an extreme
case, the secrecy and guilt parallel findings in the literature on compulsive
shopping (O'Guinn and Faber 1989). Such compulsions and obsessions in
collecting are considered further in the concluding chapter.

Another aspect of consumption that is evident in collecting is the development of desire and longing for specific material things. As a book
collector describes this longing in his childhood butterfly collecting, the
passion that defines collecting is most evident:

> After forty years I can still feel my hot anxiety as a "new" butterfly
> sailed into view, darted off over the warm summer fields, and finally
> came to rest, opening and closing its wings. This is what collecting is
> – the all but unbearable excitement when the longed-for quarry
> appears, the fierce and crafty pursuit ... [the acquisition and
> mounting], the admiring and (supreme felicity) envious visitors.

(Lewis 1946, p. 8)

Nor has this excitement declined for Lewis in forty years of collecting, for
he goes on to describe his discovery of a provincial bookstore with three
fellow book-collector friends:

> The four of us started up the narrow stairs. On the landing I picked off
> the shelves what I took to be a first edition of *Maud*. Beside it was a first
> edition of the *Idylls of the King*. The other three made equally sensational
> discoveries. Sinbad in the cave of diamonds was not more dazzled.

(Lewis 1946, p. 12)

This desire is often manifest as a "have to have it" feeling on encountering
the desired object, whether in person, or via a catalogue, or based simply

on hearing about it. One woman of 45 described this feeling to me and its consummation:

> A few weeks ago I was at a show and one of the dealers brought in a lifesize bronze of a dog – a lifesize head of a hunting dog – and I collect bronzes. And as she walked in I just walked past her and said, "How much is it?" And she gave me the price and I bought it. I never asked if she could do better. It was just, it HAD to be mine!

Collectors, even of mass-produced goods, value rarity in collected objects because it provides both more challenge and a greater feeling of accomplishment and higher status within the circle of collectors of similar objects. Accordingly, there is an even greater feeling than with normal shopping that if the collector does not seize the object when it is first encountered, it will later be irretrievably gone, most likely to a competing collector. For this reason, the urge toward immediate gratification of desires is especially strong among collectors.

There is perhaps a deeper ritualism in acquiring and possessing objects for a collection than ordinary products of use. In acquisition, in the prowling of art galleries by the Schwartzs, and of antique shops, auction houses, and flea markets by Warhol, there is a quality of sacred ritualism intended to divine treasures. There are ritual protocols within each of these sites as well. Katriel (1988/89) discusses a number of elements in the exchange rituals of Israeli child card collectors, including opening ritual phrases, the use of referees, and the recitation of "magical" phrases to make the trade revocable or irrevocable. And once the object is acquired the owner must perform the alchemy of transforming it into a part of the collection. These "possession rituals" (McCracken 1988) may again be deeper and more elaborate than those required for ordinary possessions. The bibliophile Barton Currie (1931) described his post-purchase actions in this way:

> You come out of a bookstore carrying a first edition of something or other. You cannot explain how or why you got it, or what you paid for it. But you have it; and when you arrive home with it you creep off to some secluded room to examine it. Then occurs the first little burning exaltation. Just a little glow to begin with, then by infinite gradations a consuming fire.
>
> (quoted in Rigby and Rigby 1944, p. 317)

For Freud, possession rituals involved first bringing his beloved antique statuettes to the dining-room table so he could admire them during his meal (Jones 1955). They were then moved to his consultation room and office which was crowded with such figures (see Gamwell and Wells 1989; Engelman 1976). He would often hold, examine, and fondle the pieces as he consulted with patients (Sachs 1945). And he would greet his favorite pieces with a "Good morning" as he began the day (Spector 1975).

As Freud's morning greeting to his favorite collected objects suggests, we sometimes further our passionate involvement with these objects by anthropomorphizing them. For Carl Jung, the anthropomorphized object was instead books, as he explained in *Nietzsche's Zarathustra*:

> Objects lie about heavily. They have no legs or wings, and people are often quite impatient with them. For instance, this book would like it very much better, I am sure, if it were lying near the centre of the table where it is safe, but I have put it on the edge. It is an awkward position for that poor creature of a book. It may fall down and get injured. If I am impatient, if I touch them in an awkward way, it is a lamentable plight for the poor objects. Then they take revenge on me. Because I ill treat them, they turn against me and become contradictory in a peculiar way.
>
> (quoted in Watson 1990, pp. 112–113)

The revenge of things is also seen in Guy de Maupassant's story "*Qui Sait?*" and Henry James's novel *The Spoils of Poynton*, in which maligned antiques turn on their owners (Tintner 1984). We see once again the "little world" of collectibles made as animate as toy soldiers, but without the proper rituals the objects in this world are no longer controlled but controllers. Chapter Five will suggest an explanation via the concept of fetishism.

Utz too (Chatwin 1989) anthropomorphizes his porcelains and treats them as respected "dwarfs." Watson explains the proper anthropomorphic care of books by collectors, based on their status not as dwarfs but as children:

> Books are children, and owners possessive parents who hate to be parted from their offspring. They decorate their charges with proprietary plates and exhortations to others to treat them well and send them home soon. Some owners cannot bear even to have their books touched by other people. There is horror when books are burnt and outrage at their defacement. ... The greatest sanctity is accorded to manuscripts. Next in the holy hierarchy are first editions signed, or better still once owned, by the author.
>
> (Watson 1990, p. 113)

For similar reasons, some overly protective librarians see it as their job not to provide public access to books, but rather to safeguard books from the public. Another feature of anthropomorphizing collected objects may be to name them. Thus among the two dozen automobile collectors I have interviewed, their much loved automobiles are often given names such as "My Cheree," "Candy," and "Shot Through the Heart," or referred to as "my baby" and "my child." Naming collected objects like vehicles, dolls, and weapons is a way of further individualizing, singularizing, and decommoditizing them (Appadurai 1986; Rogan 1990). A famous scene described by Clark (1963) recounts the dying Cardinal Mazarin "stumbling unobserved through his picture gallery and saying good-bye to Correggio's *Antiope*, Titian's *Venus* and Carracci's '*incomparable Déluge*.' '*Adieu chers tableaux que j'ai tant aimés*'" (p. 15). When we anthropomorphize collected objects we animate our regard for these objects so that a person–thing relationship becomes a person–person relationship. Furthermore naming, like touching or shedding blood upon something, is a possession ritual by which something is made more truly ours (Beaglehole 1932; Belk 1988a; McCracken 1988). Here too, as Chapter Five suggests, there may be an indication of fetishism.

Guilt and innocence in collectors' materialism

In two studies of collectors I completed with colleagues (Belk *et al.* 1988; Belk *et al.* 1991), we argued that collecting is socially sanctioned as a legitimate and worthwhile activity which provides collectors with a noble sense of purpose. Depending on the type of collection, we said, collecting even of such mundane objects as Mickey Mouse characters, magazine advertisements, comic books, or elephant replicas, can make collectors feel that they are part of a great tradition and are contributing in a small way to either art or science. Clifford (1985) sees the collection as a means of transforming "an excessive, sometimes even rapacious need to **have** ... into rule-governed meaningful desire" (p. 238), while Meyer (1973) sees the legitimization as stemming from a feeling that as collectors we are gathering and preserving valuable objects as "mankind's agent" (p. 187). Rehmus (1988) believes that collecting is such a good sign of a wide-ranging passionate intellect that it should supersede the Medical College Admission Test. When bibliophile Hence Bodley was besieged with requests to help the poor, infirm, widows, and orphans in the impoverished year of 1597 in London, he rebuffed them by arguing that "The preservation of the vital thoughts of great men who had gone before, of transmitting their thoughts to future generations [is] of greater value to the state and to mankind in general than charities that might appeal to other men" (Wright and Ray 1969, p. 14). But Brook (1980, p. 12) suggests that book collectors, like stamp collectors (e.g., Moskoff 1990), have been too ready to rationalize their collecting on the basis of the knowledge it provides, when the **pleasure** in collecting is their real motivation and should be reason enough. The existence of collecting communities and clubs also provides a self-justifying social nexus to sanction collecting activity. However, as the surreptitious accumulation of collectibles hidden from family and spouse suggests, collecting is still not always guilt-free. Secrecy implies that the collection has become a fetish, Stewart (1984, p. 163) suggests.

Fear of the bald indulgence and playfulness of collecting may account for the decline in the incidence of collecting after childhood. Gelber (1992) suggests that the stigma of childishness has helped make adult stamp collectors cling to notions of taxonomy in order to cloak themselves in the mantle of science and serious work-like activity. At the Collector's Club in New York, a commonly castigated subgroup of members comprised those who collect "topicals" such as stamps with butterflies or purple stamps. Such collectors were inevitably characterized as women and children. At the other end of the spectrum of respectability within the club were those with a highly academic interest in postal history. To be a respected collector of postal history one should be able to read several languages and trace developments in postal history, writing up discoveries in scholarly articles. The hierarchy that seems to exist in this traditional club (founded 1896 with a limited membership of less than 1,000 drawn from around the world) is not entirely parallel to the "seven ages of stamp collectors" suggested by Bryant (1989), but shares the criteria of specialization and scholarliness with his distinctions. Even in painting Moulin (1987) notes that there are degrees of legitimacy with the minimum cutoff being art versus craft and non-art. Within "art" there are paintings of the past consecrated by history and contemporary paintings which are not. Old masters are the blue-chip stocks, with other types of paintings arrayed in descending orders of legitimacy. Across types of collections, hierarchies of acceptability seem to be based on how adult, serious, and scholarly or scientific the collection is seen to be. Collections such as those of paper matches and brands of pins have been dismissed as "meaningless oddments" (Gelber 1991, p. 748). One book collector observed, "Most book collectors I have known or have known about have graduated to books from a brief preoccupation with lower forms of collectibles, such as stamps and coins" (Mathews 1991, p. 329). And if stamp and coin collectors object to such derogation, book collectors offer other comparisons in areas of collecting where a scholarly interest in the subject matter is more difficult to contemplate:

> The real justification of the book-collector in society, the thing that allows him to feel a bit superior to the collector of tram-tickets or matchbox labels, is that he is forming a collection that may be of real value to the scholar of the future.
>
> (Brook 1980, p. 11)

By implication, the argument is that collectors of tram tickets and matchbox labels are engaging in a wholly self-indulgent pursuit, while book collectors are performing a valuable service for future generations by creating their collections.

Guilt about collecting is often cast in religious terms. Dealers and others "tempt" collectors with their offerings (Muensterberger 1994, p. 135). Various sins might be freely admitted by collectors, since in the contemporary secular world sin seems to have lost much of its former sting

(Menninger 1973). For instance, Brook attributes the following sins to himself and fellow book collectors:

> it is well to look for a moment at the Seven Deadly Sins in relation to book-collecting. The chief of them is Pride, and is there any collector who can say that he is not proud of his collection? Then there is Avarice. Well, avarice is the whole point of collecting: the collector hoards books as the miser hoards gold. And his activities are not far removed from Gluttony; the glutton demands an excess of food for the body whereas the book-collector demands an excess of food for the mind. Wrath is the sin that you indulge in when the book for which you have sent in a bid at an auction sale is knocked down to a higher bidder. As for Envy, I indulge in that sin freely whenever I see the books of another collec-tor. It may seem that the book-collector is not guilty of Luxuria, or Lust, but many collectors are attracted by the large class of books which the Bodleian Library, permitting itself an erudite pun, classifies under the Greek letter *phi* or which booksellers describe as "curious" and keep on a shelf well within their line of vision. As for Accidie or Sloth, what else is it that causes a collector to refuse to dust his books? We can only hope that book-collecting may act as a sublimation of these various undesirable impulses. If we did not collect books we might be doing something else even more socially reprehensible.
>
> (Brook 1980, pp. 23–24)

Of this list of medieval sins, four seem clearly to be related to materialism: pride, avarice, gluttony, and envy (Belk 1983). Even if modern sin has lost some of its former sting, these are hardly considered virtuous traits.

How then to excuse, atone for, or expiate such sin? Four means seem common to collectors. The first is to blame it on human nature by invok-ing the collecting instinct or an acquisitive urge that is supposed to be basic and unavoidable. In this rationalization the collector acknowledges the acquisitiveness but sees it as natural. As Eccles argues:

> private ownership of works of art begins with the need to satisfy in some way or other the acquisitive instinct which is implanted in us at birth. What does the exercise of this instinct feel like to a man engaged in collecting? I have compared my experience with that of friends, and we agree that when we buy something the purchase makes us feel better, more secure, and in some way enlarges our personality. If we are asked why we bought this porcelain figure or that modern paint-ing, we reply that we simply had to have it. We were hungry and had to eat. We gave way to the acquisitive instinct which is in every man.
>
> (Eccles 1968, pp. 2–3)

Pavlov (1928) and Humphrey (1979) argued that the collecting instinct is biologically programmed because the ability to classify and distinguish things had a survival advantage in early food-gathering behavior. Others go farther. Mathews (1991) contends that "It is well documented that the instinct to collect is a very common positive sign of high intelligence in children," and contends that Charles Darwin's childhood collecting of beetles was indicative of his eventual greatness as a scientist. However, instinct theory does not fare well these days. Danto (1991) observes that not all cultures have "serious collectors." Beaglehole (1932, p. 281) dismisses animal analogies and the acquisitive or collecting instinct in favor of a more social and learned model channeling "the primitive impulse to grasp" into conformity with group values. In this way Beaglehole links collecting with fundamental needs, while allowing a variety of collecting or non-collecting behaviors depending on socialization and the environment.

A second defense against the guilty feeling that collecting is somehow a sinful self-indulgence is the previously mentioned tendency to cite the rational economic motive of investment. Price (1989) notes that besides claiming to collect "primitive" art as an adjunct to art or science, a number of collectors claim to do so for material gain: "the wish to employ Primitive Art for personal financial profit is, if not the loftiest of Man's motivating drives, at least a supremely understandable and acceptable one" (p. 77). This is a motive that might seem more plausible for collectors of certain types of objects such as coins or fine art, but I have heard it from collectors of beer cans, comic books, and fiesta ware as well. Even wine collectors who plan to eventually consume their collection commonly talk about the shrewd bargains they achieved in buying a wine which has escalated in price since it was young and unappreciated. It would appear, however, that most claims of investments in collections are an unfounded excuse for collecting. As Naifeh observes of collectors of New York art:

> Many collectors, perhaps most collectors, who expressed an interest in the investment value of their collections – perhaps most such collectors – would never sell a single item. Investment was a rationale, a practical excuse used by collectors to justify spending large sums of money on an indulgent pastime to individuals who did not possess the collector's urge. If the collector felt uneasy personally about devoting so much money to art, he could also use the rationale of investment to justify collecting to himself.
>
> (Naifeh 1976, p. 113)

Reitlinger (1970) concluded that "most of those who spend upwards of £20,000 on a single object or picture are not investors at all but buyers of prestige symbols and sometimes buyers of public honours as well through their ultimate benefactions, aided by various forms of tax relief" (p. 15). Similarly, Alsop (1982, p. 71) observes that it is easy to forget the essential irrationality of human collecting simply because striving for profit seems such a purposeful and understandable goal. Nevertheless, making money is anathema within most collecting circles because it leads to the charge that someone is "only in it for the money," and is thus not a sincere, devoted, passionate collector. Gelber (1991, pp. 756–757) also notes that a number of collectors who have the opportunity to earn money from their collection or collecting expertise refuse any compensation for fear that it would turn their hobby into a job and thereby erase the boundary they have drawn between work, which they do because they must, and leisure, which they pursue because it brings them pleasure. In psychological terms, they fear that over-emphasizing an extrinsic rationale for their behavior will demean or diminish the intrinsic pleasure that their collecting behavior now brings (e.g., Deci 1971). They will no longer be able to tell themselves that the only reason they collect is because it brings them joy. Nevertheless, in a consumer society in which many have come to measure success in material terms, the total estimated monetary value of a collection is a way for collectors to "keep score" or monitor growth and progress, even though they may well have no intention or even a possibility of selling the collection.

A third means to justify the self-indulgence of collecting is related to the instinctive justification, but uses the medical vocabulary of disease. This is a very commonly offered denial of responsibility that shares something with the drunk's claim of alcoholism or the obsessive gambler's claim of addiction, but with less social stigma presumably attached. Thus those who openly confess to "bibliomania," for instance (e.g., Flaubert 1836 [1954a]; Jackson 1989; Paton 1988), do not expect opprobrium of the sort offered in clinical treatments of "collector's mania" like this one:

> The collector's mania is a symptom found in conditions of weakening mental faculties, most often senility. It consists of a compulsive, panic collecting of many different objects. . . . It is very characteristic that the collector cannot bring himself to make use of the collected items, or to part with them . . . take away the treasures from the collector, he will get worked up into a state of affect, anxiety and desperation. . . . Cupidity and the collecting mania, as well as prodigality, have their correlating determinants in the infantile attitude toward feces.
>
> (Jensen 1963, p. 606)

Similarly in a 1921 paper Dr. Henri Codet concluded that both the miser and the collector suffer from "omniomania" and share "the same urge for possession, the same tendency to amass quantity" (quoted in Rheims 1961, p. 33). But rather than extreme anal retentiveness or anal expulsiveness, what is meant when collectors like Joseph Hirshhorn said "I have a madman's rage for art" or when Jacques Lipchitz said "Collecting is an illness with me" is that they have gone beyond mere passion and are possessed by the objects of their desire (Brough 1963, p. 119). Hirshhorn amassed thousands of paintings and sculptures and observed, "If you see a piece that you really like ... it hits you in the brain, and in my case, I've got to buy it" (ibid, p. 135). Other collectors use terms like "addicted," "magazinaholic," "rockpox" (chronic rock collecting), "collecting bug," "timbromania" (chronic stamp collecting), "craziness," "antique fever," "nuts," "print junkie," "Deadhead" (traveling to as many Grateful Dead concerts as possible and swapping their concert tapes), or "hooked" to describe their "afflictions." For if one is sick, bizarre collecting behaviors can be defined, only partly tongue in cheek, as being the result of forces outside of the collector's control to which they have unfortunately fallen victim. As one art collector explained:

> I labour under a very serious affliction ... I have all Callot's etchings, except one, which to tell the truth, so far from being the best, is the worst he ever did, but which would complete my collection; I have hunted after this print these twenty years, and now I despair of ever getting it; it is very trying.
>
> (Assendorf 1993, p. 51)

The passion that collectors direct toward the objects they collect means that they appear to be more prone to obsessive behaviors toward things than is the case in everyday consumption (Tuchman 1994). Nevertheless, most collectors do not appear to exhibit true obsession, compulsion, or addiction. The final chapter considers this issue further in offering an assessment of the social desirability of collecting.

The fourth rationalization often used by collectors to assuage the guilt of self-indulgent acquisitiveness is one that portrays the collector as a savior of lost, neglected, or endangered objects. This goes beyond the ennoblement of collecting as participating in art or science in that it makes the objects (and later presumably a grateful world) the benefactors of heroic efforts by collectors with the foresight, diligence, and cleverness to rescue objects from certain danger or oblivion. Eisenberg presents a portrait of an heroic New York record collector, Clarence:

> In capitalism there are first heroes of production and then (as Riesman has shown) heroes of consumption. These are people who spend on an heroic scale, perhaps, or with heroic discrimination. The collector may be heroic in either of these ways, but the true collector's heroism is closer to the ancient model. It is exploit, the dauntless and cunning overcoming of obstacles in pursuit of the prize. The prize itself is secondary to the pursuit (if this is true of men generally, as Pascal thought, it is truer of heroes). Clarence's collecting is of this heroic type. His eagerness to share his collection, which at first seems to contradict the whole idea of acquisition, is just the openhandedness of the hero who, having pulled off his exploit, is free with the proceeds.

Clarence will lend records out or give them away, but never sell one – imagine Menelaus selling the spoils of Troy!

(Eisenberg 1987, p. 18)

Assendorf (1993) too sees the sacrifice of the collector for the collection as his or her ennobling and redeeming feature. While most collectors are less generous with and more possessive of their collected treasures than Clarence, they may still convince themselves that the public will ultimately benefit from their collecting. Both Saarinen (1958) and Baekeland (1981) note that John D. Rockefeller, Jr. was such a collector:

Collecting may be an allowable pleasure for a person who finds it hard to indulge himself. . . . A famous example of this kind of collector was John D. Rockefeller, Jr., who gave the Cloisters to the Metropolitan Museum of Art. . . . He was especially fond of jewels. Collecting art was the closest he would allow himself to come to self-indulgence. He justified buying it on the grounds that the works of art would eventually go to a museum. When buying for himself as opposed to the Cloisters, he was often cautious and guilt ridden.

(Baekeland 1981, p. 53)

In an argument paralleling the New Testament doctrine of stewardship of wealth, Andrew Carnegie suggested that:

It is well, nay, essential for the progress of the race, that the houses of some should be homes for all that is highest and best in literature and the arts, and for all the refinements of civilization rather than that none should be so. Much better this great irregularity than universal squalor.

(Carnegie 1889, p. 653)

With the exception of the fine art and literature they might preserve, Carnegie argued that the wealthy should live simply and bequeath virtually all of what they gain to the public. Many less wealthy collectors also see their collections as part of a mission to save and preserve, as with one collector interviewed by Kron:

"I'm a rescue service," said Lillian Williams. "It's gratifying to find things in disrepair and then breathe life into them. I am a custodian. I have an obligation to restore things and put them in good hands." Whether or not she gets pleasure from rescuing because she still feels remorse for breaking one of her mother's antique dolls when she was five, she doesn't feel like the *owner* of her things, just the conservator. "I have chairs that are demented and twisted and broken and legless and they've all been restored because my husband and I are fanatical about restoring things. And restoring them correctly. . . . I am always desperate to find homes for my things; they're orphans, abandoned, lost. And our house is the orphanage."

(Kron 1983, p. 200)

A similar metaphor was used by a woman I interviewed who collected dolls. Besides her own collection she ran a "doll hospital" to help rehabilitate others' dolls with spare parts she had gathered in her collecting. While seeing oneself as a savior of lost objects is a rationalization for collecting, it also partakes in a broader romantic pattern of true selfless dedication in some extreme collectors. This is a pattern that is explored further in the concluding chapter.

WHY COLLECT?

If at least one-third of those in affluent nations collect something, it is likely that no single motivation will explain such a widespread phenomenon and that no single means of deriving pleasure from collecting will pertain to all collectors and all types of collectibles. Something of the range of possibilities is illustrated by these brief sketches of a half-dozen very different collectors.

Per's beer cans

Per is a 60-year-old Swedish dentist and collector of beer cans. He began collecting fifteen years ago when his wife complained about the clutter in their house of empty cans from the beer he had consumed. He told her beer cans were beautiful and decided to demonstrate this by collecting them. His specialty is Scandinavian beer cans, but he also has an international collection from eighty-six different countries. Some of the international cans are from his travels, but most are obtained by trading with other collectors. His collection consists of 3,000 cans and he says that it is quite a small collection. He drinks most of the beer from the cans that he gets new, but some are just poured down the sink. He belongs to the Beer Can Collectors of America club and has attended six of their international "Canventions," and set up displays of a portion of his collection at five of these shows. He is proud to have received two first places and two second places in the "type and brand" category (one of eight areas in which exhibiters compete). His wife eventually became very supportive of his collection, but she died four years ago. Since that time Per has become even more involved in his collection and says that his best friends are those whom he has met in these activities. Because there are only 140 or 150 beer can collectors in Sweden, most of these friends live in other countries, especially the U.S. and Canada which he tries to visit each year at Canvention time.

Mickey's nutcrackers

Mickey is the 50-year-old wife of an American stockbroker and has collected 350 nutcrackers in the past fourteen years. Her fascination with nutcrackers began at a Christmas party at the house of a friend who had half a dozen nutcrackers on display. On a trip to San Francisco that New Year's she bought several nutcrackers she found for sale and the collection was launched. It is stored on custom teakwood shelves along the walls of what was once her daughter's bedroom in her home in a fashionable suburb of a western city. The collection is arranged thematically by character's occupation, size, color, and type (e.g., handcarved). She once collected more indiscriminately but now concentrates on two exclusive and expensive German brands of nutcrackers. A local dealer assured Mickey that hers is the largest collection in the state, although one other collector has 300 nutcrackers. She knows no other nutcracker collectors personally. Besides buying locally, many of her pieces have been acquired on trips, including one to Germany and one to East Africa. Friends and family help and bring her nutcrackers from their travels, but it is hard for them to know what she has and wants. On the bottom of each piece Mickey notes the date and place of acquisition, as well as the price paid. Once a piece enters the collection it never leaves and she would never consider using one of them to crack nuts. She now buys 20 to 25 nutcrackers each year and laughingly suggested that she might have to get a job to "support my habit." Eventually she would like to donate the collection to a museum, but realizes that "It's an art form, but not to that degree; not like a collection of paintings."

Walter's art

Walter recently retired at 65 and moved from his 5,000-square-foot California home into a 1600-square-foot apartment in an upscale urban neighborhood. While he and his wife had to get rid of much of their furniture, he never thought of diminishing his collection of paintings, ivory, jade, netsukes, and oriental furnishings. He collected a few block prints when he was in Japan with the U.S. military following World War II and when he later spent three years there as an attorney specializing in international trade. He also has some paintings and porcelain that he inherited from his mother. But the biggest inspiration for his collecting is an uncle who recently donated a five-million-dollar portion of his jade and ivory collection to a local university. Walter's own jade and ivory pieces are displayed in an eight-foot-wide floor-to-ceiling glass display case with dramatic spotlighting, located in his living room. He lovingly and knowledgably explains different types of jade and design and carving techniques. His art also includes Chinese and Japanese paintings and screens, and several prominent paintings, including a Courbet that is too valuable to keep in the apartment. He is now hoping to buy some of his uncle's remaining ivories and jades which he is liquidating. He would also like to buy more Japanese block prints that a friend is selling from his collection. Otherwise he has mostly relied on New York dealers for his purchases. Although his six children's collecting interests are different from his own, they have indicated their preferences for various pieces and the allocation of his art collection is specified in his will.

Jeff's tattoos

Jeff, a 30-year-old American university chemistry instructor, keeps his art collection in a different place: on his body. As with a number of other owners of multiple tattoos (Sanders 1989), Jeff views his tattoos as a collection. His initial impetus came from peer pressure and a friend who had a tattoo. Also,

> it's a BAD GUY image – a MAVERICK image – someone trying to break the mold of accepted things to do with your body. And I guess I went into there with the idea of getting one tattoo. It was kinda neat, but it looked lonely out there. It didn't look right having [just] one.

He had the initial tattoo placed high on one shoulder. It was an image of a samurai warrior, which he found artistically appealing and symbolic of his interest in martial arts. He soon got a tiger on the other shoulder and slowly began to build his collection with mountains and "oriental" scenery linking the two tattoos across his back. "Then after a while the background started unfolding – a canvas – and pretty soon everything started to look congruent." He is proud that the tattooer, who became his friend, has been placed first and second in tattoo contests. Jeff has been getting tattooed for four years now and plans to continue, perhaps with a penis tattoo. He explains that,

> I've always been different. I had long hair when it was not really accepted. Eventually I cut it off. I hate being categorized. I never really fit a mold. I was doing way-out things, but then again I was a straight "A" student. People could not reconcile that and that was just fine. I don't like fitting people's molds.

He says he is happy with his body and the tattoos are not compensatory. His wife admires them and his two young daughters seem to think tattoos are normal. The tattoos do not show when he is wearing a shirt, so many people are not aware of them. He does feel a bond, though, with others who have tattoos.

Robert's wines

Fifty-year-old Robert is a New Zealander who also has a university teaching position. His collection of several hundred bottles of New Zealand and

Australian wines was once much larger, but to his regret, he drank it down to a small size. He says he feels a sense of personal diminishment when the collection becomes smaller and he would like to build it back to the point where he has enough to consume a bottle a day for the rest of his life (he expects to live to be 80). He has several friends who also collect and he started a wine club with several of them and edited their newsletter. He has also been in wine-tasting competitions and enjoys telling stories about his adventures and expertise in these tastings. He has visited wineries on three continents and has a remarkable memory for details of particular wines and experiences with them. Although he laments the shrinkage of his collection, he enjoys recalling stories of both acquisition (putting away wines that are undervalued and watching them appreciate) and consumption (recalling when each special bottle was consumed, on what special occasion, and with what special friends). This non-ordinary use of the wines he collects keeps his consumable collection within the definition of collecting as involving, in part, removing things from ordinary use. He has also had several other collections as an adult. He shared an interest in ornamental horticulture with his now deceased father and is proud of the success of the exotic plants he has grown in his suburban yard, often to the surprise of friends and neighbors. He knows the plants' Latin names and acquired most of them after having his house built several years ago. He also once had a collection of seven race horses which he is quite proud of having bred and raced successfully in partnership with several friends. He tells of beginning by studying stud books of Australian and American race horses and deriving a breeding theory. When his best horse had to be put down, the pain caused him to sell the other horses, although he still enjoys relating stories of his horses' success. A final collection about which he is more secretive is his extra-marital affairs. He can count nearly two dozen in recent years with his most recent passion being Asian women. While his regard for these women as a collection may seem a dehumanizing objectivization, he speaks of both them and his wines, plants, and horses lovingly and can relate moving stories about each. Thus, with the exception of ornamental plants (which are tangible but also grow and change), Robert has emphasized experiences in his collecting more than tangible objects.

Michael's postal-history collection

Michael is a 35-year-old self-educated high-school dropout. He lives in New York City and works as the librarian in a non-profit organization. He formerly modeled for classes in Renaissance drawing and helped do research for an art historian. He began collecting stamps as a child. He now concentrates on pre-philatelic postal material (letters before postage stamps) primarily from fifteenth-century Venice and refers to himself as a paleographer. He has taught himself ancient Greek and Latin, as well as Italian in his pursuit of this material, and has published several articles and book reviews in stamp-collecting journals. He previously collected Greek, Roman, and Byzantine coins, but lost money when he had to sell the collection in the mid-1980s, when the market for coins was very soft. In both stamps and coins only the very wealthy, who can afford to buy the best, are able to speculate profitably and when they do so, Michael does not regard them as true collectors. Still to have a worthy collection in an area, you need to have a few spectacular and expensive pieces. He is not well paid and tries to make up for the lack of funding for his collection with a deeper knowledge than other collectors. He goes to shows and buys some material at auctions. The highlight of his collecting was when he was able to spend a month in Italy doing research and collecting several years ago. He does not exhibit his collection and says that his ultimate interest is the synthesis of the historical knowledge he is accumulating in conjunction with it. He is single and thus does not have to hide purchases from a spouse as some others he knows do.

Diverse motivations and pleasures

As this set of collectors suggests, there is considerable diversity in what is collected, how it is collected, and the uses and benefits of collections for collectors. Perhaps the most general benefit suggested by my interviews with approximately 200 collectors is gaining a feeling of mastery, competence, or success. For both the collector and others, one evidence of these traits is in the collection itself. In a materialistic society, the quality and quantity of our possessions are broadly assumed to be an index of our successfulness in life in general. In addition, by competing for rare objects of value, we are able to demonstrate our relative prowess and the effects of superior knowledge, tenacity, monetary resources, cleverness, or luck. Luck was also prominent in Horatio Alger's stories of success (Bowerman 1979; Ihamon 1976; Scharnhorst 1976; Zuckerman 1972) and earlier stories of Dan Whittington (Piper 1972) and adds an element of chance that contributes to the challenge of collecting; anyone **might** succeed, even if some are better equipped to do so than others. Moreover, the proving ground of collecting a particular type of object is generally a choice that is self-selected and self-prescribed. Michael, the postal historian, has selected an area in which most of his competing fellow collectors are in Europe rather than the United States where he lives. Similarly, Per has selected an area, beer cans, which finds most of his competitors in the United States, rather than Sweden where he lives. Because collecting is cumulative and involves collecting more or better things over time, the older collector may have an advantage. The same is true in terms of the resources of time and money for single, childless, older, and retired collectors. Consider the sort of competencies that Robert is able to demonstrate to himself and others in his collections of wine, women, horses, and plants. In acquiring undervalued wines, exotic women, winning horses, and rare plants, all in the face of improbable odds, he is able to achieve a success that has thus far eluded him in his university career. Furthermore, he is succeeding in areas that were important to his father. And by also following his father as a great raconteur, he can engagingly repeat these successes to others. Within the narrow areas these and other collectors have chosen, there is a good chance to become an expert and gain the admiration or envy of others with a similar specialization. As is appropriate for a consumer society filled with an over-abundance of objects, the key skill shown in a collector's expertise is that of discrimination:

> The ability to discriminate (or, more to the point, to *be discriminating*) is incontestably the most essential skill of connoisseurship. A serious wine connoisseur would not easily admit to mistaking a St. Emilion for a Pomerol; a connoisseur of mushrooms would be embarrassed to confuse an Agaricus campestris and an Agaricus bisporus; a proper art connoisseur presented with two fifteenth-century paintings of the vision of Saint Augustine would not hesitate before identifying the one by Sandro Botticelli ... for everyone in our society aspires to mastery of this faculty in some areas of life.
>
> (Price 1989, p. 13)

Accordingly, even those who do not share an enthusiasm for these collecting realms may admire the dedication, passion, and discriminative abilities exhibited by the collection.

A related benefit sought by most collectors is the chance to stand out as being unique by virtue of possessing rare, valued, and unique possessions. Collectors may start out with a less specific collecting interest as with Michael's initial stamp collection and Mickey's former acquisition of less expensive nutcrackers, but eventually the tendency to cultivate one or more specialties composed of rarer and more esoteric or unavailable items provides a chance to excel and distinguish the serious collector from the more general or casual dabbling collectors. As with post-Renaissance scholarly specialization in narrower and deeper research, so too the collector pursues the unique. As Taylor (1980) points out of book collectors, "almost no collector is content merely to gather new books as they fall from the press" (p. 28). Jackson explains the irony that the usefulness of a book is superseded by its rarity:

> Natural rarity is a strong loadstone of itself, as you have heard, a great temptation: rare books, scarce or unique *copies*, pierce to the very heart of the bibliophile, and they are desired and coveted inordinately by the bibliomane, who dotes on scarcity before utility; there is no greater allurement; rarity makes desire, 'tis like sauce to their meat; if they but hear of a unique copy they are mad for it; they care not for

beauty, truth, art, wisdom, charm. If the book be rare, then it is fair, fine, absolute, and perfect; they burn like fire, they dote upon it, rave for it, and are ready to mope and fret themselves if they may not have it. Nothing so familiar in these days, and in past times, as for a bibliomane to sacrifice all for a piece of scarcity; and though it be a dunce's album, and have never a wise thought to its pages, neither good writing, nor good seeming, an empty piece, but only rarity, it will have twenty bidders in an instant.

(Jackson 1989, p. 540)

Rarity is prized because it is not enough to succeed if everyone else succeeds as well. The desire for uniqueness in collectibles is the desire for uniqueness among people (Fromkin and Snyder 1980; Snyder and Fromkin 1981), even though this desire may be stronger in more individualistic cultures (Weisz *et al.* 1984). This parallels the finding that we are not pleased by an increase in income if others gain as well, but are greatly pleased if our income increases relative to others (Easterlin 1974).

Another related benefit of collecting is in enlarging the collector's sense of self. While it may be clearest in the case of Jeff's tattoos, the perceptual fact that collections become a part of the owner's extended self (Belk 1988b) is also evident in Mickey's emphatic declaration that she would never part with any of her nutcrackers and in Robert's sense of diminishment as his wine collection dwindles in size. To say that collectors like these are attached to the objects in their collections is like saying they are attached to their arms and legs. However, unlike arms and legs, the choice and assembly of objects to form a collection is ostensibly a self-expressive creative act that tells us something about the collector. After having observed and interviewed a number of automobile collectors at *concours d'élégance*, I agree with Dannefer (1980) who observes, "In show competition, participants voluntarily present their vehicles (and thus themselves), for inspection and evaluation" (p. 399). But a similar concern with evaluation of our self-symbolizing collections is found at baseball-card and comic-book shows in which amateurs nervously and hopefully bring their collections to be appraised by the experts (Belk *et al.* 1991). Among art collectors like Walter, the concern is sometimes whether they can really measure up to the quality of the art they buy, whether they are "good enough" to own a particular painting (Greenspan 1988). In Baudrillard's (1981) terms, the art lover's hubris is to believe "He is the equal of the canvas itself" (p. 118). Similarly, Stewart (1984, p. 159) suggests that the surest way to undermine a collector is to observe that the collectible or collection "is not you." This is the opposite of the situation faced by Joseph Duveen, the art supplier to the turn-of-the-century robber barons, who had to convince his customers that the art he recommended was good enough for them and their ambitions to immortality through art (Behrman 1952). By buying the family portraits and other artworks once owned by aristocrats they hoped they too would be ennobled. The masculine metaphor of extended self is consistent with the focused attachment typical of collecting rather than the more diffuse absorption implied by the feminine metaphor of incorporation. In Freudian terms, the process is seen as one of cathexis (Rook 1985; Secord and Jourard 1953), directing libidinal energy (Gamwell 1989), or investing psychic energy (Csikszentmihalyi and Rochberg-Halton 1981) in the object. In each case both possessive attachment and concentrated focus on the object are involved in order for it to become a part of extended self. Such attachment and focus are very characteristic of collecting.

Rather than royal provenance, Walter Benjamin's (1968a) concern with the aura of a collectible focused more on the contagious magic of a work that had been touched by a great artist. As Cameron speculates of early collections:

> The collection may have said, "See how rich I am," or "Look at this. Look at how I surround myself with beautiful things. See what good taste I have, how civilized and cultivated I am." It may have said, "Oh! I am a man of the world who has traveled much. Look at the places I have been. Look at all the mysterious things I have brought back from my adventures. Yes! I am an adventurer."
>
> (Cameron 1971, p. 15)

As with the non-verbal language of clothing, collections can say things about us that it would be socially unacceptable to express aloud (McCracken 1988). But in such claims the implication is also that the collector's self truly is extended and enlarged by his or her collection. It is thus more understandable that many collections like Per's beer cans, Robert's wines, and Freud's antiquities seem to be initiated or stimulated by the loss of a loved one. In Wicklund and Gollwitzer's (1982) terms what these collectors may be attempting is "symbolic self completion" at times when they have lost a significant human part of their extended self. In this sense too the drive for completing a collection, while feared for threatening a cessation of active self-defining collecting, is also a drive toward self completion. The drive for completion also helps explain Assendorf's (1993) account of the collector who was driven to obtain the worst etching of Callot because it was the one he did not have.

The self-extending aspect of collections is also seen in the feelings of warmth and comfort that Pons obtained in standing among his porcelain dwarfs. Others (e.g., Gulerce 1991; Muensterberger 1994) have compared this feeling of security to that supplied by the child's transitional object. It is not material security, but psychological security that is most critically supplied by a collection. Rigby and Rigby note that this feeling involves ownership rather than acquisition:

From the small boy to the great connoisseur, the joy of standing before one's accumulated pile and being able to say, "This belongs to me!" is the culmination of that feeling which begins with the ownership of the first item. Over our possessions we exercise a definite control; and when we "love" them, it is in part because they are fallen to us and become of us.

(Rigby and Rigby, 1944, p. 35)

And the merging of the collection and the extended self helps explain the thematic relevance of some collections to personal and occupational history, as with Walter's collection of Asian art and his prior personal and business connection to Japan and China. Because he acquired little of his collection while in Asia, he too is pursuing a program of self completion.

Formanek (1991) also finds a number of collecting benefits to the self in her survey of collectors. It is noteworthy in this regard that the historic rise of collecting and consumer culture in Europe occurred at the same time that "self"-prefixed words and phrases such as "self-regard" and "self-consciousness" were entering the English vocabulary (Bruner 1951). Tuan (1982) provides further evidence of this historic emergence of the self through such evidence as the increase in autobiographies, the proliferation of family and self-portraits, the growing popularity of mirrors, development of the concept of personality, the replacement of benches with more individuating chairs, increasingly private and specialized areas in homes, more introspective drama and literature, and the birth of psychoanalysis. While it is likely that personal identification with and ownership of artifacts is fundamentally human (Belk 1982), this does not mean that they have always been a part of symbolic self-definition. Rather the development of widespread consumer culture and widespread collecting seem to have been interwoven with the rise of possessive individualism and the symbolic self (Belk 1984; Clifford 1990; Duby 1988; Macfarlane 1978; Macpherson 1962). Mickey's wistful desire to leave her nutcrackers to a museum and Walter's will specifying which of his children will inherit his various works of art may both be seen as part of a desire for immortality through a collection. Unfortunately for collectors few can aspire to have a memorial wing of a museum built for their collection as Walter's uncle has accomplished with his donation to a university museum.

There is still another way in which collecting contributes to the sense of extended self and that is by contributing to the collector's sense of past (Belk 1991b). Robert's ability to recall when and where he acquired each of hundreds of bottles of wine and the price paid, his ability to taste an unidentified wine and be transported back to the time and place he first tasted it, and his ability to look at a vacant space in his wine cellar and recall the occasion and company with whom it was consumed, all speak to this sense of past. So do Walter Benjamin's (1968b) reflections on his book-buying adventures as he describes lovingly unpacking each volume. In fact most collectors see the items in their collections not as objects occupying a cell in a taxonomy, but as packages of memories. Thus Jeff recalls the circumstances of each tattoo in vivid detail. While talking to Mickey, I pointed at random to one of her 350 nutcrackers and asked her what came to mind when she saw it. Without even glancing at the identifying label on the bottom of the piece she replied, "I got that one in San Diego. I remember the store and I remember how excited I was when I saw it, because I'd never seen it before. And now it was mine." "It's fun to remember them," she added.

A related benefit derived by most collectors has been referred to as the thrill of the hunt. A part of what makes travel an interesting and meaningful experience for Mickey is the chance to find new nutcrackers. Her son and husband collect duck replicas, so they too have a purpose in their travel that makes it more exciting as well as purposeful for them. The hunt for new postal material and information was the sole purpose of Michael's month in Italy. And Robert relishes his trips to America, France, and Australia in no small part because of the winery tours he is able to make in these countries. For Freud, whose anxiousness for new finds was betrayed by his misreading of shop signs as "antiquities," the artifacts he brought back from annual travels to the ruins of Italy and Greece served to remind him that "after the long winter in Vienna he could return" (Bernfeld 1951, p. 109). And when he traveled to New York to give lectures in 1909, Freud was preoccupied with his study of the antiquities at the Metropolitan Museum (Walter 1988, pp. 102–103). Andy Warhol's daily shopping expeditions offer another example of the thrill of the hunt. The relationship of the hunt to the sense of autobiographical past is explained by Stewart:

> it is not acceptable to simply purchase a collection *in toto*; the collection must be acquired in a serial manner. This seriality provides a means for defining or classifying the collection and the collector's life history, and it also permits a systematic substitution of purchase for labor.
>
> (Stewart 1984, p. 166)

Yet the metaphor of the hunt implies more than just the systematic substitution of purchase for labor. "At its most committed," Muensterberger (1994) observes, "it assumes the proportions of a kind of aggression with masculine potential, if not dominance or an all-consuming, sensuous activity surpassing rational ends" (p. 240). Formanek elaborates on this view in terms of traditional psychoanalytic libidinal and aggressive drive theory:

> In many respects collecting resembles hunting: one locates the prey, plans for the attack, acquires the prey in the presence of real or imag-

ined competition for it, and feels elated. The prey becomes a trophy – a symbol of one's aggression and prowess.

(Formanek 1991, p. 277)

Challenge and mastery in the hunt metaphor obviously relate back to the benefit of feelings of accomplishment and success as well. In pursuing this commonly applied metaphor Clark (1963) suggests "just as no one would go out to shoot a cow in a field, so a true collector enjoys the length and difficulty of the stalk, and the uncertainties which attend it up to the moment of the kill" (p. 15). While it is not necessary to hypothesize a derivation from some "hunting instinct" (Rigby and Rigby 1944), it is easy to appreciate why collectors like Michael find auctions of postal materials exciting and why a collector like Mickey finds some dilution of her pleasure when she receives nutcrackers as gifts rather than finding them herself. To return to the "instant collectibles" discussed in Chapter Two, the foregone benefit of collecting such items is the thrill of the hunt. For as McCracken (1988) notes, when their acquisition is uncertain, "collectibles make it possible once again to dream" (p. 113). This is the imaginative desire that Campbell (1987) characterizes as modern hedonism.

While some collectors like Mickey and Michael are solitary and somewhat introverted in their collecting, others like Per and Robert find the interpersonal part of their collecting activity the most rewarding. In addition to interviewing Robert and hearing his stories about his adventures and successes in collecting, I also interviewed Curtis, a friend of about the same age with whom he has shared both wine-collecting interest and a joint investment in their seven race horses. Through triangulation it was clear that their stories about their past collecting adventures, while largely true, also carried an element of dramatic exaggeration. Fine (1987) found a similar playful exaggeration in the stories of mushroom collectors, and noted the function of these stories in providing the folklore that helps build a sense of community among collectors. The same is true of the specialized vocabulary and knowledge with which collectors in many areas are able to speak to each other. In the case of wine, for instance, knowledge of wine varieties, qualities, and characteristics provides a terminology that quickly separates vinophiles from others and makes it possible to establish a community of friends that is easily defined (Lehrer 1983). Similar phenomena exist in many types of collecting including art (Baekeland 1981), automobiles (Harrah 1984), and stamps (Christ 1965; Gelber 1992). These communities may interact through collectors' clubs, at shows, with dealers, artists, and museum personnel, and in chance encounters with others for whom collecting is a passion shared. There is a widespread belief among collectors that a common collecting interest is a great leveler and that blue-collar workers, white-collar workers, professionals, and aristocrats all share a common status among fellow collectors. Given social-class patterns in collecting (Belk *et al.* 1991; see pp. 99–100 below), there is exaggeration here too, but the claim seems essentially true. This is not to say that such feelings of community lessen the rivalry and envy that many collectors in an area feel toward one another. But the fellowship that Per enjoys when he attends a Beer Can Collectors of America Canvention is real. He feels no reluctance to leave his valuable exhibit because he knows others will watch it and he joins the general flow of people between hotel rooms at night as they trade conversation, beer cans, and related collectibles.

But perhaps the deepest benefit of collecting to most collectors is one they find most difficult to articulate: that of providing contact with self-transcending sacredness or magic in their lives. If, as argued in Chapter Two, the locus of sacredness in contemporary life has shifted from religion to science to consumption, collecting epitomizes the sacralization of consumption in the contemporary world. Although the locus may have changed, the need for something that is transcendent, numinous, or magical in our lives remains. It has already been suggested that collecting can be ritualistic and that collectors may act as sacred priests able to transform an ordinary object of use into a sacred object in a collection. The ritual of bringing them into the collection decommotitizes, singularizes, and sacralizes these objects. The non-use of most collectibles is another indicant of their extra-utilitarian status. The primary exception to this among automobile collectors is those who drive their cars in special vintage-car rallies complete with period costumes. This is clearly a non-ordinary use. Others bring their cars to *concours d'élégance* on trailers and wrap the tires in plastic lest they get a blade of grass in the treads as they roll them into their show positions. Among gun collectors it is not uncommon to find large collections of weapons that have never been fired (Stenross 1987). Per does not mind pouring beer down the drain because it is the can that is important. Robert does consume his wines, but a special wine demands a special occasion and special guests. Thus he saved key bottles for his son's twenty-first birthday, for his own fiftieth birthday, and for dinners with other vinophiles. As Fuller observes of wine tastings:

> A wine tasting, like a religious service designed to give rise to a felt sense of the holy, leads individuals through a series of ritualized behaviors that are designed to bring individuals face to face with that which is deemed perfect or exquisite.
>
> (Fuller 1993, p. 40)

Robert's visits to wineries on three continents may well be seen as pilgrimages. His wine cellar can be regarded as holy territory and only the initiated may enter there. He was recently burglarized, but was much relieved to find that the burglars had not profaned this territory.

The sacred role of collections helps further explain too why the collector who is primarily interested in profits and investment is not generally regarded as a true collector. For money threatens to profane something which should be above such considerations. Even art dealers, Moulin (1987) finds, try to deny the monetary aspect of their business. But paradoxically when a painting is sold for an unfathomably large amount of money this may be sacralizing as well, for it signals the huge esteem in which the object is held (Belk and Wallendorf 1990). Both because of the increasingly large sums it commands and because it is a collectible object that is clearly non-utilitarian, fine art has for centuries remained at the top of the pantheon of collectible objects. For most people the most revered artworks have left the realm of commodities entirely and become cultural icons that are truly above price. Clark (1963) notes that in the presence of a Rothschild collection he found himself "whispering as if I were in church" (p. 15). Baekeland (1981) observes, "if museums are the churches of collectors, then the auction houses and art galleries are ecclesiastical merchants who purvey the objects necessary for domestic shrines" (p. 50). The prepositional phrase that opens this comment is based on Rheims (1961):

> Museums are the churches of collectors. Speaking in whispers, groups of visitors wander as an act of faith from one museum gallery to another. Until the end of the nineteenth century it was customary to visit the Hermitage Museum in Leningrad in a white tie. The almost ritual habits practiced in the sales-rooms in London and Paris have been the same for two hundred years. The Hôtel Drouot in Paris is a sort of temple. It has fixed ceremonies, and its daily hour from ten to eleven has a completely religious atmosphere.
>
> (Rheims 1961, p. 29)

An eighteenth-century porcelain collector claimed that his "passion for Dresden amounts to worship" (Rheims 1961, p. 4). And the phrase "true collector" often found in discussions of collecting (e.g., Clark 1963, p. 15; Eisenberg 1987, p. 18) is the secular equivalent of true believer in a religious context (Hoffer 1951).

Because the sacred is mystical, it is enhanced by collecting objects that are distant in time or space from the owner. Antiques, old masters, ancient artifacts, foreign and old stamps and coins, and exotic artifacts from "primitive" people are all likely to have a mystique that makes them pre-singularized (Appadurai 1986). Such "otherness" offers the collector "a means to escape the limits of one's own individual life" (Assendorf 1993, p. 53). For antique collectors interviewed, this escape was sometimes powerful and captivating enough that they believed the antique's resonance for them must signal a connection to the object in a prior life. Similarly, Tooley suggests that collections of coins, seashells, or baseball cards may act as talismans and tokens:

> Talisman and token must provide evidence of a link between reality on the one hand and romance and sentiment on the other. Tokens in

romantic literature are unarguable proof that the shepard's daughter, possessor of the ruby ring, is indeed the long lost daughter of the king.

(Tooley 1978, p. 180)

The pull of romanticism is equally strong for many collectors and Muensterberger (1994) contends that collected objects "allow for a magical escape into a remote and private world" (p. 15).

Sacredness in a collection may also be imparted or enhanced through the contagious magic of the objects' creators or of prior owners of objects with special provenance. In Walter's case it is the famous painters of some of his art that provides these paintings with the aura of which Benjamin (1968a) spoke. For baseball-card collectors it was the signature of famous ball players that made some cards extraordinarily sacred. At one show a bat broken by Babe Ruth as he hit a home run was revered as reverently as any holy relic might be. Among contemporary antique collectors, just as with the robber barons ransacking the aristocratic collections of Europe, the prior ownership or provenance of antiques has special magic (Stillinger 1980). Thus for an owner of a music box that once belonged to Winston Churchill, the object held sacredness far beyond that imparted by time and quality. This concern extends to collectors of books and paintings as well so that art collectors may refer to prior owners as well as original artists: a Walferdin Boucher, a Weil-Picard Fragonard, or a Gangnat Renoir, for instance (Rheims 1961). Provenance can enhance reverence for collectible cars as well, as Dannefer explains:

> There are actually often two strands of tradition giving a sacred meaning to the car: 1) the general tradition of the marque and/or of this particular model; and 2) the specific tradition of this individual car. The later is not always invoked, but often it is, and in many ways. If the car has belonged to a celebrity or moderately famous person, or to a wealthy person or even merely an eccentric person, this will become an oral or perhaps written tradition following the car and giving it a unique significance.
>
> (Dannefer 1980, p. 410)

In the case of family heirlooms, however, the provenance most likely has sacred meaning only to the owner. Thus in one *concours d'élégance* a man who was restoring his deceased father's recent model Dodge automobile was an unfathomable enigma to other automobile collectors. Had it belonged to a famous person or if it had been pre-singularized by a famous marque such as Ferarri or Bugatti, they could have readily understood his devotion to the car. But in this case the Dodge will most likely remain a private shrine only.

WHO COLLECTS?

A final consideration before we leave the individual collector is the demo-
graphic profile of the collector. It was emphasized in Chapter Two that
with the development of consumer culture and the spread of affluence, collecting as well as other forms of luxury consumption were democratized.
Relatively speaking this is true, but there is still an upscale and male bias
among adult collectors. As the studies reviewed near the end of Chapter
Two attest, nearly all Western children collect, and boys and girls are
equally likely to be avid collectors before their teenage years. During ado-
lescence collecting declines for both sexes, but especially for girls.
Furthermore, there is a tendency for men to renew collecting in middle
age; a tendency that does not find a parallel among middle-aged women
(Ackerman 1990). The male dominance in most collecting areas has also
been true historically, despite the fame of some women collectors including Catherine de'Medici, Catherine the Great, Queen Christina of Sweden,
Madame Pompadour, Isabella Stewart Gardner, and Peggy Guggenheim. As
noted in Chapter Two, in nineteenth-century France, women were disparaged as "mere buyers of bibelots," while for men "collecting was perceived
as serious and creative" (Saisselin 1984, p. 68). It may seem surprising in
light of the stigma sometimes attached to collecting as being a childish or
feminine activity that males should dominate most collecting areas. But the
work-like, competitive, and aggressive characteristics of collecting also
accord well with traditional masculine gendering (Belk and Wallendorf,
forthcoming). Furthermore, with greater economic resources, men have historically been in a more advantageous position to collect than women, as
Rigby and Rigby (1944, pp. 326–327) have observed. Psychologically it has
also been suggested that since women have the creative potential for child-
birth, men may compensate through the creation of collections (Baekeland
1981). Moreover, collecting may be one of the few socially sanctioned
opportunities for men to be expressive, while at the same time being aggressive and competitive (ibid.).

Still, there are many female collectors. According to one American study,
approximately 41 percent of coin collectors and 49 percent of stamp collectors are women, while the majority of collectors of instant collectibles such
as those of Bradford Exchange and Franklin Mint are women (Crispell 1988).
This suggests that there are sex differences in **what** is collected. Characteristic
collector traits include both "masculine" aggressiveness, competitiveness, and
desire for mastery, and "feminine" preservationism, creativity, and nurtu-
rance (Belk and Wallendorf, forthcoming). Nevertheless, there is continuing
disparagement of women as collectors, Baekeland suggests that:

> we rarely think of accumulations of dresses, shoes, perfumes, china
> and the like as collections. . . . Men's collections, however, be they of

stamps, cars, guns or art, tend to have clear-cut thematic emphases and standard, external reference points in public or private collections. Thus, women's collections tend to be personal and ahistorical, men's impersonal and historical, just as, traditionally, women have tended to have a relatively greater emotional investment in people than in ideas and men to some extent the reverse.

(Baekeland 1981, p. 47)

As with male-biased models of scientific research (e.g., Benston 1989; Keller 1983), the distanced, impersonal, logical, serious, and mastering traits thought to be typical of men are those most venerated in collecting. The caring, personal, artistic, playful, and sentimental traits thought to be typical of women are those thought to be least conducive to "real" collecting. Studies of children's collections (Danet and Katriel 1989; Durost 1932; Whitley 1929; Witty and Lehman 1931) show that sex biases show up in pre-teen years. Girls have been found to be more likely than boys to collect decorative objects (e.g., flowers, pictures, household objects), jewelry, personal reference objects (e.g., souvenirs, Valentines, dance favors), dolls, school objects, and games. Boys have been found to be more likely than girls to collect animal and insect parts, salable objects, tobacco merchandise, weapons, game objects (e.g., marbles, tops, kites), and building and repair objects (e.g., nails, radio parts, lumber). Among adults, one guide to men's antiques (Revi 1974) suggested that men should collect objects such as weapons, toy soldiers, snuffboxes, railroad artifacts, relics of early aviators, musical instruments, and chessmen. Another guide for men (Hertz) suggested that:

decorative articles or those whose primary use is decorative are essentially feminine antiques; operating and functional articles are for the most part inherently masculine antiques ... women are more inclined to the fragile rather than the substantial ... while men lean toward more substantial materials such as iron and tin ... women usually collect with decorative values or a definite decorative purpose in mind; men for study from a technical standpoint.

(Hertz 1969, pp. 6, 8)

Based on a study of one husband's collection of fire engines that had been converted into a personal museum and his deceased wife's collection of mice replicas that had been posthumously converted into another personal museum, colleagues and I (Belk *et al.* 1991, pp. 189–190) inferred the following symbolic contrasts where the female collection trait is represented on the left and the male collection trait on the right:

Tiny : Gigantic
Weak : Strong

Home	:	World
Nature	:	Machine
Nurturing	:	Extinguishing
Art	:	Science
Playfulness	:	Seriousness
Decorative	:	Functional
Inconspicuous	:	Conspicuous
Animate	:	Inanimate

To this I would add that there is an association of the female collection with consumption and the male collection with production. Consistent with this, Gelber (1991) finds that men are more interested in the investment rationale or rationalization for collecting than are women. As a form of consuming, collecting is socially constructed as feminine, while as a form of capital accumulation and work, collecting is able to be socially constructed as masculine (Belk and Wallendorf, forthcoming; Gelber 1992). Based on the non-representative set of collectors I have interviewed, men are more likely than women to collect guns (see also Olmsted 1988b, 1989), automobiles (see also Dannefer 1980, 1981), stamps, antiques, books, tattoos, beer cans (see also Soroka 1988), wines, and sports items, while women are more likely than men to collect jewelry, housewares (e.g., dishes, silverware), and animal replicas. There are exceptions to these patterns, but collecting is most often a highly gendered activity with the greatest social sanction for those collections and collector traits that fit masculine sex-role stereotypes.

Because collecting objects sold on the market requires money and even collecting found objects requires resources to travel to collecting sites, transport collectibles, and store them, the very poorest are precluded from most collecting realms. Because collections consist of non-functional objects or objects taken out of use, they remain a luxury even in an affluent society. And generally speaking the most widely revered areas of collecting are those that are the most expensive to pursue, just as the most revered collections in any area generally consist of the most costly pieces. Baudrillard (1981) refers to art auctions as an "aristocratic measure of value" (p. 113), with the price of the artworks being conflated with the value of their new owner. The status hierarchies that are generally encoded in visible consumption are similarly encoded within collecting worlds, although the range of people who can decode the status of collected objects and who care about the result is narrower. The committed collector has not opted out of the sort of consumption-based status competition that goes on in consumer societies more broadly, but has instead elected to focus intently on status within a prescribed collecting realm and, most likely, a narrower specialty within it. Collecting as masculine status competition for collectible trophies does not characterize all collectors, and many are in it just for the fun of it. But most collector shows, whether they involve stamps, minerals, tattoos, or beer cans, are likely to have awards for the "best" collection as well as lesser prizes in a number of special categories. Within collecting circles, these awards are a reification of the more pervasive process of assigning higher status to those with bigger and better collections.

If the lowest-income segments of society are precluded from collecting in most areas, the middle classes are not. A survey of subscribers to an American collecting magazine found that median income was about 30 percent above the U.S. overall population median and that 70 percent of the sample had white-collar jobs (Treas and Brannen 1976). The middle classes form the major portion of collectors of stamps (Bryant 1989), baseball cards (Rogoli 1991), model airplanes (Butsch 1984), beer cans and related objects (Soroka 1988), and instant collectibles (Roberts 1990). Over 40 percent of coin collectors and over 44 percent of stamp collectors are white-collar managers, or professionals (Crispell 1988). As with gender, there appear to be social-class differences in **what** is collected. Rochberg-Halton (1979) found in a study of favorite possessions in Chicago that upper-middle-class informants were the most likely to cite visual art. Cost is a significant factor that restricts collecting of fine art to higher social classes (Marquis 1991; Moulin 1987). However, there are also significant differences in the "cultural capital" of the dominant classes that make collecting certain types of fine art an important status marker that is far less accessible outside of these classes (Bourdieu 1984; Halle 1993). Collectors in areas that are more broadly regarded as lower-status, such as tattoos, baseball cards, and beer cans, proudly point out the members of high-status occupations such as medicine and law among their numbers. Such claims are sometimes true, as illustrated by Per, the Swedish dentist who collects beer cans. For the most part, however, they are exaggerated attempts to elevate the status of their collecting area. Even though the wealthiest collectors in any area tend to have an advantage in being able to afford the most admired and status-imparting objects, other collectors' knowledge, time, persistence, and luck can compensate to some degree. Along with choosing an affordable and narrow collecting area and specialty within this area, these factors make it possible for a large number of people from all but the lowest social classes to find opportunities for success in collecting.

PROBLEMATICS OF INDIVIDUAL COLLECTING

The understanding of individual collecting offered in this chapter has emphasized the linkage of collecting to issues that concern a consumer society more generally. I have raised the issues of materialism (including acquisitiveness and possessiveness), self-indulgence, sex bias, and class bias in collecting. I have sought to distinguish between rationalizations given for collecting and deeper benefits that help to explain the popularity of collecting. Still these issues have not been fully evaluated. Before attempting to do so in the final chapter, it is important to consider various trends in institutional collecting that are relevant to collecting and to consumerism.

CHAPTER FOUR

INSTITUTIONAL COLLECTORS

——— •◆• ———

INSTITUTIONS THAT COLLECT

Prominent types of institutional collections have included religious, royal, commercial, governmental, and non-commercial business collections, in approximately that sequence of historical emergence. Some of the same psychological processes involved in individual collecting are involved in institutional collecting as well. For instance, our extended selves are affected by institutional collections as well as by our individual collections, except that broader and more aggregate levels of the extended self are implicated. Instead of the individual or family level of self, it may be the community, regional, or national level of self that is extended by an institutional collection (Belk 1988a; Delaney 1992). Thus, for example, a loss to the Smithsonian collections would be a loss to the American sense of self, just as a loss to the Louvre collections would be a loss to the French sense of self. We might well seek an answer to the question "What does it mean to be American/British/Dutch/French?" at the Smithsonian, British Museum, Rijksmuseum, or Louvre. If we are part of an ethnic minority it might be harder to find our identity in these museums, but this may be changing and there may be more specialized museum collections that provide a better answer. There are other differences between individual and institutional collecting besides the levels of self they affect. Since public institutions are usually corporate entities, the individual feelings of acquisition and possession of objects may be lacking in institutional collections. Furthermore, an institution involved in collecting can affect the marketplace for collectibles more than an individual collector can. This is true both in terms of the institution's buying power and in terms of the ability of some institutions, especially museums, to legitimize and sacralize certain objects as being worthy to be collected. And cultural institutions like museums mediate between groups within society such that their collecting policies may enfranchise some and disenfranchise others. In this chapter I explore the nature of institutional collecting. I am particularly concerned with the effects of consumer culture on collecting institutions and the effects of collecting institutions on consumer culture.

The rise of institutional collecting

Not surprisingly, the rise of consumer society that precipitated mass individual collecting also precipitated massive institutional collecting during the same periods. This is seen in the founding dates of public museums, most of which correspond well to the rise of consumer culture in these countries traced in Chapter One and the rise of collecting in these countries traced in Chapter Two:

Piakotheke in the Propylaea of Athens – 5th century BC
Library in the Sanctuary of Athena at Pergamum – 2nd century BC
Rebuilt Temple of Concord in Rome – 1st century BC
Porticus Octaviae in Rome – 32 BC
Ashmolean Museum at Oxford – 1683
Uffizi Gallery in Florence – 1739
British Museum in London – 1753
Louvre in Paris – 1793
Conservatoire National des Arts et Métiers in Paris – 1794
   (now Musée National des Techniques)
Rijksmuseum in Amsterdam – 1808
National Gallery in London – 1824
Smithsonian Institution in Washington, D.C. – 1835
Hermitage Museum in St. Petersburg – 1852
Bavarian National Museum in Munich – 1855
South Kensington Museum in London – 1852 (now Victoria and
   Albert Museum and Science Museum)
Xujiahui Museum in Shanghai – 1868
Museum of Fine Arts in Boston – 1870
Metropolitan Museum of Art in New York – 1872
Ministry of Education Museum in Tokyo – 1872
Educational Museum in Tokyo – 1875 (now National Science
   Museum)
Art Institute of Chicago – 1879
Imperial Museum in Tokyo – 1889 (now National Museum)
Field Museum of Natural History in Chicago – 1894
Palace Museum in the Forbidden City, Beijing – 1925
History Museum in Wu Gate of the Forbidden City, Beijing – 1926
Chicago Museum of Science and Industry – 1926

The greatest number of foundings of important museums occurred during the nineteenth century, which Bazin (1967) calls the Museum Age and Alexander (1979) calls the Golden Age for museums. Like the development of consumer culture, museum development in the modern world began with a few isolated developments that became more and more sustained in the nineteenth century. For the few modern museums built earlier, the nineteenth century was a time of great growth in collections. When individuals in a consumer society acquire sufficient wealth and leisure time, they are inclined to collect and display luxury goods. The same appears to be true of cities, states, and nations. The two phenomena are also correlated because of the desire for immortality by having one's collection institutionally memorialized. The fact that some private collections have been accepted by museums helps to legitimize collecting as a whole, as Harris explains:

> When our [American] millionaires began ... to ransom great European masterpieces, the newspapers all assumed that the community itself was the residuary legatee. Thus museums legitimated the pursuit of private pleasure, suggesting that collecting goals and object accumulation were public benefactions.
>
> (Harris 1990, p. 136)

Museum formation is also more likely when a nation has nationalistic tendencies and imperialistic ambitions it wishes to assert. The rise of world's fairs and department stores during the latter half of the century of museum foundation is more than coincidental (Lewis 1983). All celebrate an abundance of material things. And with better transportation, it was not lost upon communities that museums are an important incentive for tourism and, in turn, increase local business (Horne 1984).

The primary exception to the general correspondence among the rise of consumer culture, the rise of individual collecting, and the rise of public museums is in China and Japan. Malraux (1967) suggested that the idea of art collecting is antithetical to non-possessive Asian ideologies, but this fails to explain the rise of individual collecting during these periods (e.g., Brook 1993). The museums of these two countries began to emerge not only after individual collecting and consumer culture proliferated, but also in very different periods of their histories. The height of consumerism and collecting in the Tokugawa period in Japan and in the late Ming dynasty in China were both times in which these countries (especially Japan) were relatively closed to the outside world and international trade. New consumer wealth was instead generated internally. With the Meiji restoration that followed in Japan after 1868, Western influence came suddenly after over 250 years of being effectively shut out. It was only during this era that museums began to sprout in Japan (Konishi 1987). Similarly in China, contact with the West influenced the idea of museums. The Xujiahui museum in Shanghai was set up by French missionaries (Feng 1991). Other early Chinese museums were also in coastal areas with greater outside contact, such as Jinan and Tianjin (Hamilton 1977). A variety of cultural, political, and economic factors are likely to be involved in a full accounting for these differences, and there is no doubt that Western countries themselves were also influenced by each others' museum ideologies. But unlike the West, consumer culture did not continue to grow without major disruptions in the East. Furthermore the lack of outward orientation to "the other" in China and Japan during their closed periods led to a lack of necessity for public museums to reinvent a sense of national self. And the more collectivistic, less individualistic values of China and Japan may have resulted in less desire to define national uniqueness. To an inward-looking nation that knows itself as superior, there is less need to glorify that greatness in public museums or to contemplate the culture's relative place in the world. All of these factors seem important, but more detailed research is needed.

Chapter Two described some of the early museums in England and the United States. In England the first public museum, the Tradescants' Ark transformed into the Ashmolean, was an expansive cabinet of curiosities that grew from a private collection to a commercial venture and finally became a public museum. The largest three of the museum's ten rooms were public and early visitors described them as crowded with country folk on market day (Welch 1983). The collections themselves were in the hands of scholars and the wealthy, but as a public museum the Ashmolean could, in principle, be visited by all (MacGregor 1983). Cambridge and Harvard too had their repositories of curiosities, with Harvard's lasting only from its inception in 1750 to its loss in a fire in the 1760s (Bazin 1967). Like the Royal Society's cabinet in England, the American Philosophical Society maintained a cabinet of curiosities in Philadelphia following its merger with the American Society for Promoting Useful Knowledge in 1769 (Bell 1967). The commercial museum of Charles Peale grew from his private collection and freely mixed fine art and curiosities. But it never became a non-profit public museum. Neither did the Western Museum of Cincinnati, which, like Peale's, was established in 1820 with the lofty ideal of being educational, popular, and commercially successful all at the same time (Dunlop 1984). John James Audubon was the Western Museum's first artist and taxidermist. But within two years of its opening, bankruptcy threatened and the museum became more and more driven by the principle of novelty. As Tucker (1967, p. 74) describes it, "Vulgarized and converted into a freak and horror show, the Western Museum became one of the best-known entertainment sites in the United States and the first Disneyland of the West." Indeed besides stuffed animals, rocks, insects, coins, and Indian artifacts, the museum had a mermaid made from the top half of a monkey stitched to the bottom half of a fish, the tattooed head of a Maori chief, a charade known as "The Invisible Girl," and, most popular of all, an electrified and mechanized depiction of Dante's Hell (Dunlop 1984). The Western Museum, which lasted until 1867, caused one English visitor to remark:

A "Museum" in the American sense of the word means a place of amusement, wherein there shall be a theatre, some wax figures, a giant and a dwarf or two, a jumble of pictures, and a few live snakes. In order that there may be some excuse for the use of the word, there is in most instances a collection of stuffed birds, a few preserved animals, and a stock of oddly assorted and very dubitable curiosities; but the mainstay of the "Museum" is the "live art," that is, the theatrical performance, the precocious mannikins, or the intellectual dogs and monkeys.

(quoted in Tucker 1967, p. 74)

Eventually the Western Museum, Charles Peale's museum, P. T. Barnum's museum, and numerous imitators such as the "dime museums" of the Bowery in New York City, were supplanted by non-profit public museums. Furthermore, as with collections in general, museums became more specialized. The eclecticism of the *Wunderkammern*, the Ashmolean, and the early private American museums eventually gave way to the specialized public museums of art, natural history, ethnography, history, science, and industry (Alexander 1979). Some of the reasons for these splits are traced in Chapter Two and include the transfer of sacred power from religion to art, science, and commerce. But more than this was involved. As observed by Durkheim and Mauss (1963), the classification of objects often recapitulates the classification of society. That is, museums which began with mixed objects and mixed social-class audiences came eventually to segregate both. This is clearly seen in the Museum of Fine Arts in Boston (DiMaggio 1982a, 1982b).

Prior to the 1870 establishment of the Museum of Fine Arts, Boston's museums were commercial and modeled on Barnum's in New York. The Boston Museum was one of these, founded in 1841 by Moses Kimball and exhibiting "works by such painters as Sully and Peale alongside Chinese curiosities, stuffed animals, mermaids and dwarfs" (DiMaggio 1982a, p. 34). When the MFA was first established, it too mixed both objects and classes. It featured a few original works of art as well as various curiosities, including mummies, a buffalo horn, an old sled, Zulu weapons, and numerous reproductions of paintings, sculptures, and architectural decorations (DiMaggio 1982b; Harris 1962; Levine 1988). It also exhibited works of local amateur painters, wood engravings, Christmas cards, and colored glass. And it was mandated to be open to the public free at least four days each month, resulting in an especially diverse audience on free weekend days. Spiess and Spiess explain the rationale for such a charter:

The emergence of great public museums at the beginning of the nineteenth century demanded a new rationale for maintaining private collections at public expense. While the private collection of the eighteenth century began as entertaining diversion, the public museums were premised on the belief in the benefits of research and education. As a public institution, the museum could not merely collect objects; it had to preserve them. As an educational agency, the museum could not merely display objects; it had to invest them with meaning through interpretation.

(Spiess and Spiess 1990, pp. 144–145)

Implicit in the educational mission of the museum is the promise that museums are for everyone. Gradually, however, the upper-class board of directors of the MFA exerted itself and drove popular art, reproductions, and lower-class patrons from the museum. The reproductions were desacralized and relegated to the basement as the museum's collection of original art grew and as it explicitly changed its mission from one of education about art to communion with selected sacred art by the favored elite of Boston society. It moved to a more exclusive location in Boston and expelled those whose dress and manners were considered inappropriate. Just as the Boston Symphony Orchestra erased popular music from its repertoire and relegated it to the Boston Pops, DiMaggio (1982b) finds that the MFA sacralized and purified its collections and audience by removing all that was not deemed high culture and high society. What happened at the MFA also happened at other museums, including New York's Metropolitan and Washington's Smithsonian (Levine 1988). While the progress has not been strictly linear, the course of early American museums from carnivalesque freak shows to elite showcases of high culture has been motivated by the opposition of two arguments: the democratic critique of elitism and the professional critique of kitsch popular culture. With the professionalization of the sciences, the nineteenth century became an era of increasingly more rarefied and less populist museums and museum collections (Orosz 1990).

Further classification of objects occurred within art museums as they moved to order paintings chronologically, nationally, and according to school of art (Holdengräber 1987). Art historians created a science of artwork (and perhaps aesthetics) that became a part of the cultural capital of the upper social classes (Bourdieu 1984; DiMaggio 1987). This is Foucault's (1970) Classical episteme mobilized for the sake of class hegemony in an age of consumer democracy. What sumptuary laws failed to protect, and what democratized consumption in an affluent consumer society took away, was regained by the elite, at least for a time, in the sacred temple of the museum. As Zolberg (1984) detected, Benjamin (1968a) feared, and Malraux (1967) urged, the same mass-production forces that create consumer culture have the potential to also eliminate privileged access to luxury collectibles by reproducing them in the form of photographs, prints, casts, and books. But by stressing the importance of the authentic original as the only vehicle capable of preserving the sacred aura of the creator, by relegating such objects to the collections of the very wealthy or to ostensibly public museums, and then by monopolizing control of these museums, the elite is able to preserve its hegemony in a way that is no longer possible in ordinary consumption. This is done in a number of ways in the museum, including becoming a patron, being in a position to donate important private collections in the future, being appointed to positions on museum boards, and embracing the romantic cults of authenticity and artistic genius. Museums for their part became "temples of authenticity" (Handler 1986). This explains why the Boston Museum of Fine Arts' plaster casts, like those once housed in the Metropolitan and the Victoria and Albert museums, could not be tolerated by the Brahmins of Boston society. French and British museums have had somewhat different histories of private influence, but the result of increasing museum control by higher social classes has been largely the same.

The unequal distribution of cultural capital facilitating an understanding and appreciation of the mysteries of high culture has also long made museum audiences disproportionately dominated by members of higher social classes (e.g., Bourdieu and Darbel 1990; Merriman 1989). While Bourdieu (1984) attributes these attendance patterns, as well as the tendency of higher-class visitors to spend more time in museums, to their greater class-based access to stylistic knowledge and classification principles and Zolberg (1984) cites greater willingness to "work" at developing a faculty for "difficult art," a simpler explanation is found in the mere exposure hypothesis which states that we like that with which we are more familiar due to prior exposure, whether or not we understand the abstract principles used to elevate these works to the status of high culture. Experiments manipulating the amount of prior exposure to works of art offer support for this hypothesis (Zajonc *et al.* 1972). In addition, the grand and imposing temple architecture of museum buildings, their traditional glass-case hands-off distanced displays, and their solemn tomb-like demeanor are intentionally off-putting for members of lower social classes. While the architecture of the palatial department stores constructed in the latter half of the nineteenth century was nearly as imposing, these stores had a more actively helpful and deferential manner toward visitors and their merchandise and displays were participatory and invited contact. Glass display windows, multiple entrances, and readily accessible merchandise all invite the department-store shopper to touch and participate. Such features are notably absent in museums. Department stores actively challenged the elitism of the museums and counter-positioned themselves as the democratic alternative to the snobbish seclusion of the museum (Harris 1978).

Thus, however broad the initial vision for museums like the Louvre and Boston Museum of Fine Arts were, a large part of the support for and direction of these museums was provided by the upper classes. In America the nouveau riche had a significant role as well in founding, endowing, and bequeathing collections to public museums. They include Andrew Carnegie in Pittsburgh, Paul Melon in New Haven, Henry Francis Dupont in Delaware, William Thompson Walters and Henry Walters in Baltimore,

Marshall Field in Chicago, Henry Huntington, Armand Hammer, and J. Paul Getty in California, and a host of others. At the Metropolitan Museum of Art in New York, besides J. P. Morgan and John D. Rockefeller, Jr., prominent merchant princes instrumental in building the museum collections also included Benjamin Altman, Henry Osborne Havemeyer, and Robert Lehman (Tomkins 1970). As McCracken (1992) distinguishes, whereas old wealth attempts to demonstrate the justice of its social standing in the museum, new wealth attempts to launder its image in the profane world of commerce through the sacred world of art. Besides these benefactors, another prominent link between museums and consumer culture was the world's fair (Ferguson 1965). Museums founded on the basis of materials or buildings from these fairs included the Victoria and Albert Museum and Science Museum in London, the Field Museum in Chicago, several San Diego museums in Balboa Park, the St. Louis Art Museum and History Museum, the Smithsonian's Arts and Industries Museum, the Leiden Museum in the Netherlands, and the Musée de l'Homme and the Palais de la Découverte in Paris. World's fairs were also influential in stimulating new, more theatrical, display techniques in museums (Harris 1978). As museum directors and department-store owners both came to realize, they were competing with each other and with world's fairs for "customers."

Just as there are hierarchies of collectible objects, as discussed in Chapter Three, there are also hierarchies of museums. It is no accident that the higher social classes and robber barons were most prominent in fine-art museums while the museums established from world's fairs were more likely to be museums of decorative arts, ethnography, industry, and science. These museums also reached their peak in the nineteenth century, although Bedini (1965) argues that many seventeenth-century *Wunderkammern* can be considered science museums as well. Jonaitis (1992) specifies a "continuum from popular to exclusive: world's fairs, natural history museums, fine arts museums" (pp. 40–41). Museums of science and industry are closer to the world's-fair end of this continuum and are intended to foster a mass appreciation of science and technology and a belief in continual progress (Ettema 1987). Natural-history museums stress similar values by emphasizing evolutionary patterns, which for a time also included racist eugenics (Rydell 1993). The commercial museums of Peale, Barnum, Kimbell, and the Western Museum would be at an even more extreme point on the popular end of the continuum along with other commercial attractions. As Handler (1986) observes, fine-art museums are taken to represent "our own culture," while ethnographic museums are established, like the colonial exhibitions of the worlds fairs, to represent "the less advanced cultures of others." The empowerment and legitimization of one culture at the expense of another parallel the social-class hegemony within the museum (Breckenridge 1989; Jordanova 1989; Karp and Lavine 1990). One serves to establish social distance from others of different cultures, while the second serves to establish social distance from others within the same culture. In both cases we symbolically enact our dominance. As Chapter Three contends, private collections help us to gain a sense of mastery and control over "the little world" of objects we collect as individuals. But museum collections help us, and particularly those among us of the higher classes, to gain a sense of mastery and control over the natural, human, and artificial worlds around us.

Changes in the character of institutional collecting

While the nineteenth century was the golden age of museums in which most countries of the Western world established prominent national and regional collections, the twentieth century has seen the proliferation, privatization, and re-emergence of democratic commercialized institutional collecting. In the early 1960s a new museum was constructed every 3.3 days in the United States (Hendon 1979). By 1989 mansion museums alone were being constructed at this same rate in the U.S. (George 1989). Throughout the 1980s an average of 230 museums opened each year in America (Vander Gucht 1991). In Britain museums are emerging at the rate of one every fortnight, and France, Germany, and Japan are enjoying a similar boom in museum growth (Lumley 1988). Contrary to the pattern in most of the world (except Japan), less than half of the museums in the U.S. are government- or university-sponsored and only 6 percent are federally operated (Lurie 1981). But this is not a basis for the conclusion that democratic commercialized institutional collecting has re-emerged. Rather, the trend toward commercialized institutional collecting exists more broadly than just the U.S. and involves a multifaceted set of links between museums, corporations, collectors, dealers, artists, and the public. As these linkages arose the former boundaries between high culture and popular culture, sacred and profane, profit and non-profit, and art and commerce have all become blurred.

One of the ways in which museums like the Boston Museum of Fine Arts and the Metropolitan Museum of Art rarefied themselves, in addition to relegating their reproductions to storage, was to avoid buying works by living artists, especially when the artists seemed to be profitable. For this would destroy the romantic myth of the starving artist/genius whose work is only appreciated posthumously. It would hint at profane intrusions of money into the sacred realm of museum art. Whereas the supply of art by artists of past generations is finite, the supply by living artists continues to expand. It was for this reason that Joseph Duveen refused to sell such work to his nouveau-riche clients and J. P. Morgan refused to buy such work. But there was a significant development in the art world that changed the nature of art collecting: the development of the avant-garde. One of the key advantages of relying on old masters as a source of art-collecting prestige is that there exists a stable pool of cultural symbols that can be purchased in order to extract the status that is culturally attached to these artworks. But the avant-garde, born of the French Revolution and steeped in romantic revolutionary political fervor, is dedicated to upsetting the status quo, bringing down the elite, and challenging traditional symbols of power (see Calinescu 1987). Deriving from the same romantic spirit as the consumer revolution, the avant-garde desire for novelty parallels that of consumer culture. Prominent among avant-garde artists are the French Impressionists who painted the informal leisure and recreation activities of late-nineteenth-century France as well as scenes of exotic "primitive" life (Clark 1985). For this first generation of avant-garde visual artists it was the everyday and the simple that most challenged the canons of the academy and the elite. As a romantic and revolutionary movement, avant-gardism was also opposed to capitalism and embraced, at least ostensibly, the model of the artist starving in a garret (Greenberg 1957). The Cubists, Futurists, and Dadaists were prominent among the second generation of avant-gardists (even if they felt it was avant-gardists their work repudiated) and began also to include even more humble everyday objects and bits and scraps of advertising in their sculptures, collages, and paintings (Benson 1987; Varnedde and Gopnik 1990). By the time of the New York Armory Show in 1913 and the opening of the Museum of Modern Art in 1929, the avant-garde had won the day. But a third and fourth generation of revolutionary artists emerged in the 1950s with Abstract Expressionism and Pop Art and in the 1980s with Neo-Geo, Neo-Conceptual, and Simulation art, offering still further avant-garde challenges and even more blatant uses of the commercial, the branded, and the popular. Just as the 1984 MOMA show "'Primitivism' in Twentieth Century Art" recognized and celebrated tribal objects as art, the 1990 MOMA show "High and Low: Modern Art and Popular Culture" recognized and celebrated the transformation of consumer goods, mass media, and advertising as art. And this work too has been assimilated by art museums, in ways that would have once shocked. As Calinescu (1987, p. 143) observes, the avant-garde is an elite movement committed to destroying all elites, including itself. It has succeeded and is now supplanted by a postmodernism which is largely classless and removes barriers between the high and the low. As art moved closer to the market, this may have been inevitable if Weber (1975) and DiMaggio (1982b) are correct that the market declassifies culture. Market declassification of culture is suggested by the earlier era of commercial museums as well as their modern counterparts by Madame Tussaud, Guiness, Disney, and Ripley. But declassification is increasingly found in large public museums as well. The vulgar market has invaded the sacred temple.

The marketization of museum collections and collecting has taken a number of forms since Pop Art first emerged. All of these things would have been unthinkable in early public museums, despite their roots in

Wunderkammern and commercial freak shows. And all of them would have horrified Benjamin (1968a), for they suggest that the work of art in an age of mechanical reproduction **is** a mechanical reproduction. As early as 1794 with the establishment of the Conservatoire National des Arts et Métiers in Paris, industrial machines began to find their way into museums, but only in the 1970s did consumer goods such as automobiles, radios, and televisions begin to appear in the revamped museum, now called the Musée National des Techniques (Danilov 1976). Following the Armory show, the New York branch of John Wanamaker's department store featured a Futurist Cubist fashion show, taking out a full-page ad in the *Sun* newspaper with the show's logotype (a pine tree) and motto "The New Spirit" featured at the bottom of the page (Lynes, 1955, p. 209). In 1928, Robert W. deForest, who succeeded J. P. Morgan as president of the Metropolitan Museum of Art in 1913, published a monograph through the Museum entitled *Art in Merchandise: Notes on the Relationships of Stores and Museums* (deForest 1928). In it he described the services of the Met to consumer-goods producers over the previous ten years:

> How ... dormant artistic traits have been awakened and marshalled to rescue beauty from the beast of stark utility is an open question. ... Certainly some advertisements have become a pleasing feature of our periodicals, and just as certainly this beneficent influence has extended to great improvements in the appearance of the package and containers in which so many of our manufactured products are now sold. In some cases, perhaps, and assuredly in the case of automobiles, this influence has reached the design of even the product itself. ... Every progressive museum in recent years has felt it to be an essential public duty to serve commerce by making available for study and inspiration the cultural resources of its collections. Special exhibitions of industrial art are a feature of this service and have a stimulative effect with ever-widening response. The Metropolitan Museum of Art, for example, held its tenth annual exhibition of this nature last winter and is now preparing for a successor for a growing public.
>
> (deForest 1928, p. 3)

DeForest goes on to describe the Met's assistance to and endorsement of Macy's in the store's exposition of the latest in tastefully designed consumer goods. He also praises Henry Ford for employing fine artistic design in the still secret Model A to replace the ugly utilitarianism of the Model T. In doing so, deForest elevates that mass reproduction to aesthetic virtue:

> Handwork has always been considered as superior artistically to the products of any machine, yet one of the most important factors in this alleged superiority is quite foreign to the question of good design. That is the factor of rarity or exclusiveness. The human hand cannot

repeat exactly, the machine cannot deviate. .... This may cheapen the product from the viewpoint of rarity but it enhances the aesthetic influence of that particular design if it is good in the model made for reproduction in quantity.

(deForest 1928, p. 7)

DeForest concluded with praises for the Parisian department stores Bon Marché, Galleries Lafayette, Louvre, and Printemps, each of which had pavilions at the 1925 Paris Exposition, as well as departments featuring "all kinds of material conceived in the modern spirit" (p. 10).

It is hardly surprising then that it was the Met which contributed to the various promotions of consumer fashions in the 1980s as chronicled by Silverman (1986). Each of the shows of note was initiated by Diana Vreeland, former editor of *Vogue* and *Harper's Bazaar* who was hired by the Metropolitan's Costume Institute in a successful effort to attract new people and new money to the museum. Her grand exhibitions began with the 1980–81 Met show of Ch'ing dynasty robes of the Chinese court. Not only did Bloomingdale's and Bonwit Teller's department stores capitalize on the exhibition by marketing mass-produced imitations of these robes and a host of related artifacts, the show was also sponsored by fashion designers Yves Saint-Laurent, Bill Blass, Oscar de la Renta, Adolfo, and Halston, who used the gala opening of the show to display their own new fashion lines on a number of the most prominent guests. And when visitors entered the exhibition hall they were overwhelmed with the smell of Yves Saint-Laurent's new perfume Opium, with which Vreeland had drenched the room in neocolonialist celebration of exotic China. The China show was followed by "The Eighteenth-Century Woman" sponsored by Merle Norman Cosmetics; "La Belle Epoque" sponsored by Pierre Cardin and also embraced by Bloomingdale's to market their new line of French fashions, perfumes, art, and furnishings; "Twenty-Five Years of Yves Saint-Laurent" during which the Met gift stores sold YSL merchandise and also promoted Diana Vreeland's new autobiography, *D.V.*; and the Polo/Ralph Lauren-sponsored "Man and the Horse." As Silverman (1986) incisively notes, the latter show abandoned all pretext of historicism in order to conflate the horsey set of British and French aristocracy with Ralph Lauren's Polo logo, his Thoroughbred line of home furnishings, and his line of equestrian fashions that followed the show. The benefit of each of these shows to the designers, department stores, and cosmetics firms involved was manifest in the contagion of enhanced image and accelerated sales, while the Met itself benefitted from expanded attendance and significant donations from those involved as well as their friends.

While the Met has been prominent in enshrining and ennobling consumer goods and their producers and purveyors, it has hardly been the only museum to do so. In 1987–88 the Victoria and Albert Museum in London staged a special exhibition, "Salvatore Ferragamo: The Art of the Shoe, 1927–1960." The poster for the exhibition was soon prominently displayed in Ferragamo shoe stores. By the time the show came to the Los Angeles County Museum of Art in 1992 it was accompanied by a lavish and highly complimentary catalogue filled, as was the exhibition, with photos of famous movie stars wearing Ferragamo shoes (Ricci 1992). Ferragamo contributed $100,000 to the museum whose gift shop sold Ferragamo handbags, scarves, and jewelry during the show, and Ferragamo retail stores in the area enjoyed a 20 percent increase in sales (Jacobson and Collins 1992). In 1991 the Stedelijk Museum in Amsterdam mounted a show of the work of industrial designer Raymond Loewy, including Studebaker automobiles, the Coca-Cola bottle and soft-drink dispensers, and the Lucky Strike cigarette package. There is a certain irony in the fact that while the showman-like Loewy was willing to take credit for designing the Coca-Cola bottle, he had nothing to do with its design (Bayley 1990). During November and December of 1991, Coke was involved in another exhibition at the Royal Ontario Museum in Toronto entitled "The Real Thing at the ROM." This seasonal exhibition included twenty-six of Haddon Sundblom's paintings of Santa Claus for Coca-Cola advertising from 1931 through the 1960s. Coke furnished the paintings and offered a discount on the entry fee into the exhibition with proof of purchase of its products. The critical response to the exhibition was summarized by Jill Savitt of the Washington, D.C. Center for the Study of Commercialism:

> It is sad that an august institution like the Royal Ontario Museum would put its imprimatur on junk food. . . . This further links the birth of Christ with Santa Claus, with consumption, and kids might understandably think for that reason Coke is really good for them. You expect greater objectivity and context in a museum show.
>
> (Godfrey 1991 p. 61)

Coca-Cola justified the show by suggesting that these Santa images transcend the soft drink and concern the creation of a modern legend. I interviewed the curator Howard Collinson nine months after the show's close and he said the critics unfairly expected the show to take a critical rather than an objective stance toward paintings which show the role of a corporation in creating our image of a popular cultural icon (see Belk 1993b). He saw nothing wrong with the exhibition or its inclusion of thirty other advertising paintings for Coke depicting the idealized world of Coke drinking. He felt that it was an objective portrayal of the role of the corporation in molding Santa Claus in this idealized image, complete with Coke's red-and-white color scheme.

These are just a few of the now commonplace appearances of branded consumer goods in museums. Museums like the Smithsonian have rules about what is and is not allowed commercially (since 1991 it has allowed corporate logos of exhibition sponsors), but so do corporations like Coca-Cola which insists that the first and last words of its name always appear on the same line and that any mention of the brand must be prefaced by the word "enjoy." Abiding by the Met's rules, in exchange for his corporation's $350,000 donation to the "Man and the Horse" exhibition at the Metropolitan Museum of Art, Ralph Lauren was granted the right for his logo to appear on all promotional material for the exhibition (McGill 1985). Such policies do not preclude controversy. Nevertheless, in the face of soaring art prices and dwindling government support, corporate sponsorships are an increasingly attractive option for museums. The initial assumption was that corporate sponsorship of museum exhibitions and the performing arts was a form of philanthropy:

> Some share the views of economist Milton Friedman that a corporation is to produce profits. ... Undoubtedly someone has to pay for corporate social projects – shareholders through lower dividends, customers through higher prices, workers through foregone wage increases. Yet, there has been surprisingly little resistance from all three groups to corporate philanthropy toward health, education, and welfare.

> (Chagy 1973, p. 79)

More recent discussions of such sponsorship make it clear that corporate sponsors expect these efforts to build favorable corporate culture within their organizations (French 1991), to perform the public-relations work of enhancing their prestige (McKay 1988), and to improve public attitudes toward companies in industries which threaten health and the environment. Thus it is no coincidence that some of the biggest corporate sponsors are cigarette companies such as Philip Morris, Rothmans, and Benson & Hedges, and oil companies such as Mobil, Texaco, Exxon, and Imperial Oil. By affiliating with prestigious art museums and events, a halo of sanctity is sought and perhaps acquired. In 1983 Philip Morris was doubly assured of their halo when they paid $3 million to sponsor the Metropolitan Museum of Art's "Vatican Collections: The Papacy and Art." And Mobil explained that they sponsored an exhibition of Maori art at the Met because it gave them a chance to foster good relations with the New Zealand government with whom they were pursuing a joint venture, and to entertain businessmen, politicians, and important customers from both countries at the opening-night gala (McGill 1985). The down side of this from the museum and public perspectives is that in seeking art to "match corporate image," the resulting exhibitions may be "safe" rather than provocative or adventurous. Furthermore, congruity theory holds that when two disparate images are paired, they both move in the direction of convergence (Osgood and Tannenbaum 1955). Therefore, if Mobil's image improves through association with the Metropolitan Museum, the Met's image will decline, with the stronger of the two changing least. Some corporations have formed lasting alliances with museums by opening museum branches in their corporate offices. Prominent among them are the New York headquarters of Equitable Life Assurance, Philip Morris, and Champion International, which have all opened branches of the Whitney Museum of American Art in their offices. Whitney supplies a rotating series of paintings and sculptures while the corporations provide the gallery space and cover associated costs (Danilov 1986). The institutions' positions are reversed from corporate sponsorships in traditional museum buildings to a museum's name embedded in a corporate setting.

A still more direct form of corporate involvement in the arts is through corporate collecting. In the United States there were over 1,000 corporate art collections in 1989 (Martorella 1990). By building corporate collections that are dispersed throughout corporate offices or housed in a corporate gallery that is open to the public, the firm enhances corporate morale, builds public and community prestige and support, and maintains a good financial investment at the same time. IBM began collecting corporate art for its pavilion in the 1939 world's fair (Zukin 1991). Now, like many other companies, it has a corporate art museum in its Armonk, New York headquarters. Other corporate art museums include those of Charles Saatchi (of Saatchi and Saatchi) in London, American Express and AT&T in New York, General Mills in Minneapolis, Minnesota, and Yasuda Fire and Marine Insurance Company in Tokyo. Of 379 museums in Japan in 1988, fully 60 percent were owned by businesses (Chapman 1990). Corporations have been called modern Medici because of the power they are coming to wield in the art world (Joy 1993; McKay 1988). For instance, in addition to housing a branch of the Whitney Museum, Equitable Life Assurance spent over $7 million on art for its corporate lobby in the mid-1980s, including commissioning a huge Roy Lichtenstein mural and a sculptural seating complex by Scott Burton (Stephens 1986). In this case an added intent of the art collection is to draw tenants to its high-rent office building. Cassullo (1988) overstates only a bit in claiming that "Thanks in part to corporate involvement, art has finally become a commodity to be traded like soybeans and pork bellies" (p. 137). This is an interesting, if unintended, extension of the metaphor of market commodities that Joseph Choate, the first president of the Metropolitan Museum of Art, used in 1880 in appealing to wealthy merchants for contributions to the museum:

> Think of it, ye millionaires of many markets – what glory may yet be yours, if you only listen to our advice, to convert pork into porcelain, grain and produce into priceless pottery, the rude ore of commerce into sculptured marble, and railroad shares and mining stocks – things which perish without the using, and which in the next financial panic shall surely shrivel like parched scrolls – into the

glorified canvas of the world's masters, that shall adorn these walls for centuries.

(Tomkins 1970, p. 23)

What has not changed is the sacralizing, elevating, and cleansing power of art. Where once merchants sought to launder their individual reputations through ownership and eventual donation of art to public museums, now corporations seek to sanitize their reputations by ownership and display of art which they also hold as an investment. Such collections do for corporations what museums do for municipalities and nations (Buck and Dodd 1991). But as with corporate sponsorships, Joy (1993) finds that corporate collections in Canada insist that "art objects cannot be controversial, make political statements, or be explicitly sexual" (p. 40). At the same time, such corporate galleries do make art accessible to a larger or at least a different public. And if the art is often used as part of interior decoration in order to gain, claim, or display status, the same may be said of the original Medici and centuries of art collectors before and since. Based on her study of 234 corporate art collections, Martorella (1990) concludes, "It is unfortunate that some of the finest examples of contemporary American art are found in the office corridors of Fortune 500 companies not accessible to the public" (p. 178). But here too, the same may be said of individual collections of art. The difference may be that the collections of on-going corporate institutions will remain inaccessible to the broader public for a longer period of time than individual collections. Rather than the Medici, a more apt comparison for corporate art collections may be the robber barons:

Ideologically, art in the workplace could undermine the reality of an economic condition of mass production that encourages sameness and conformity rather than the individuality fostered by the creative process. This process of co-optation is further enhanced by recent developments in the economy that encourage the short-term profiteering that predetermined corporate collecting. This period of rapid growth is analogous to the building boom of the mid-nineteenth century, which became the subject of Thorstein Veblen's well-known critique of culture and society. Similarly, many corporate headquarters are shockingly vulgar expressions of the profits made by their mergers and junk bond departments. Postmodern façades use expensive marble, glass, and steel; interiors glitter with mirrors and cloth wallcoverings, marble-covered atriums; huge, vacuous spaces indicate affordable yet horrifying waste. Collections are abundant and express the arrogance of wealth and power. They are ostentatious by their quantity and size, as well as by their ability to be expediently and rationally used in an unabashed way to improve the marketability of corporate products.

(Martorella 1990, p. 184)

There is little doubt that corporate decor and lifestyle are more opulent than most of us can afford. While corporations have generally not been asked to justify their art collections and opulence, Andrew Carnegie's (1889) defense of robber-baron art collecting as advancing the nation would probably not be an unlikely response.

Another type of corporate museum collection that is generally less opulent and more directly tied to public relations and promotion is the museum of the corporation or its industry. Examples are Conoco's oil museum, Campbell Soup's museum of antique soup tureens, General Foods' museum of food utensils, N.V. Philips's "Evoluon," the Corning Glass Center, Goodyear's "World of Rubber," Nippon Telephone & Telegraph's Telecommunications Science Hall, and Hershey's "Chocolate World." There are over a hundred such museums in the United States and at least thirty in other countries (Danilov 1986). Some are less blatantly self-promotional than others. For example, unlike the Ferragamo shoe exhibitions, the Bata Shoe Museum in Canada and the Bally Shoe Collection in Switzerland feature historical shoes with the sponsoring corporations appearing only in the names of the exhibitions. A prominent recent corporate-museum opening was the $15-million World of Coca-Cola founded in Coke's corporate home city of Atlanta, Georgia in 1990. A brief look at this museum highlights the way in which such museums may operate to enhance corporate images.

As Pendergrast (1993) observes, the Coca-Cola museum is a fantasyland geared to corporate myth-building, inaccurately invoking the American success myth of Horatio Alger novels. But there is more to the carefully crafted museum (attracting a million visitors a year) than this. The central exterior feature of the museum is a twelve-and-a-half-ton two-sided neon Coca-Cola/Coke disk rotating inside a globe. As the title of the museum implies, a central theme expressed is that Coke is a world-wide beverage. Indeed, Coca-Cola is the quintessential multinational corporation, doing business in nearly every country in the world. But globalism is also a part of the appeal in this U.S. museum. Visitors see numerous advertisements for Coke in foreign lands, as well as photographs of Coke in exotic contexts, for example with camel drivers in front of Egyptian pyramids, in a Japanese tea room, and cases of Coke being carried on a bicycle and by rustic boat in Thailand. There is a wall-size composite high-definition television version of the "Hilltop Reunion" bringing together in 1991 the original participants in the popular 1971 "I'd Like to Buy the World a Coke" commercial for a remake with their children. And Coke proudly touts its Haddon Sundblom Santa Claus ads not only in English, but in other languages from around the world. I have even seen a version in Thai in a hill-tribe village in northern Thailand. And near the end of the self-guided tour, there is a tasting room to sample all of Coke's beverages (besides its classic version) sold in various parts of the world. The appeal of Coca-Cola in most of the world is that it represents modern America (e.g., in Romania and other Eastern European countries, Coke makes it a point to advertise in English). But in The World of Coca-Cola, the appeal to the largely American visitors is the exotic otherness of the places in which Coke is globally marketed. There is a corporate neo-colonialism expressed here that is reminiscent of the colonial exhibitions of native villages in the world's fairs of the nineteenth and early twentieth centuries.

The other major thrust of the Coke museum is one that is common to many museums: the appeal to nostalgia. Not only are there numerous Coca-Cola advertisements and merchandising materials from the past, but the visitor is able to select and watch five-minute video clips of a variety of historical topics from each five-year period from Coke's 1886 founding to 1940. The newsreel-like coverage has nothing to do with Coca-Cola per se, and its only rationale is to associate Coke with nostalgically remembered periods in the past. But despite an emphasis on exotic cultures in less economically developed parts of the world and antique advertising and memorabilia, the museum is not at all tawdry. Its clean-cut red-jacketed employees, its simulation of an endlessly moving automatic bottling line, and its use of the latest in high-tech media, all give a sanitary, cheerful, and lively feel to the museum. We leave the museum feeling that there could be nothing untoward or sinister about this corporation and its innocuous request to buy the world a Coke. The Coca-Cola bottle that Raymond Loewy did not design is a pan-cultural icon and this museum is a monument intended to venerate it (Gilborn 1982). Lest the pilgrim leave without a souvenir to memorialize the visit, the tour concludes in the gift shop which is filled with Coca-Cola logos festooned on a wide variety of red-and-white products reiterating the themes of nostalgia and exotic otherness emphasized in the museum. The museum is a monument to a quintessential symbol of consumer culture: a temporarily arousing elixir providing pleasure that quickly fades and is infinitely renewable in the spirit of modern hedonism. The consumer uproar when Coke tried to change its "classic" formula for something that tasted better shows the strength of Coke's symbolic iconic meaning.

As Zembala (1990) points out, the "grandfather" of corporate museums is Henry Ford's Greenfield Village and Henry Ford Museum in Dearborn, Michigan. Now independent of the Ford family and Ford Motor Company, the museum for years was crowded with Ford automobiles and historical and grand automobiles from around the world, as well as other forms of transportation, and products of mass production. In the automobile portion of the museum, its Curator of American History, Robert Casey, explained in an interview that the cars were all lined up in chronological order to reflect Ford's vision of the march of progress. This changed in 1987 when the museum opened its first interpretive exhibition, "The Automobile in American Life." In preparing for the $6-million permanent exhibition that occupies one-fourth of the museum's floorspace, the Ford museum deaccessioned nearly 800 cars and added about 40 others in order to concentrate on approximately 100 primarily American cars, with Ford playing little more than a representative role (Hyde 1989). Perhaps more than any other consumer good, the automobile is a key symbol of consumer society, so I was interested in how it was portrayed as shaping consumer desire. In one of seven major sections, the exhibition does a good job of detailing the role of the automobile as a symbol of success, individuality, youth, power, freedom, and personality. Another section at least implicitly acknowledges the role of the automobile in changing the roadside landscape from independent tourist cabins and diners to corporate chains such as McDonalds and Holiday Inn. And a section on advertising and promotion effectively details the various appeals of automobile advertising and promotions at auto shows and world's fairs.

Still, as Robert Casey recognizes, there is a celebratory tone to all of this. The automobile is represented nostalgically with an emphasis on glamour, fun, and escape. Automobile exterior design is presented as art. But there is little attention to traffic deaths, pollution, stultifying production lines, or even the growth of suburbs and shopping malls. When the exhibition does deal with problems (emissions, the decline of the American automobile industry, fossil-fuel shortages, safety), it deals with them as problems tackled and mastered by American industry. Nor is there any kind of ethnographic evidence drawn from automobile consumers. As with most museums, the objects are thought to need only curatorial interpretation, and the voices of those who use these objects are ignored. Rather the cars are "heroic artifacts" (Corn 1989). Nevertheless, the exhibition is not as celebratory of the brand (make) as corporate museums like Coca-Cola's are. Nor is it as obsequious as some museum exhibitions with corporate sponsors. Casey cites the Chicago Museum of Science and Industry's recent reliance on corporations and trade associations which essentially build the exhibitions for which the museum acts as a shill. But in the Henry Ford Museum's collaboration with *Popular Mechanics Magazine* in staging an exhibition, "Possible Dreams: Popular Mechanics and America's Enthusiasm for Technology," running from 1992 to 1994, the exhibition poster featured sixty-six covers of *Popular Mechanics* (Wright 1992) and the exhibition is as celebratory of technology as "The Automobile in American Life" is of cars.

The criticism of the Chicago Museum of Science and Industry appears well founded. In 1993 the museum featured in its entry forum a large Erector Set (Meccano) model of the Ferris Wheel with a notice that Meccano products are sold in the museum shop. Another exhibition "Wheels of Change" was presented by General Motors and featured that firm's cars. A Marshall Field's store operates in the museum. At the Star Trek Federation Science exhibition, visitors can see highlights from twenty-five years of *Star Trek, Star Trek: The Next Generation*, and the *Star Trek* movies, and a Starfleet

Store is set up to sell Star Trek memorabilia. There is also a Business Hall of Fame in the museum paying tribute to numerous business leaders and their companies, most of which have some links to the museum, and an exhibition on the advantages of natural-gas energy. What has been said of this museum might as easily be said of a number of other science and industry museums, which in fairness were established in order to promote technology, science, and industry, although perhaps not individual corporations. Increasingly as well, numerous exhibitions might be cited from other types of museums which also feature branded consumer goods. These include the permanent "A Material World" exhibition at the Smithsonian's National Museum of American History (Friedel 1988; Horrigan 1992; McDaniel 1989), the same museum's O. Orkin (Pest Control) Insect Zoo at the Museum of Natural History, the 1984–85 "25 Years of Barbie Dolls" exhibition at the Indiana State Museum in Indianapolis, various computer exhibitions including those at the Chicago Museum of Science and Industry, the National Museum of American History, Boston's Computer Museum, and San Jose's Tech Museum of Innovation (Abbate 1993; Rash 1990), the 1993 Ferrari exhibition (and numerous past automobile exhibitions) at the Museum of Modern Art, and the 1993–94 "Mechanical Brides" exhibition at the Cooper-Hewitt National Museum of Design in New York (Lupton 1993). The 1993 "George Carlson Dignity and Art" exhibition at the Gene Autry Western Heritage Museum in Los Angeles goes a step further by offering the bronzes and prints for sale at prices ranging from $2,600 to $250,000. Museums **do** sometimes reject certain work and exhibitions as being too commercial as with the Philadelphia Museum of Art's rejection of the lifesize bronze of Sylvester Stallone which was installed in front of the museum for the film "Rocky III." In this case, however, the commercial tie-in was less a concern than the fact that this particular film series was representative of popular culture rather than fine art (Rice 1992).

In other cases, museums have embraced popular culture and openly celebrated branded consumer goods as something integral to everyday twentieth-century life and therefore worth presenting as historical subject matter. One of these is the Museum of Modern Mythology in San Francisco, which recognizes the mythological character of anthropomorphic advertising icons such as Colonel Sanders, Speedy Alka-Seltzer, Pacman, and the American Express Centurion (Dolan 1988; Rapoport 1989). At the Strong Museum in Rochester, New York, there is a large permanent exhibition of "Selling the Goods: Origins of American Advertising, 1840–1940." The museum itself is funded by the estate of Margaret Woodbury Strong, an inveterate collector of popular culture (Sandler 1989). Rather than "upgrade" the collection to one of high culture, director H. J. Swiney has pruned the collection of anything that would not be found in a middle-class Victorian household (Moynehan 1982). And as a part of the SAMDOK project in Sweden, the Nordiska Museet of Stockholm has devoted a portion of its yearly budget to surveying the contents of contemporary Swedish homes, interviewing the residents about the meanings of the objects found there, and acquiring a number of their rooms, complete with contents, for the museum (Nyström and Cedrenius 1982; Rubenstein 1985; Stavenow-Hidemark 1985). When I visited the archives of this program in 1988, the researchers had begun to return to some of the families interviewed earlier in order to collect longitudinal data on their material lifestyles and artifacts. A part of this program, also being carried out in offices and factories, is based on the philosophy that it is less expensive to collect contemporary objects now than to try to find them years later as antiques. Various advocates have urged the collection of more objects of popular culture by museums (e.g., Schroeder 1981). But more than this, rather than the mute testimony of objects, the SAMDOK project gathers ethnographic data from everyday consumer life. The same is true of an exhibition by Grant McCracken at the Royal Ontario Museum's Institute of Contemporary Culture in 1992, entitled "Toronto Teenagers" and featuring for each of a number of teen subcultures, representative clothing, music, and videotaped interviews on issues of the day (Noorani 1992). Unfortunately this first exhibition by the Institute may have been its last due to funding problems. And the consumer was silent in the V & A's 1994 "Streetstyle" (Polhemus 1994).

Three final aspects of consumer culture in museums that have developed or accelerated in the past decade are the museum shop, the blockbuster show, and the "Disneyfication" of museums. The most successful of the museum shops are those of the Metropolitan Museum of Art and the Smithsonian Institution, which grossed $65 million and $52 million respectively in 1988 (Levine 1989). Of this the Met earned about $6.2 million in tax-free profit. Besides its main shop and thematic boutiques throughout the museum, the Met has outlets in Macy's department store, the New York Public Library, and upscale shopping centers in New Jersey, Connecticut, and Ohio. It also sends out its catalogue six times a year to almost three million people (Levine 1989). As museums scramble for funds, few can aspire to the success of these giants ($1million a year in sales is more typical), but museum retailing is becoming increasingly like that of other marketers. Chicago's Field Museum of Natural History has hired a manager from Lord & Taylor department store, the Art Institute of Chicago has hired a shop manager from Nieman-Marcus, and the Los Angeles County Museum has hired a general manager from Gump's department store (Rudolph 1985). As if in oxymoronic tribute to Benjamin's (1968a) fears about the work of art in an age of mechanical reproduction, these museums specialize in offering "authentic reproductions." At the Met, the head curators of each museum department are in charge of approving reproductions from their departments and exclusive distribution assures that the reproductions will not show up at other mass merchants. The museum is also careful to supply authenticating descriptions of the original work with each piece and reports that customers balk if such documents are missing. This may seem a bit like the pedigrees of the plates and miniature collectibles sold by firms like the Bradford Exchange and the Franklin Mint (Boniface and Fowler 1993, p. 116), except that in this case the museum's prestige and possession of the original is better than the gold that once backed paper currency because it helps transfer to the buyer the aura with which Benjamin was concerned. And like the *Treatise on Superfluous Things* in Ming China and the magazines and manuals of more recent times in Europe and America, the fact that something comes from a prestigious art museum assures the would-be social climber of his or her good taste.

The blockbuster show represents the museum's adaptation of another marketing technique that can be traced to the Crystal Palace and the development of consumer culture: the spectacle (Debord 1970). The spectacle is all surface with no depth. Blockbuster shows like a giant show of Picasso, Impressionists, King Tut, or Georgia O'Keefe, are, like corporate collecting, "safe," profitable, and accessible, but they don't break any new educational or scholarly ground (Marquis 1991, pp. 327–328). They provide "spectacular though often superficial entertainment, with the disadvantage of creating disruption and crowding" (Zolberg 1984, p. 389). Similarly, the widely expressed concern with the "Disneyfication" of museums is grounded in a fear that the museum, in order to remain economically viable, must increasingly pander to the entertainment desires of a public raised on television, shopping malls, and theme parks. A Disneyfied museum, critics charge, sacrifices education and enlightenment to superficial entertainment based on illusions. It offers little more than the smoke and mirrors of Dante's Hell in Cincinnati's early Western Museum. In order to compete for visitors, the museum creates an illusionary hyperreality (Baudrillard 1988a; Eco 1986) like that of Disneyland and Disney World where the presentation is sterilized and romanticized in order to make it more visually appealing; more appealing than reality; a hyped reality. Hooper-Greenhill (1992) expresses the concerns raised by such spectacles: "What is the use of the museums in the age of the 'experience', the unified total approach to knowledge? Where museums seek to emulate theaters, cinemas, pageants, and funfairs, what is left of unique and specific value?" (p. 215).

Some of the more commonly cited examples of hyperreal Disneyfied museum presentations are the Jorvik Center in York, Plymoth Plantation in Massachusetts, and Colonial Williamsburg in Virginia (Vander Gucht 1991; Lumley 1988; Mills 1990). In each case the charge is that these historic locales have been sanitized, glorified, and made into consumption-oriented entertainments rather than something more authentic and substantive. Whereas Bazin (1967, p. 257) describes Williamsburg as "an enchanted world where all is as it was two centuries ago," the pristine conditions, the initial lack of any indication of slavery, and the romanticized cuisine in the reconstructed village's restaurants and taverns, lend themselves to the charge of hyperreality. While for most museum curators Disneyland represents the evil of market-driven pandering to the lowest common denominator of public tastes (e.g., Terrell 1991), Margaret King (1990, 1991) has been a champion of the thesis that museums have much to learn from Disneyland, Disney World, and EPCOT Center. By making exhibitions more accessible and enjoyable, she suggests, museums reach a broader public in a more effective way. Instead of remaining a bastion of elite culture, museums on the Disney model are more egalitarian, full of life, and dynamic rather than forbidding. No doubt to the horror of many museum directors and curators, King (1991) suggests that the museums of Charles Peale and P. T. Barnum recognized these truths far better than modern museums. Disneyfication is a controversial topic within the museum community (Ames 1992). When I raised the issue with Robert Casey at the Henry Ford Museum, he offered a familiar defense of the museum against such practices: authenticity. "Disney is an illusion. The whole attraction is how good the illusion is. You come to a museum to see real stuff, not an illusion." Since only museums have the "real stuff," their collections are seen, in this view, as containing sacred objects with an aura of authenticity. Thus, despite the many inroads of consumerism and the market into museums, we are back to Benjamin's objection to reproductions. To begin to sort through these contradictions the next section asks what is unique about institutional collecting.

THE NATURE OF CONTEMPORARY INSTITUTIONAL COLLECTING

Institutional collecting versus individual collecting

One starting point for understanding institutional collecting as discussed in this chapter is to ask how it differs from the individual collecting discussed in the previous chapter. I began this chapter by suggesting that many of the same psychological processes found in individual collecting can also be found in institutional collecting, with modifications such as those concerning the levels of extended self involved. Another difference may be found in the notion of possession that underlies the collection. While a curator may be possessive toward a collection and regard it as "mine," the fact remains that unlike an individual collector, a museum curator does not own the objects in a collection and lacks the individual collector's total control over their fate. This is not an insignificant difference. Price relates one dealer's summary which

> placed museum curators in the same category as men whose only knowledge of women derived from reading pornographic magazines; collectors, by possessing the objects, are the ones who know how to

make love. Just as headhunters have always known, he proposed, "Knowledge is founded upon possession."

(Price 1989, pp. 101–102)

Furthermore, while an individual collector may sometimes feel compelled to justify a collection falsely in terms of its contribution to art, science, or history, a museum curator is implicitly or explicitly bound to acquire, maintain, and present objects for the benefit of others. This is generally taken to mean inspiring and educating the public, or some segment of it at any rate. It is far more likely, for instance, that the individual collector can justify collecting as a playful, fun activity. Museum collecting, on the other hand, even if it involves psychedelic posters such as those Howard Collinson collected for the ROM, is serious. Although individual collecting is sometimes redeemed by casting it as serious rather than playful, this seriousness is often claimed in terms of the collection's supposed investment potential, even if the collector only offers this as a rationalization. This seriousness is also demonstrated by documentation in the museum: "What distinguishes a museum collection from [a] private collection? We hope a sense of purpose. We hope a sense of responsibility to document in the finest detail the things that are collected" (Neal 1980, p. 26). Herrmann elaborates on these traits versus those of the avid amateur collector:

> There is a curious antithesis of objectivity between the professional art historian or museum curator on the one hand and the private collector on the other in the purchase of what may be virtually the same pieces. The professional regards taste as a vague, ambivalent characteristic; he tends nowadays to profess scientific detachment, he must shun prejudice . . . to fill his gaps, to be representative, ultimately to educate. The collector's considerations are far more personal. Does the object appeal to him; does he think it beautiful; is it sufficiently different from what he already owns; will it "go" with the rest of his belongings?
>
> (Herrmann 1972, pp. 20–21)

While this portrait exaggerates the extent to which curators are emotionless and detached from the materials they collect, it captures the criteria on which a curator is expected to rely. The museum collection may not invoke the investment criterion of private collectors either, although the corporate collection may. What is legitimately left to the museum curator is an intellectualized and distanced view of the collection. Furthermore, museum visitors are used to such presentations and expect labels (or audiovisual presentations) to tell them what they are seeing. This may result in a staged authenticity (MacCannell 1989) in which the signs and labels are more important than the objects, site, or event (see Kirshenblatt-Gimblett 1990). In these intellectualized institutional collections that produce such exhibitions, what is most likely to differentiate museum objects from objects in individual collections is the emotional response of both visitors and those in charge of the objects (Hendon 1979). In part this is due to the intellectualized framing of these objects, in part it is due to the museum-goer's prior expectations, and in part it is due to the curator's lack of the individual ownership which allows the collector to manipulate his or her little world of objects for personal pleasure.

Some museums confound these expectations. For instance, the Explora-torium in San Francisco has many hands-on exhibitions and encourages visitors to explore and discover rather than read labels. In Germany, the Insel Hombroich near Düsseldorf has a series of buildings linked by paths beside a river on a partially wooded former farmstead (the former farm buildings join newly constructed buildings as exhibition space). Some of the buildings have art, others are acoustic experiments. None of this is labeled. Unidentified artwork is mixed rather than being grouped or chronologi-cally arranged and folk art, fine art, and popular art are mixed indiscrimi-nately. Although the music memorabilia collected and displayed by the Hard Rock Cafe chain are all labeled, there still exist bars with unlabeled eclectic mixes of nostalgic objects that do not differ greatly from the collections in apothecaries, taverns, and barber shops of an earlier era (Dewhurst and MacDowell 1986). And in 1972 Marcel Broodthaers mounted the exhibition "The Eagle from the Oligocene up to the Present Day" in the Städtische Kunsthalle in Düsseldorf, showing 266 representa-tions of eagles on or in such diverse objects as jewelry, bottles, fossils, suits of armor, paintings, comic strips, and typewriters (see Buchloh 1983; Crimp 1993; Grasskamp 1983). While these objects were each carefully numbered and labeled, these labels said, in French, German, or English, "This is not a work of art." By juxtaposing eagles from such diverse contexts and by repeating this variant of Magritte's "*Ceci n'est pas une pipe*," Broodthaers played with the notion of a museum in a way that nicely differentiates individual and most contemporary institutional collecting. For while such eccentricity and diversity is tolerated in individual collecting or even institutionalized private collections such as a mouse museum (Belk and Wallendorf, forthcoming) and an elephant museum (Wallendorf and Belk 1987), we do not expect to see it in a "serious" museum. It defies the Classical episteme that Foucault (1970) suggests has held since the Enlightenment. We might find such objects scattered among museums of ethnography, fine art, modern art, history, natural history, and industry perhaps, but not mixed together like this. The taxonomic rules separating museums from *Wunderkammern* and legitimizing them as sanctuaries for art, history, or science have been violated. The audience may be baffled, amused, enraged, or delighted, but these are responses we have learned to suppress in our reaction to the left-hemisphere presentations of serious museums. Even art museums are not places for aesthetic enjoyment as much as for learning about art history. Weil illustrates this by asking us to imagine a National Toothpick Museum,

> heavily endowed, well situated in a prime downtown area, installed in its own large, modern and climate-controlled building, and wholly and exclusively devoted to the collection, preservation, study, interpretation and display of toothpicks ... this is a ridiculous endeavor, a venture that might be acceptable enough as a hobby but which becomes grotesque and preposterous when inflated to the level of a large scale museum.
>
> (Weil 1990, pp. 43–44)

Thus, while there are some serious intellectual individual collectors and some frivolous emotional institutional collectors, we are most likely to pair these adjectives in just the opposite way.

Museums versus department stores

Perhaps predictably, a reviewer of the recently opened Andy Warhol Museum in Pittsburgh compared the experience to that of "a rather exhausting department store" (Adams 1994, p. 129). Appadurai and Breckenridge frame the historical linkage of the emergence of department stores and museums discussed in Chapter One and earlier in this chapter:

> Museums in Europe and the United States have been linked to department stores through a common genealogy in the great nineteenth-century world's fairs. But in the last century, a separation of art and science and of festivity and commerce has taken place in these societies, with the objects and activities in each category fairly sharply distinguished in terms of audience, curatorial expertise, and visual ideology.
>
> (Appadurai and Breckenridge 1992, p. 39)

If the department store, the shopping mall, and the theme park, despite their feared intrusions into the museum, are anathema to traditional museums, what are the critical factors that keep museum collections distinct? Or are they distinct? One obvious difference is that in department stores everything is for sale. Several prominent Japanese department stores in Japan and the United States have further blurred the boundary by opening galleries and museums in their stores (Buck and Dodd 1991). But even museums with the most aggressive museum shops have not come to the point where the collections exist merely to lure people into the shop (although a recent Saatchi and Saatchi promotion did refer to the Victoria and Albert as "An ace caf' with quite a nice museum attached"). In one Philadelphia Museum of Art exhibition of "Design Since 1945," the installation of primarily household objects explicitly sought to distinguish itself from displays in department stores such as Macy's or Bloomingdale's. The solution for curator George Nelson was to emphasize the historical and educational mission of the museum exhibition. This was done in three ways:

> First, the exhibition is arranged in a linear progression – you enter and follow a designated route, as opposed to the department store's random, horizonless layout intended to encourage impulse buying. Second, the objects on exhibit are arranged by subject group or materials, such as lamps, furniture, glass, ceramics, and textiles, in chronological order; discrete designs within these groups are given equal treatment. A department store, on the other hand, arranges objects according to environments or settings meant to simulate the home and the objects are arranged in their subordinate position as accessories. Third, the exhibition attempts to inform us of the history, design, and manufacture of these objects, where a department store would highlight style and function.
>
> (Bodine 1983, p. 25)

In other words, the underlying principles are order, taxonomy, decontextualized (or recontextualized) highlighting of the object as art, and an educational and historical emphasis on factual information. Just as collectors typically take objects away from their normal uses, rather than classify goods by function as in a department store, museums arrange them by more abstract, presumably scientific criteria. Museums are also typically places of guards and glass cases where we are kept at a distance from the objects, whereas we are welcome to handle the merchandise in a department store, as Assendorf distinguishes:

> touching the goods, trying them on, the pleasure of rummaging about in the materials bring to the visual a tactile component in the presentation of commodities, which minimizes the distance, necessary in the museum but disturbing in the department store, between people and the things. Touching allows for a provisional participation in the paradise of commodity plentitude, which only intensifies the desire for possession.
>
> (Assendorf 1993, p. 103)

Museums are also traditionally places with old objects which have both a nostalgic appeal (Harris 1978) and the status derived from a patina of age (McCracken 1988). Department stores, on the other hand, have objects whose prestige lies in their price, newness, novelty, and fashionableness. Museum objects are only novel by virtue of their anachronistic qualities and otherness. In this sense Harris (1962, p. 130) calls department stores, shopping malls, and markets "the true museums of everyday life." In a 1972 study of nearly 2,000 people in Germany, 57 percent considered going to a museum to be improving/informing, but only 6 percent considered it to be entertaining/relaxing (Alexander 1979, pp. 168–169). Asked what a museum reminded them of, this sample replied: a palace (30 percent), a monument (19 percent), a school (12 percent), or a church (9 percent). Only 2 percent said a department store. In a 1985 study in Great Britain based on nearly 1,000 respondents, 35 percent said a museum was similar to a library, 34 percent chose a "monument to the dead," 11 percent a school, 10 percent a church or temple, and only 1 percent a department store (Merriman 1989).

However, in recent years, especially in the United States, the differences between museums and commercial businesses may be declining. Silverman compares the differences between the China shows at Bloomingdales and at the Metropolitan Museum:

> Significantly, in the months before the Met show opened, many of the same precious Chinese robes to be exhibited at the Met had been on display at Bloomingdale's, where a special museum had been established for the duration of the China sales campaign. The Metropolitan exhibition was on the surface very different from the Bloomingdale's project. At the department store the real Chinese robes had been difficult to distinguish from the panoply of reproductions offered for sale in close proximity; the Met show focused only on the rare, authentic robes, lifting them out of the marketplace into the citadel of scholarship, connoisseurship, and historical explication. Yet despite the presumed difference between the consumerist and high cultural versions of China, the 1980 Met museum show shared the themes and selectivity of the Bloomingdale's packaging of China. ... The Metropolitan's Chinese robes show emerged as a perfect pendant to the Bloomingdale's presentation of China preceding it; it projected fantasies of wealth, power, and leisure attached to an ancient imperial civilization and displayed them in the form of a fashion show.
>
> (Silverman 1986, p. 31)

As Silverman's account suggests, not only has the museum moved in the direction of and in compliment to the high-end department store, these stores have also adopted some of the techniques of the museum, including appropriating its prestige and patina status associations (see Zukin 1991). As Urry (1990) observes, high-quality shops provide increasingly museum-like displays where people can wander and gaze. Furthermore, many restaurants, pubs, and shops have become "museumified." Besides Hard Rock Cafe, other chains like TGI Friday, *Planet Hollywood,* and the Bubble Room have followed this path. As the museum increasingly competes for private funds, it feels itself increasingly in competition with the department store, shopping mall, and theme park. Morton suggests that this competition may not always be good:

> Some of the contemporary pressures operating on museums come from the growth of tourism and the industries devoted to leisure. For

instance theme parks compete directly with museums as alternative places for visitors to go. A shopping mall sets out to attract consumers and to occupy their free time with the pleasures of consumption in a public space whose architectural features are reminiscent of those found in museum buildings. . . . The greater the success of these malls and theme parks, the greater the pressure on museums to emulate these in various ways; to mount spectacular and expensive displays (to compete with, say, the Disney organization's EPCOT in Florida) or even to place a museum "shop" in a prominent site.

(Morton 1988, pp. 137–138)

More than merely placing shops in prominent locations, the directors of these shops in museums like the Metropolitan and the Louvre have experience in department-store retailing and are sophisticated merchandisers (Costa and Bamossy, forthcoming). Besides shops, which now sometimes even form the entry and exit to the museum, museum cafés and restaurants, special Omnimax cinema presentations, and in the case of museums like the Metropolitan Museum of Art, renting out galleries for cocktail parties, dinners, corporate gatherings, and other events at prices of $30,000 and up, all expand the marketing emphasis of the museum in ways that some find horrifying. In the concluding section of this chapter, I explore whether this response is warranted.

MUSEUMS AS MARKETERS

Paradoxically in light of the role of the rise of consumer culture in stimulating mass collecting by both individuals and institutions, the increasing involvement of museums as marketers seeking to win consumers away from commercial competitors has caused significant consternation in the museum community. As Harris observes,

> some of the effort to gain government grants and to tap private sources through membership drives, gift shops, innovative entertainments, and popular exhibitions has had beneficial results. But in the eyes of some critics these financial pressures have also introduced a vulgarized and distorting set of institutional goals, diverted attention and energy away from ongoing curatorial and administrative responsibilities, introduced a commercialized ethic and vending vocabulary, and generally exaggerated museums [sic] expectations and anticipated benefits to a point where they have been inevitably disappointed.
>
> (Harris 1990, p. 143)

Consider a relatively minor incident at the Victoria and Albert Museum in 1988. From its inception following the Great Exhibition of 1851, this museum, along with its sister institution, the Science Museum, which was also an offshoot from the original South Kensington Museum, was intended to promote British decorative arts, science, and technology, partly as a reaction against the growing military and industrial strength of Germany (Morton 1988). It also exhibited a consumer orientation early on, opening the world's first museum restaurant in 1863 (Bazin 1967). The 1988 incident involved substituting a Wedgwood vase from the museum's collection for the famous Portland Roman vase from which Josiah Wedgwood made his copy only 200 years ago. While this vase is a technically admirable copy and was appropriately labeled when it replaced the original which then underwent restoration, Wernick (1991) demurs because Wedgwood was "a mass manufacturer of high-grade kitsch" (p. 9). In addition, Wedgwood played an important role in the development of consumer culture in England by means of then revolutionary (though now commonplace) marketing techniques (Forty 1986; McKendrick *et al.* 1982). These techniques included product differentiation, branding, limited distribution, periodic fashion changes, direct advertising, market segmentation, and multiple product lines (price lining) such that the more exclusive lines that were marketed to the elite (often friends of Wedgwood) made the more affordable lines more prestigious to the masses. In Wernick's (1991) view, there are a series of ironies here. The V & A uses the original Portland Vase as a symbol to promote itself. Yet, by featuring the Wedgwood vase, which unlike the original is a reproduction and a product of a corporation that still makes a profit from ceramics, it helps to promote Wedgwood. Added to this, the pivotal role that Wedgwood played in introducing the marketing techniques that helped fuel the consumer revolution in England makes the vase a sacrilegious substitution in Wernick's eyes.

Because U.S. museums have depended heavily on private funds for a longer period of time, there is a partially accurate perception that the U.S. led the way in consumer-oriented museum marketing (Wersig and Shuck-Wersig 1990). Art museums in the U.S. are not unique in their involvements with dealers and artists and these relationships currently have less strength than many imagine (Becker 1982; Naifeh 1976), but Marquis suggests that in comparison to Europe these relationships have taken on a unique U.S. character since World War II:

> The shift of the art market's capital from Paris to New York after the Second World War was of far more than mere geographic significance. It also meant a profound change of sensibility: from European elitism to American populism; from Old World suavity and discretion to New World merchandising and flimflam. European artists cherished the bohemian myth of the inarticulate, alienated avant-garde; American artists called press conferences and stormed the grand stairway of the Met. European dealers inhabited drawing rooms and wore

morning coats; American dealers advertised and gave away free samples. European patrons discreetly bought works for private appreciation; American collectors flaunted their acquisitions in museum exhibitions and auction rooms. Along with the new art made in America came cultural values unique to the New World: the democratic mingling of high and low arts; a yearning for superstars; flamboyant emphasis on money; zeal for self-improvement; uncritical affection for "art"; a conviction that bigger is better; and long-standing ties between commercial art and fine art.

(Marquis 1991, p. 338)

While this characterization exaggerates the situation on both sides of the Atlantic, it is useful in fleshing out the objection to marketing in a museum context. As with the rise of consumer culture in general, it is not accurate to attribute the increased consumerism in individual and institutional collecting to just buyers (individual collectors, corporate collectors, museums), just sellers (producers, artists, galleries, dealers, auction houses), or just gatekeepers (media, critics, curators, academics, funding agencies, corporate sponsors). Rather, it is the joint and not altogether coordinated actions of all of these parties that constitute the production, marketing, consumption system for collectible goods. There are also other special interest groups, like those McCracken (1992) calls the politically correct, who have a voice in museum collections and museum marketing practices. "Politically correct" subcultural groups seek to reappropriate objects of their culture within the museum, in order to control and tell their own story with these objects (e.g., Gaither 1992; Jones 1992). But this systemic view of the changes taking place in museum collecting and exhibition does not negate the fact that individual museums can and increasingly do employ marketing strategies and see themselves in broad competition with the more commercial institutions of leisure, recreation, and shopping.

Exactly what is a marketing orientation? In the most popular marketing view, it is more appropriately labeled a consumer orientation, generally referred to as "the marketing concept." The marketing concept became fashionable during the mid-twentieth century and replaced "the selling concept" that in turn had replaced "the production concept." The production concept was popular when consumer goods were in short supply and focused on increasing production efficiency. Once this was generally accomplished, the primary business problem became how to make more consumers buy the product. That is, once supply caught up with demand, the emphasis shifted to how to increase demand. As a result, selling and advertising techniques were the major focus of marketers. Eventually some enlightened marketers began to realize that rather than make a product and then try to make consumers want it, it made more sense to reverse this process; to find out what consumers want and then make it for them. This entailed marketing research in order to discover what consumers want. Once marketers began to attempt to do this, they realized that not all consumers wanted the same thing. Therefore the way to serve consumers better and thereby increase profits was to segment the market and offer different products to different segments large enough to justify a separate offering (an offering comprising not only the product, but the price, promotions, and physical distribution that go along with it). The next step called for was "broadening" the marketing concept, so that it could be applied not only to profit-seeking corporations but to such non-profit institutions as hospitals, symphony orchestras, universities, and museums as well (Kotler and Levy 1969). In a museum context the customer is the potential museum-goer (or sometimes the potential donor or sponsor), the product is the museum experience derived from exhibitions, facilities, brochures, restaurants, and shops within the museum, the price is the admission and other contributions or support paid by the customer, promotions include publicity, advertising, exhibition banners, and other efforts to attract visitors, and physical distribution includes the location of the museum, museum branches, special exhibitions, and community outreach programs, as well as hours and days of operation. Each of these variables are to be designed to reach certain target markets comprised of segments to which the museum as a whole or specific exhibitions and programs might appeal. Rather than maximizing profits, the goals in a museum might be to broaden the audience, increase frequency of attendance, lengthen visits, and enhance the visitor's experience based on the desires of selected market segments. In addition, the museum might seek to make itself more attractive than the perceived competition, whether it is other museums, other cultural experiences, shopping malls, sports events, television, cinema, or theme parks.

If this, from a marketing perspective, comprises an application of the marketing concept to make museums more consumer-oriented, what then is the basis for the objection to such an orientation? Isn't giving museum goers more of what they want a good thing? To a degree it is, but there are shortcomings in the wholesale adoption of this concept. One objection that is especially relevant for public institutions, but should be relevant to private and commercial organizations as well, is that what people want may not be what they need. A symphony orchestra that simply plays the music most popular with its audience is failing in its presumed mission to nourish the development of symphonic music and to educate and expand the tastes of its public. Similarly, a museum that simply recycles one blockbuster Impressionist or Cubist exhibition after another, or one that provides only nostalgic portrayals of history as visitors might like to remember it, or one that entertains without enlightening, invigorating, or challenging, is also failing. Second, consumers may not know or be able to explicate what they want. Rather than ask an art-museum audience what art it likes best, what art it would like to see, and how it would like to see it presented, curators or other exhibition specialists may be in a better position to appreciate possibilities and creatively design exhibitions. And third, what consumers want may not be good for them or for the culture. If a significant social class, ethnic group, gender, occupation, or other group wants to see itself glorified in the museum at the expense of other groups, the museum has an obligation to object. Besides recognizing consumers, marketing also recognizes competition. It is for this reason that Weber (1975) and DiMaggio (1982b) may be correct that the market declassifies culture. That is, it pushes offerings in the direction of what is popular in order to attract a larger market. This larger audience is also likely to be broader; more declassified. This is not inevitable according to marketing logic, because market niching suggests choosing a segment of the market that is underserved, because no organization can successfully be all things to all people. Nevertheless public museums are likely to resist this because they are charged with serving the public as a whole and because the holdings of a museum provide substantial ballast or constraint for what it is able to do. For these reasons, museum marketing is likely at least to move the institution in the direction of popularization, in the direction of Disney.

While these are practical reasons why we might object to a wholesale application of marketing in a museum context, there are also deeper philosophical reasons why we might object to such practices. As McCracken argues when the marketing concept is applied to museums, it may distort our view of the museum visitor, the museum collection, and the interaction between the two:

> The marketing concept was developed to comprehend the marketplace transaction. . . . For good and bad reasons it has made itself heir to eighteenth century concepts of the individual as a gain-seeking, advantage maximizing creature . . . the marketing concept suppresses our vision of the individual as a culture-bearer and asks us to see him or her as a "consumer" driven by a benefit-calculating, information-processing rationality. Second, it suppresses our vision of the object as a cultural artifact, as an instance of material culture charged with cultural meaning. It asks us to see the object as a "product," a need-satisfying bundle of utilities. Finally, the marketing concept suppresses our vision of the interaction between individual and object as a complex and social and cultural event. It becomes instead a "purchase," an uncomplicated underspecified act of getting, having, and consuming. . . . If the great objective of the ethnographic museum (once it has satisfied its responsibility to conserve and study its collection) is to create that astonishingly difficult interaction between an individual with his or her many interpretive frames and an object with its many symbolic properties, it is hard to see how the marketing model advances this process in any very detailed way. There is reason

to think that it may even obscure some of the very things we need most to understand and manipulate.

(McCracken 1990, pp. 41–42)

What McCracken laments is the simplistic views of the museum-goer as a utility-maximizing consumer and of the museum as a benefit-providing product. He concludes that we should instead view the marketing concept as a metaphor rather than an operational prescription, lest we lose sight of the rich way in which people relate to objects in museums.

But is this how most people relate to objects in museums? I readily agree with McCracken that to view museum-goers, or for that matter car buyers, as rational information-processing utility-maximizers is simplistic and wrong-headed. A growing minority of consumer researchers would also concur (see Belk, forthcoming; Sherry 1991). But it may also be simplistic and wrong-headed to view museum-goers as necessarily engaging in a deeply meaningful ritual of communion with and through museum objects. Kelly (1987a, 1987b, 1993) has conducted observational studies of museum visitors at the University of British Columbia Museum of Anthropology, the Met and MOMA in New York, the Royal Academy and the British Museum, the Louvre, Musée D'Orsay, the Rijksmuseum, and the National Museum of Thailand. He consistently finds that about 30 percent of visitors never enter the museum galleries. Instead, this substantial minority typically visits the museum gift shop, acquires a souvenir to authenticate and memorialize their having been to the museum, and leaves. They may also seek the status of "having been" to a prestigious museum by eating at the museum restaurant. And even for those who do enter the galleries, Kelly finds that they may seek out the most revered museum pieces – *Night Watch, Mona Lisa, The Scream* – and then leave. Kelly and others (e.g., Horne 1984; MacCannell 1989) use the concept of pilgrimage to explain this sort of museum visitation. This provides further insight into the reaction against the marketing concept encapsulated by McCracken (1990). It brings us back to the regard for museums as sacred sites and the objects in their collections as aura-laden sacred icons. What we see with Kelly's description of many museum visitors, however, is that this is more of an ideal model than an actual one. Rather than humble awed pilgrims rejoicing at the font of knowledge, museum-goers are more often tourists playing a game of "been there, done that." The museum, like the church before it, has lost much, though not all, of its sacralizing power (see Leach 1993, pp. 164–73). Seen in this light, the reactions against marketing, against the Disneyfication of the museum, against the inclusion of everyday objects in the museum, against corporate sponsorships, and against Pop Art's veneration of such objects, is a reaction against threats to the privileged power of the museum as the cradle of the sacred.

THE POSITION OF A MUSEUM IN A
CONSUMER CULTURE

In the mid-1980s, before the fall of communism in Hungary, among the museums occupying the former palace on Castle Hill above Budapest was the Museum of the Hungarian Working Class Movement. It contained an exhibition of Hungarian Socialist Realist Art and a series of reconstructed worker rooms to show the impoverished consumer lifestyles that prevailed before the Hungarian Social Democratic government in contrast to the larger rooms, complete with awkward Soviet televisions, that followed. Next door in the National Gallery (Nemzeti Galéria) the art on display included two interesting pieces by American artists. One was a nearly life-size Andy Wharhol print of Elvis Presley in cowboy garb drawing his sixguns. The other was a lifesize Duane Hanson sculpture of an overweight woman in loud polyester casual clothing and with her hair in curlers. She is pushing a supermarket shopping cart full of frozen dinners and convenience foods with a cigarette dangling from her lips. What are we to make of these consumer-culture depictions that stood in such glaring contrast to the Socialist Realism next door? The official line apparently was that these were depictions of the decadence and ludicrousness of consumer lifestyles in capitalist America. But given the prominent placement of these works in the museum and the fascination they seemed to have for Hungarian museum visitors, a nearly opposite subtext seems to have dominated: these were the desiderata of modern consumption; the forbidden pleasures of the West; the longed for good life. Indeed, a number of analysts have suggested that the overthrow of communism in the former Soviet Union and in Eastern Europe had more to do with consumption desires than it did with any craving for democracy (e.g., Kohák 1992; Kozminski 1992). Slavenka Drakulić (1991) recounts first coming from communist Yugoslavia to New York City and entering Bloomingdale's department store. At first, like Dreiser's Sister Carrie, she was overpowered with the feeling of raw desire for all that she saw:

> First you discover an immense greed, a kind of fever, a wish to buy everything – the primordial hunger of consumerism. Then you discover powerlessness – and the very essence of it, poverty. Moreover, you start to realize that Bloomingdale's for you is a museum, not a real store where you can buy real things for your real self.
>
> (Drakulić 1991, p. 121)

In a consumer culture a museum may not function as a temple of consumer desire precisely as it did in the National Gallery in Budapest, and our department stores may not be museums of unreachable goods, but there is a clear and yet grossly underexamined role of the museum in consumer culture. This is the role of museums in the glorification of goods. In talking with Robert Casey at the Henry Ford Museum, he stressed that one reason why it was difficult to present a critical view of the automobile in the museum was that "The stuff is just so neat! You'd really have to hit the visitor over the head with it to make any impression at all, because the stuff is just so neat that it blows people away." Whether the stuff is automobiles, Impressionist paintings, Kwakiutl carvings, Greek sculpture, Washington's wooden teeth, birds of paradise, mastodon bones, mummies, Samurai helmets, eighteenth-century waistcoats, Calder mobiles, or silver-age comic books, it seems clear that we continue to be fascinated by museums because they are full of "neat stuff." Ettema has observed of museums that:

> they simply reinforce the idea that goods are inherently beneficial because objects contain desirable qualities. These qualities, it seems, will accrue to us if we buy the objects; they will have the power to make our lives more fulfilling. Thus history comes to be the story of material progress. Although they no longer aim specifically to reinforce genteel standards of behavior, museums still promote the interests of the business and manufacturing classes because they celebrate the ownership of objects. In short, museums teach materialism.
>
> (Ettema 1987, p. 72)

Harris suggests that not only have museums celebrated and taught materialism, they have made it seem noble and valuable to acquire objects like those in museums:

> by presenting museum displays portraying the evolution of artistic form, including its expression in textiles, furniture, glass, silver, and china, museums apparently justified heavy expenditures of the rich on antiques and personal possessions. With their presence the tycoons were not simply parading their wealth in a crude grab for attention but apparently participating in a long-standing, valued activity, working variations on collecting patterns established by connoisseurs and royalty centuries earlier.
>
> (Harris 1990, p. 136)

Ettema (1987), along with Carson (1978) and Horne (1992), suggests that rather than simply revere consumer culture and thereby endorse materialism, museums should critically examine the role of materialism in our lives. Horne (1992, pp. 192–193) suggests that the emergence of window shopping should be given all the attention in museums that we give, for example, to the Bronze Age. How does materialism affect interpersonal relations, class relations, work relations, generational differences, sex roles, identity; our daily lives? These are critical questions that elude a formalist presentation and interpretations that offer little more than a contextualized functionalist understanding of the history of things. This non-critical functionalism is the same orientation that McCracken (1990) objects to in the marketing concept, but in this case applied to museum presentations of stuff. In the concluding chapter I will try to apply such a critical perspective to collecting behavior and attempt to analyze how collecting affects our everyday lives and the consumer culture in which we are immersed.

CHAPTER FIVE

COLLECTING IN A CONSUMER SOCIETY: A CRITICAL ANALYSIS

―― •◆• ――

As the preceding chapters have shown, it is natural, if not inevitable, that collecting things and displaying things should flourish among individuals and museums in a consumer culture. It is also natural, if not inevitable, that the things we collect and exhibit, whether as artifacts or art, should also increasingly come from the consumer culture in which we are embedded. Just as it was natural to paint madonnas and seek relics of saints in a time and place when Christianity was the center of sacred power, and to assemble cabinets of automata, wonders from the New World, and natural curiosities in a time and place in which science was emerging as the sacred center, so too is it natural to collect and revere mass-produced objects and artistic depictions of such things in a consumer society in which consumer goods have become the central focus of our dreams and desires. It is little wonder that our museums now hold cars, corporate icons, and Coke cans (not only at The World of Coca-Cola, but also in independent museums like MUBO in the Netherlands – Turner 1992). At least since Marcel Duchamp's readymades, increasingly humble consumer goods have crossed the sacred museum threshold to become art. Paintings, prints, photographs, and sculptures have produced or reproduced images of our most quintessential consumer brands (Cornfield and Edwards 1983; Sudjic 1985), as well as our advertising (Varnedde and Gopnik 1990), and money (Nygren 1988). Further images of prestigious and fashionable brands are proudly portrayed on T-shirts (O'Flynn 1990; Sayre 1992). People are more likely to collect mass-produced objects today than they are to collect objects of nature, antiquity, or fine art, or hand-crafted artifacts. In a Larry McMurtry (1982) novel about a "scout" who finds objects for diverse collectors, the scout deals with collectors of bumper stickers, chess sets, punch cups, masks, bird nests, patent models, tricycles, cowboy boots, hubcaps, nineteenth-century lightbulbs, truncheons, and magazines. With such a wide range of collected everyday objects, largely from consumer culture, some have asked, "Is nothing junk anymore?" (Ashton 1966), or conversely, "Is everything becoming junk?" in this age of "the creeping ascendancy of objects" (Estes-Smith 1972). As Soutif (1989) correctly observes, the museum is no longer a corrective to the market, because the same objects may be found in both. While Soutif worries that as this happens the museum will become desacralized and art may disappear, a more congenial assessment is that we are merely putting those things we most highly venerate in the sacred museum or personal collection where we can more effectively worship them. Because they already have power, mana, or aura instilled by advertising and society, they do not profane the museum, and may actually add to its sacredness. But there is another and more fundamental concern I wish to raise in this chapter, and that is whether collecting in a consumer society is good for us. The focus here is not so much what happens to goods when we revere and collect them, as what happens to us when we do so. To begin to answer this question we must return to the notion of materialism.

MATERIALISM, CONSUMERS, AND COLLECTORS

As defined in Chapter Three, materialism is the importance we attach to possessions. It involves an existential emphasis on having over doing or being (Fromm 1976; Sartre 1943). However, as was also demonstrated in Chapter Three, besides its emphasis on possessive having, collecting also involves an emphasis on acquisitive doing. This at least leaves open the possibility that collecting may not be as materialistic as it first appears. If so, collecting may not necessarily be adverse to well-being, even though materialism has consistently been found to be so (Belk 1985; Dawson and Bamossy 1991; Mehta and Keng 1985; Richins 1987; Richins and Dawson 1992). Csikszentmihalyi and Rochberg-Halton (1981) distinguish between terminal materialism in which possessions are sought for the sake of having them, and instrumental materialism in which possessions are sought as a means of doing something else. They argue that terminal materialism is negatively related to happiness while instrumental materialism is positively related to happiness. Collecting would seem a reasonably clear case of terminal materialism since the objects acquired are generally not intended for use or else are placed beyond use in the collection. The never ending cycle of excited anticipation, brief elation upon object acquisition, rapid dissipation of pleasure, and reformation of anticipatory desire, which Campbell (1987) characterizes as the modern imaginative hedonism typical of consumer society, seems to have much in common with the collector's pattern of endlessly hunting for new objects for the collection. But the analysis of collecting as terminal materialism is complicated by the fact that the objects collected might still be seen as means to other ends: building the collection, investing, leading to the more perfect objects the collector desires, or gaining feelings of aesthetic pleasure, achievement, purposefulness, mastery, or status. Once objects enter a collection they may become memory cues that recall the stories of their acquisition or conjure up associations with a more distant past. And as a part of extended self (Belk 1988a), possibly contributing to symbolic self completion (Wicklund and Gollwitzer 1982), collections may help us to feel better about ourselves. Thus, while collecting is undeniably materialistic, it does not necessarily involve terminal materialism. Its nature leaves open the possibility that collecting may be good for us as individuals.

It is as pointless to ask collectors if they enjoy collecting as it is to ask new car buyers if they like their new cars. An enthusiastically affirmative answer is inevitable. Furthermore, with perhaps a third of us in consumer societies actively collecting something, blanket characterizations of collecting as good or bad for the individual are very likely too simplistic. And what is good or bad for the individual collector may not be comparably good or bad for the collector's household or for society as a whole. Therefore, I plan to examine each of these levels of self – individual, household, and society – and to pursue a two-sided assessment considering both good and bad aspects that apply to some collecting. We should then be in a better position to make a summary assessment of collecting's role in a consumer society.

HOW COLLECTING AFFECTS THE INDIVIDUAL

Negative aspects

In defining collecting in Chapter Three as the process of actively, selectively, and passionately acquiring and possessing things removed from ordinary use and perceived as part of a set of non-identical objects or experiences, I distinguished collecting from hoarding, miserliness, possessive accumulating (the "packrat" tendency), and simple acquisitiveness. While these behaviors are generally evaluated negatively as aberrant forms of consumerism, collecting is generally evaluated positively. I also argued that for most collectors who describe themselves as suffering from a disease (a mania, madness, addiction, obsession, or compulsion), the use of such terms is only half-serious hyperbole intended to justify their ostensibly selfish and indulgent collecting behavior as something they cannot help. Thus, in a survey of 1,300 American collectors (members of collecting clubs and participants at collectors shows), Travis (1988) found that more than 40 percent agreed with the statement, "I regard myself as a compulsive collector in that collecting is an obsession with me," and more than 70 percent agreed with the statement, "As far as my interest in collecting is concerned, you might say I am addicted to this particular hobby." Since these particular collectors have committed themselves to their collecting activity through public display of themselves or their collections, it is doubtful that most of them think of their collecting as truly deviant. But just as some consumers become addicted to drugs, alcohol, tobacco, or gambling (Burns *et al.* 1990; Hirschman 1992), obsessively spend money (Bergler 1959; Hallowell and Grace 1991), and compulsively buy things (Kaufman 1976; O'Guinn and Faber 1989), some collectors engage in obsessive, compulsive, or addictive collecting behaviors as well. In fact, Faber *et al.* (1987) find that collectibles are one of the common areas of expenditure in which compulsive buyers indulge. Faber (1992) attributes this to the importance of collecting for self-esteem, inasmuch as compulsive buying is commonly believed to be an effort to shore up sagging self-esteem. Even though the items purchased may not be needed or even wanted, the compulsive shopper enjoys a momentary, if often guilty, pleasure in the act of purchase. It is the acquisition and not the possession that provides pleasure or relief, just as the obsessive-compulsive hand washer gains relief from the act of washing and not from having clean hands. Similarly, when compulsive collectors are frustrated in an acquisition, they may become dysfunctional until they are able to make another acquisition. Lord David Eccles explores these feelings:

> If ... I have been done out of a picture because it was shown to someone else the day before the private view, or my bid left with the auctioneer has been narrowly beaten, or I have put through a trunk call to secure an item from a book catalogue and hear the book has already been sold, the rage enters my heart, and there is only one way to calm it and that is to go out and buy something else. Every dealer listens with sympathy to the tale of a collector who has just been frustrated. He knows that the wounded man, caught on the rebound, can be sold almost anything his eye lights on.
>
> (Eccles 1968, p. 7)

There is also an echo here of the theme of the wounded lover, a theme which will be explored in the following section.

The terms addiction, compulsion, and obsession have not been used in a consistent manner in medical, sociological, and psychological literatures. For instance, some would limit the term addiction to physiological dependence on a chemical substance, while others apply it to psychological dependence on behavioral rituals as well (see Belk *et al.* 1991). There is an increasing tendency to view impulse control disorders and addictive, compulsive, excessive, habitual, abusive, and adjunctive behaviors as related (O'Guinn and Faber 1989). The link between them is that they are repetitive and problematic for the individual. It is the latter problematic character that distinguishes "normal" collecting from excessive collecting, since collecting is by definition a repetitive activity. But what is considered problematic for the individual is also dependent upon the social milieu in which the collecting activity is carried out. Normal and excessive are socially constructed categories. Thus, normal collecting has been defined as "an obsession organized" (Aristides 1988). Similarly, Clifford specifies:

> The inclusions in all collections reflect wider cultural rules – of rational taxonomy, of gender, of aesthetics. An excessive, sometimes even rapacious need to *have* is transformed into rule-governed, meaningful desire. Thus the self that must possess but cannot have it all learns to select, order, classify in hierarchies – to make "good" collections.
>
> (Clifford 1990, p. 143)

When the collector is inattentive to these rules, he or she may be labeled a manic hoarder or accumulator rather than a collector (Jensen 1963; Phillips 1962).

There are also other reasons why a collector may be judged to be pathologically excessive and as engaging in problematic behavior. The record collector Clarence recounted by Eisenberg (1987) was mentioned in Chapter Three (pp. 81–2). Clarence had inherited a fourteen-room mansion and a modest sum of money, but has spent it all on records, to the extent that his heat has been turned off. Eisenberg describes his quarters:

> Clarence opens the kitchen door and you enter, but just barely. Every surface – the counters and the cabinets, the shelves of the oven and refrigerator, and almost all the linoleum floor – is covered with records. They are heavy shellac discs, jammed in cardboard boxes or just lying in heaps; crowning one pile is a plate of rusty spaghetti. . . . "Wilfred has at least two hundred thousand classical records I gave him to keep for me. Paul's got at least ten thousand of my records. But most I keep myself. The fellow from the church – he brought the spaghetti – said it looks like a record store in here." Clarence takes me outside to see the shedlike garage, which is packed with records. . . . The basement, too, is packed with records, but in a more industrial way. Cardboard cartons are stacked within inches of the hanging racks of bare-bulbed light fixtures.
>
> (Eisenberg 1987, pp. 1, 4–5)

Clearly Clarence would be judged by society to be engaging in problematic behavior. So, at one time, would a Mickey Mouse memorabilia collector whom I interviewed (Belk *et al.* 1988, 1991). At one point he had been a heroin addict. When he quit heroin he turned to alcohol. And when he gave up alcohol he turned to collecting Mickey Mouse toys. At that time he was working as an assistant manager of a supermarket in New Jersey. He described leaving work in the early evening and driving in to New York City to get his "Mickey fix" at an antique toy shop open in the evening. He would often do this three times a week, thus spending rent money and neglecting his family. He spent every cent except what he calculated he needed for gas and tolls to get back home. He described finally "kicking the habit" by becoming a dealer in such toys and selling to other addicted collectors whom he knows are spending more than they can afford. Such serial addiction is common in the addiction literature and also falls in the category of individually problematic behavior that society is likely to condemn. Similarly, Danet and Katriel (1986) describe a woman who spends money on her pipe collection that she realizes should have been used for pressing family and household needs. And Gelber (1991) notes cases of collectors of stamps, minerals, and glass whose children and spouses resent the expenditure of both time and money on the collection instead of on them and the family. Instances of collectors hiding their purchases from spouses, like the toy-vehicle collector mentioned in Chapter Three, also indicate collections that have gone beyond the bounds of what is considered acceptable.

As these last cases suggest, the individual and private nature of most collecting can also be judged problematic because it rechannels the collector's attention away from family. In extreme cases, the collector becomes a virtual recluse. In literary examples like Chatwin's *Utz* and Pynchon's *The Crying of Lot 49*, collections stand between lovers as a rival third party. Family problems often become evident when the collector tries to find an heir for the collection. In the families of the collectors I have interviewed it is rare that a child or spouse is willing to take over a collection. When collectors treat the objects in their collection like children a sibling rivalry with the human children in the family is a common consequence. And when collectors lavish love and attention upon these objects, a spouse may well have reason to feel jealous. The tendency to anthropomorphize objects collected only exacerbates these family tensions.

There is a related consequence of extreme devotion to the collection at the expense of human relationships. As Goldberg and Lewis explain:

> Fanatic collectors turn away from people as a potential source of affection and security and seek gratification instead through possessing things. And being afraid to love other humans, they bestow love and devotion on these same inanimate objects. From earliest childhood, fanatic collectors found they could not depend on their parents for the love and security they needed. ... Their only source of identity was through their possessions.
>
> (Goldberg and Lewis 1978, p. 93)

The tendency of many collectors either to begin or greatly to add to collections following the death of a parent may also be seen as compensatory security-seeking. Muensterberger (1994) too sees security-seeking as a pervasive motive in collecting and one that can get out of hand when the objects become more important than people. He gives as an example Sir Thomas Phillips, a well-known British book and manuscript collector in the nineteenth century. After his father's death he married and devoted all of the fortune his father left him, and more, to his collecting. When his wife died, Muensterberger finds, there was no evidence he felt any sadness except at the added burden of taking care of his daughters. He subsequently inquired of friends about finding a wife, but not out of desire for someone with whom he could share affection.

> "I am become now a fortune hunter, do you know any wealthy body who wants a husband." ... Phillips's efforts to find a wealthy wife had nothing to do with love or attraction. Everything was governed by his all-consuming passion for adding more and more acquisitions to his already considerable collection. To him, no woman held the spell of a rare manuscript or could measure up to an old map or a fine book. A woman was desirable to him only to the extent that her material position would enable him to add to his holdings. ... The documents, manuscripts, and topographical and genealogical source material he collected readily substituted for human relationships, while distorting and coloring his entire sense of values and his obligations to anyone, including his own children.
>
> (Muensterberger, 1994, pp. 91–93)

He eventually found such a wife and their marriage predictably suffered from his devotion to his collecting. Not surprisingly, both Goldberg and Lewis (1978) and Olmsted (1988a) report a number of divorces precipitated by collections.

Excessive devotion to objects may, then, be determined by comparison with the collector's relationships with people and with everyday affairs of life. Goldberg and Lewis make this distinction:

> People who collect as a hobby find a sense of satisfaction in their search and in their acquisitions. Obsessed collectors, however, are driven. The acquiring of a certain oil painting or a rare jade carving becomes a matter of life and death. Their obsession overrules every other aspect of their lives and they devote every waking minute to thinking and planning how to obtain the next object for their collection or how to display it. Objects ultimately become more important than people, and fanatic collectors progressively alienate themselves from friends and family, occasionally even becoming suspicious that others will take away their prized possessions. They tend to withdraw from interpersonal relationships and often do not concern themselves with everyday problems like paying bills or getting the car serviced.
>
> (Goldberg and Lewis 1978, pp. 94–95)

Balzac's Cousin Pons and Connell's Muhlbach are borderline cases, but they both progress steadily in the direction of increasing obsession and decreasing attention to family and others.

In attaching strong affection to things rather than people, Muensterberger (1994, p. 9) suggests there is a parallel to the "fetishes of preliterate human kind." Fetishistic collecting is also detected in other analyses (Belk 1991a; Pearce 1992) and linked not only to anthropological notions of fetishism, but also to the sexual fetishism discussed by Freud and the commodity fetishism discussed by Marx. The underlying notion of fetishism shared by all three of these perspectives was explicated by Ellen (1988) as involving four features:

1 Concretization,
2 Animation or anthropomorphism,
3 Conflation of the signifier with the signified, and
4 An ambiguous relationship of control between person and object.

Concretization involves reifying abstract concepts through concrete objects. This is something that Pomian (1990) sees as the essential feature of collections and the reason that collected objects are set apart from ordinary use. They provide a connection between the visible and invisible, generally transcendent, concepts like beauty, god, and love. The element of anthropomorphism has been found to be common with a number of collectors. We are reminded of Freud's practice of saying "Good morning" to his Chinese statuettes each day and of Jung's anthropomorphic regard for books, as described in Chapter Three. In conflating the signifier with the signified, the fetish object is believed to have the power of that which it merely represents. The saints' relics of medieval Europe are a prominent example here, but the belief of collectors of autographs, baseball cards, and relics of rock stars (O'Guinn 1991) that these things possess the aura of those they represent, are parallel cases. It is the final element in Ellen's (1988) synthesis of fetishism that seems most critical to distinguishing the normal and excessive collector. For when the collector can be seen as being driven or controlled by the collection rather than controlling it, we are likely to judge this boundary as having been crossed. This is something we think of more commonly among individual collectors, but museum curators sometimes may also be prone to fetishizing collected objects (Gathercole 1989; Jordanova 1989). Any collector who insists too strongly in the mystical status of the objects in his or her collection may be subject to the charge of fetishism (Jhally 1987). Dorfles worries that museums as a whole are prone to this sort of fetishistic mystification of objects:

> The present tendency to "fetishize" the excavated object, the most humble instrument discovered as a result of historical or archaeological investigations, and to raise it to the dignity and value of a work of art, most of the time only in virtue of its archaicness, must make us reflect seriously. ... We can easily imagine fragments of old steam engines, rusted gears of turbines or electric trains, minute elements of old transistors or of "electronic brains" religiously kept within glass

cases, and considered important "pieces," precious testimony of twentieth-century art.

(Dorfles 1966, p. 6)

The more recent critique of Soutif (1989) suggests that we have already gone far beyond this to the "hyperfetishization" of the everyday consumer good in the world of art and museums. Within art a popular technique for doing so is the monumental giganticism of artists like Claes Oldenburg and his soft objects, with his *The Store* acting as the epitome of hyperfetishization. It is a tendency that Handy (1988) referred to as "the objectification of objects," by rendering them oversized, out of context, and in luscious detail, much like pornography. Also like pornography, Pop Art has depersonalized, clichéd, and dehumanized images (Barthes 1989). Stewart (1984) adds that besides giganticism, miniaturization is another fetishistic tactic commonly found in collections.

But these criticisms, relevant as they are to understanding the boundary between acceptable and unacceptable collecting, may take us too far from fetishism as Ellen (1988) discusses it. After all, contemporary advertising is an inherently hyperreal, hyperfetishized medium, and yet we have accommodated such presentations and regard them as so normal that they fade into the background of the daily media barrage. This suggests that what we regard as fetishistic, like what we regard as addictive or obsessive, is a matter of socially constructed and shifting definitions. We generally regard museum collections as normal and accept that they legitimize objects that are acceptable for individuals to collect; if it's good enough for the Met, no further questions need be asked. Still, if the public were given sufficient information, it is likely that many museum collections would also be judged to be excessive. With the exception of a few contemporary open collections like that of the Museum of Anthropology at the University of British Columbia, the bulk of current museum collections are kept out of public view in storage. The U.S. Smithsonian Institution, for example, in 1982 had 100,000 bats, 2,300 spark plugs, 24,797 woodpeckers, 82,615 fleas, 12,000 Arctic fishing tools, 14,300 sea sponges, 6,012 animal pelts, 2,587 musical instruments, and 10 specimens of dinosaur excrement in its warehouses (Dowd 1982). More recently it acquired a collection of hundreds of different air-sickness bags. It might well be argued that this is the equivalent of Clarence's record collection, but on a much more massive scale.

Positive aspects

Most collectors do not cross the socially constructed lines of normal behavior. Most collectors are not addicted or obsessive to the point that they cannot help themselves and buy objects they do not even desire simply because the act of purchase provides momentary relief from insecurity, anxiety, or depression. Still, collecting is not the same as ordinary consumer behavior. It is extraordinary primarily by virtue of its passion, focus, and commitment. Collecting has been termed a "positive addiction" (Glasser 1976), a "blessed obsession" (Purcell and Gould 1992), a "magnificent obsession" (Tuchman 1994), or a "glorious obsession" (Rheims 1975). Perhaps the best analogy for this kind of behavior is not drug addiction or alcoholism, but romantic love. In a study of dating behaviors and feelings (Belk and Coon 1993) I identified two very different paradigms (exchange and agapic love) among heterosexual dating partners. In the exchange paradigm, the dating partners' behavior was closer to the investment view of collecting discussed in Chapter Three. In fact some, primarily male, daters said they expected a "fair return" on their "investments" in a relationship. They also seek control and calculate benefits in a rational, pragmatic, and egoistic fashion. Gifts in this context are instrumentally chosen and purposive, they are given to reciprocate or in the expectation of reciprocation, and their monetary value is important, at least as a symbol of commitment. On the other hand, in the agapic-love paradigm (which includes romantic love, familial love, neighborly love, and love of God), the dating partner is emotional rather than rational, idealistic rather than pragmatic, and altruistic rather than egoistic. Gifts are spontaneous non-binding celebratory expressions and their cost is irrelevant. The giver abandons control to passion and idealizes the beloved as totally unique.

Many of these characteristics of agapic love can be found in the behavior of some collectors. Passionate emotion is a chief characteristic that differentiates collecting from other types of consumption. Many collecting purchases are spontaneous with money being largely irrelevant. Collectors idealize their collections and are more prone to use logical explanations as rationalizations than as actual motives for their behavior. And when collectors act from a spirit of heroically saving items from abandonment and decay, there is often more altruism than egoism in these actions. Just as the lover cannot stand to be without the beloved in interpersonal romance, such a collector cannot stand to be without the beloved object (Grasskamp 1983, p. 138). Both romantic love and passionate collecting are self-transcendent, dreamlike, mystical rituals. The romantic lover and the passionate collector both abandon themselves to overwhelming emotions and close off attention to the world outside. Nothing else matters. As Muensterberger (1994) notes, "the attitude of a devoted collector toward his objects is similar to a lover's passion and, further, that overevaluation is, after all, a well-known trait among lovers and collectors alike" (p. 231). He also recounts the case of Martin G.: "In his infatuation with the objects in his collection, he led a separate and almost romantic existence, simultaneous with his day-to-day obligations but in contrast to them, as if part of his critical faculties had been put aside" (p. 141). Freudian theorists tend to see such devotion as a sublimation of sexual desires transferred to the objects collected. Based on his treatment of art collectors, Baekeland reports:

> To a man, they report that they usually know immediately whether or not a piece really appeals to them and whether they want to possess it. They often compare their feeling of longing for it to sexual desire. This suggests that art objects are confused in the unconscious with ordinary sexual objects, an idea that gets some confirmation from the fact that many collectors like to fondle or stroke the objects they own or to look at them over and over from every angle, both up close and at a distance, activities that are impossible in a museum. The only other context in which looking, fondling and caressing loom so large is sexual foreplay.
> (Baekeland 1981, p. 51)

We are reminded too of Freud's reported tendency to stroke his ancient statuettes as he was talking to patients (Gay 1989, p. 18; Sachs 1945, p. 101; Spector 1975, p. 21). And Karl Abraham (1927) comments about the collector that the "excessive value he places on the object he collects corresponds completely to the lover's overestimate of his sexual object. A passion for collecting is frequently a direct surrogate for a sexual desire" (p. 67).

When collecting passion is driven from a selfless love of the things themselves, "ridiculous" expenditures and efforts on behalf of the collection come to be seen as sacrifices, perhaps even noble ones. Mukerji (1978) describes this heroism succinctly: "Collectibles seem to be commodities on the brink of extinction, saved by people who saw in them some lasting importance" (p. 353). The apotheosis of objects entering a collection ennobles their collector as the "savior" of these objects. Whether in its religious context or as romantic love, passion involves suffering, and collecting is no exception. Pons and Utz are among the literary collecting figures who have suffered such passion. As described in Chapter Two, the French dentist Maurice Girardin is revered in this light for the artwork he saved and ultimately bequeathed to the French people. We may be less likely to call the sacrifices of passionate collectors of more humble objects like beer cans noble, but even in this case we may admire the sacrifice. As Purcell and Gould (1992) reflect, "In an age of passivity, where Walkman and television bring so much to us and demand so little in return, we must grasp the engaging passion of these collectors" (p. 12). As a result of the passionate collector's sometimes heroic devotion to his or her collection, parting from these objects may be as painful as the death of a loved one. We saw in Chapter Three, Cardinal Mazarin's farewell to his artworks as he was dying. The reflections of the autograph collector Adrian Joline as he faced death show his continuing concern for the fate of his autographs:

> No one will ever be as fond of my pets as I have been, and at no distant day they will be scattered among the bidders at the inevitable

auction-sale which awaits all collections save only those consigned to perpetual burial in some library. My own association with them will be lost and forgotten. I look upon them almost as one might upon the children whom he must leave behind him. . . . Some one will preserve them, and perhaps may fondle them as I have done. I trust that they may come under the protecting care of a true collector, a real antiquary – no mere bargain-hunter, no "snapper up of unconsidered trifles," but one endowed with the capacity to appreciate whatsoever things are worthy of the affection of the lover of letters and of history.

(Joline 1902, pp. 306–307)

Thus, paradoxically, although collecting may be the quintessence of acquisitive and possessive materialism in a consumer society, it may at one extreme also be a selfless labor of love. Eisenberg captures this paradox:

The true hero of consumption is a rebel against consumption. By taking acquisition to an ascetic extreme he repudiates it, and so transplants himself to an older and nobler world. (In the same way the true hero of production, the chivalrous captain of industry or reckless entrepreneur, rebels against production.) To write such behaviour off as conspicuous consumption is to miss its point.

(Eisenberg 1987, p. 15)

The heroic collector is also engaged in a struggle against conspicuous waste. "In our consumer and wasteful society, the collector is perhaps in his own way a reactionary – worried by the accumulation of attractive though valueless objects . . . he likes to gather some of a more personal nature to save them from his constant and uneasy destruction" (Caxton Publishing 1974, p. 185).

If the obsessive-compulsive or addicted collector lies at the negative end of the collector continuum and the heroic passionate collector lies at the positive end, what then of the majority of collectors who fall between these two extremes? There are some more mundane pleasures than a life of passionate commitment to be gained from collecting. Although Chapter Two presented Stebbins's (1979, 1982) and Gelber's (1991, 1992) explanations of why collectors often position themselves as engaged in "serious leisure," Olmsted (1991) reminds us that collecting can be a form of play. In terms of Clifford's (1990) specification of principles for "good collections," collecting is normally a rule-governed game. Learning and playing by the rules of the game for making a good collection help the collector gain a sense of mastery and competence that may not be as forthcoming from his or her paid employment (Belk *et al.* 1991; White 1959). By virtue of having a continually enlarging or refining collection, the collector also gains from an expanded sense of self (Belk 1988a; Rigby and Rigby 1944, pp. 35–36). Furthermore, success in competition with other collectors further enhances prestige and feelings of self-esteem (Storr 1983). Like following the same sports team, whether through actual interaction or through a more tacit sense of community, a sense of fellowship with fellow collectors may also develop (DiMaggio 1987; Friedman *et al.* 1993). Also in contradistinction to normal consumer materialism, the collector, even of mass-reproduced marketplace commodities like stamps, beer cans, and baseball cards, is exercising creative control in an otherwise alienated marketplace (Miller 1987). By remaining constant to a collecting theme rather than following each new consumer novelty that comes onto the market, the collector pursues a corrective to the alienation of the general market, even while participating actively in a sector of the market. By decommoditizing and sacralizing items that enter the collection, the collector also transcends the profane commodity market. "His possession of objects strips things of their commodity character" (Abbas 1988, p. 220). For many collectors, the collection may be the closest he or she comes to the numinous in a secular age of consumerism. And after a lifetime of collecting, the objects of a collection may be memory cues for a wealth of experiences. Thus as Benjamin (1968a) reflected on the books in his collection, each was, like Proust's madeleines and lime-blossom tea, the key to a wealth of memories that came flooding back. In the same way that writers, poets, playwrights, and artists may look back upon their creative productions in answer to the question "what has my life been?" so may collectors look back upon the collections they have produced. In all of these ways the collector may find meaning and purpose in life through collecting (Smith and Apter 1977). None of this should be taken to diminish the potential problems of collecting in creating family strife, cutting the collector off from broader participation in the world, and substituting a focus on things for a focus on other humans. But within the wide spectrum from obsessive to heroic collecting, the broad middle ground appears, in balance, more benign than malignant. Even though the public may not go as far as legitimizing most collectors as participating in a serious artistic, historic, or scientific endeavor, there is in most contemporary cultures a tolerance and implicit support of collecting by those who themselves do not collect. For if collecting is the epitome of consumerism and involves deriving pleasure from acquiring and possessing a large number of objects, to condemn collecting would be to condemn the consumer ethos to which most of us subscribe. So long as collecting is not too patently wasteful, excessive, or opulent, we would rather sanction such indulgence than to question our own consumer indulgence.

HOW COLLECTING AFFECTS CULTURE

It is possible for a behavior to be helpful and constructive at the individual level and yet be problematic and destructive at the cultural level.

Automobile driving may be an example of such a behavior, taking us comfortably to our individual destinations while at the same time contributing to pollution, highway death, and over-use of limited resources at a global level. How is culture affected by individual and institutional collecting? The greatest advantage most collectors and museums cite is that collectors have saved innumerable works of art, books, and historical treasures that would otherwise have been lost. There is undeniable truth in this claim, although it is a legacy of the past that has passed through a selective filter that not only saves the best and most exquisite, but also that which best reflects the upper classes (Lipsitz 1990; Radley 1990). A parallel process of sorting occurs in our family photo albums (Boerdam and Martinius 1980; Chalfen 1987; Sontag 1977). The photos are typically only taken during happy family occasions, to show off new possessions (cars being common), on holiday trips, and when our homes are clean and as posed as the people and pets shown. We then further cull the unflattering photographs, keeping only those that show us to best advantage. As a result, our photo albums are in no way representative archives of family life. Collector and museum filtering also occurs at several levels. Before the development of consumer societies, only the rich could afford to collect. As their collections were dispersed and passed down to others, further selection occurred in accord with changing standards of beauty and science. And when museums developed, they were controlled by an elite which helped to narrow further the standards of selection. Curators also tend to have reasonably high-social-class backgrounds (Lavine 1992). As a result of these various filters, we receive a very non-representative portrayal of past lives through collections and museums. Art in particular is a luxury good as well as a sign of taste and prestige. Non-prestigious art and popular art of the past has largely disappeared (Clark 1970). The non-representativeness of museum collections is even found, for instance, in the open-air folk museums of Scandinavia and Northern Europe, which have saved only the finest of folk architecture and handiwork, brought together in "villages" that are unlike anything that ever existed. These are biases that persist in museums today, especially among curators who employ "aesthetic" rather than "historic" or "ethnographic" perspectives. Adrienne Hood, a curator at the ROM in Toronto, spoke proudly of acquiring a tattered and humble Cajun quilt, which she did not intend to restore. She had to fight long and hard with the selection committee of the museum to acquire this example rather than "finer" (but less representative) ones that were available. Even ethnological collections intended to be scientific are not immune from such aesthetic criteria (e.g., Thomas 1991, p. 168). Movements away from hyperreality through actions like Adrienne Hood's may be increasing, but they are still fighting against long-standing patterns. By virtue of primarily collecting and displaying objects that once belonged to the rich, we celebrate and pay homage to a system of status based on material wealth.

As with many of the heritage sites that have recently been developed in Britain, collectors, curators, and visitors all have a nostalgic preference for a past that is romanticized, polished, and stylized (Belk 1991b). This is not to say that what has been collected and remains to help inspire and instruct us today is not valuable; only that it presents a very distorted view of the past through an elite filter. In the Stuhr Museum of the Prairie Pioneer in the American midwest, the depiction of artifacts suggests that pioneers had spinet pianos, fine porcelain, and stained-glass domes in their homes (Lowenthal 1989). A nostalgic film at the museum, narrated by Henry Fonda with romantic music appropriate to period depicted, fondly remembers warm family scenes and simple pioneer virtues. As the music swells the narrator reminds us that "the choke of nostalgia grips us at every turn." Any hint of hardship in the museum or its recreated village has been carefully removed. As McCracken (1988) notes, we "displace" cultural values we hold dear to other times and other places because the gap between the real and the ideal is otherwise too large to sustain belief in these values. In displacing such meanings to a past golden age or an exotic other, we keep our belief in these values intact; they exist somewhere, if safely just out of reach. The strategy of collecting itself, McCracken suggests, is a strategy of keeping our imagined but impossible hopes of a fulfilled life barely out of reach. Because collectibles are scarce and rare, and because we can continually invent new and more challenging collecting goals, the ultimate disappointment of realizing that all we hope for is not enough is kept forever at bay through collecting. There is also a further explanation of the upscale biases in collecting implicit in this argument. Because we are prone in a consumer society to believe that both the past (or future) and the rich reflect the good life far better than the present and the poor, we are more likely to seek the baubles and artifacts of the past rich than of the present poor. It is these prior rich, we believe, whose material lives come closest to touching the sacred ideal of happiness. This reinforces and nourishes the belief that perhaps we will be happy too, if we only have the finest and the best.

There is also a racial and cultural bias in surviving collections. Museums create and reinforce notions of cultural identity, but often at the expense of other cultures. The artifacts of other cultures, regardless of whether they were gathered through military, religious, or financial power, may be seen as trophies of conquest. Because museums first emerged in colonial periods and in the most developed consumer societies they, like the world's fairs, participated in defining self at the expense of others. Consider the words of one ethnographic film-maker in Papua New Guinea in the 1920s:

> We had discovered treasures beyond bonanza! Human heads! Stuffed heads! What luck! Skulls painted and decorated had grinned from every niche, but heads – stuffed heads! Glorious beyond words! Had we raided a bank and carried off the bullion we could scarcely have

been more pleased than with such desireable objects. . . . I have never seen objects more ghastly and horrible than these grim trophies. What sort of people could these be that so callously made toys of their victims? Infinitely barbarous, ferocious, and cruel, with no feeling nor thought for human agony and suffering, and I shuddered to think of the ghastly scenes that had taken place in the small clearing by the gloomy bamboos.

(Hurley 1923, pp. 380–383)

Elsewhere in his book, the author says of the Papuans "it is difficult to believe them human" (Hurley 1923, p. 352). The tendency to define the other as completely different from ourselves in order to reinforce our presumed superiority is the essence of Said's (1978) Orientalism. It is a tendency that has also been evident in the art world's discovery of the "primitive" (Torgovnick 1990). However, this Orientalism has not consistently been a racist characterization of the other as nasty and brutish. Rather, we have been more inclined in certain periods including the present, to regard "primitives" as noble and free; Rousseau's noble savage (Davis 1985; Kreamer 1990). The men's movement and New Age movement are recent examples of this nostalgic use of displaced meaning. So too is the 1984–85 MOMA exhibition "'Primitivism' in 20th-Century Art: Affinity of the Tribal and the Modern." There have also been a number of other MOMA exhibitions of this sort going back to the 1933 "American Sources of Modern Art" exhibition of Aztec, Maya, and Inca art (see Rushing 1992). Thus it is possible for objects in museum collections to be reinterpreted in a less racist way (Kavanagh 1989), although the objects collected (e.g., Hurley's "human heads!") limit the possibilities. A growing number of ethnic museums and ethnic groups are finding a greater voice in the museum world (e.g., Cohen 1989), but it is a still small voice, as illustrated by the escalating protests by Toronto's people of color during the 1989 ROM exhibition, "Into the Heart of Africa." While attempting to be culturally sensitive, certain depictions in the exhibition were seen as celebrating colonialist racism and the exhibition tour that was to follow was canceled (Ames 1992; Jones 1992). There are as well many historic cases of racial prejudice and curatorial greed that led to little more than outright theft of artworks and artifacts from traditional peoples (e.g., Cole 1985; Thomas 1991). Collector greed continues to cause widespread looting of archeological sites (Kaiser 1990), and numerous claims for repatriation of such works held by museums remain unsettled (Lowenthal 1988; Messenger 1989; Palmer 1989). It is sadly ironic that many of the finest cultural treasures of developing nations are in the museums of Europe and North America. Not only prior colonial power, but also prior histories, events, periods, persons, and styles that characterize our nations are commemorated in our collections, museums, and monuments (Horne 1984, 1992). With museums like the Whitney Museum of American Art, the Baseball Hall of Fame, Williamsburg, and the Smithsonian's National Air and Space Museum we make shrines to other manifestations of national greatness. Myth-making flourishes in venues ranging from the clean, orderly, and odorless folk village reconstructions to the corporate icons in the Museum of Modern Mythology and the corporate collections of Coca-Cola. We take our school children to these museums to inculcate a message that Carl Sandburg characterized with the incantation, "We are the greatest city, the greatest nation; nothing like us ever was."

If there are class, racial, and national biases in collections, it is likely that there are gender biases as well. In Chapter Three I outlined some of the forces that seem to drive many women out of collecting after childhood and some of the gender differences encoded in men's and women's collections. Torgovnick (1990, pp. 191–192) suggests that museums encode a series of power imbalances that are associated with one another: western "civilization" over "primitivism," colonizer over colonized, higher social classes over lower classes, and men over women. These power relationships are expressed in the objects that are collected and displayed, the way they are represented, and in the content of representational artwork. Thomas (1991, pp. 237–238, fn. 6) sees this expressed in collecting and collections by a distinction "between the masculine work of reason and infantile or feminine curiosity (grounded in the passions)." This bias is sometimes subtle as well as pervasive. It includes the serious scientific guise of the most highly revered collections and museums, positivist scientific methods, taxonomies, the aesthetic objectification of art history, the dominance of male curators and museum directors, the lack of personal ethnographic voice for those whose objects are displayed in museums, the remaining reluctance to include objects of popular consumption, the lack of attention to the home, the investment rationalization for collecting, and the general emphasis on facts and numbers over emotions and relationships. The irony is that collecting is an essentially aesthetic, passionate, consumerist activity, although these may be the very reasons such pains are taken to provide a disguise of rationality. Only in children's museums is curiosity on the part of the visitor and novelty in the displays much encouraged.

While collectors and museums did not invent power-based hierarchies of social class, race, nationality, and gender, they do more than simply reinforce them. By collecting and exhibiting artifacts of prestige and power we concretize and sanctify these inequalities. "Museum quality" more often than not also means museum inequality. In museums and collections we consecrate not just taste, but the taste of the elite and powerful. Although various others have addressed the question of whether a museum needs objects or could perhaps focus instead on ideas (e.g., Ames 1992; Ferguson 1965; Finlay 1977), and various defenses of object-focused museums have been offered, often related to Benjamin's (1968a) idea of an aura inhering in the original object, they miss an essential point. Collections and museums, as Pomian (1990) argues, make invisible ideas visible. The broadest message reified by these collections is that material objects matter. We venerate materialism by collecting not ideas or concepts, but things (MacDonald 1992). These are not just ordinary things, but the very finest, most expensive, best things. In the words of Robert Casey of the Henry Ford Museum, "the stuff is just so neat!" Where we once built temples to make manifest the idea of God, we now build museums to allow ourselves to worship "neat stuff."

MUSEUMS IN A CONSUMER SOCIETY

If, as I have argued, the development of consumer society has been the key event precipitating the spread of collecting and museums, both individual and institutional collecting have been just as slow to fully embrace consumerism as to critically address it. Given the class biases of institutional and individual collecting and the threat that consumer objects have seemed to pose to the sacred temple of the museum, there has been reluctance to allow branded objects in the highest collecting and exhibiting spheres. This is changing, however, with individual collecting leading the way. Mass-reproduced objects from Hummel figurines to baseball cards are now well accepted in their broad individual collecting circles, even if they are still unlikely to appear in museums' regular collections. By occasionally bringing such collections into the museum through special community collector shows, there is an opportunity to begin to critically analyze consumer culture, but museums have been reluctant to do so. Museum collections and exhibitions have started to become more populist and to reflect more multicultural, global, and multiply gendered perspectives, but for someone interested in learning about consumer culture a visit to a shopping mall is far more revealing than a visit to a museum. With the vested interests of sponsors, patrons, and the merchant classes supporting them, museums have done far more to promote materialism than to examine it. This is true not only in science and industry museums that glorify production, but in the general glorification of goods that the object-centered presentations of museums embrace. The concept of market segmentation allows room for such uncritical celebratory presentations, but the cultural role of museums also demands that other presentations begin to examine the other half of the Industrial Revolution: the consumer revolution that accompanied it.

In a parody on the tendency of anthropologists to study only other cultures, Horace Miner (1956) wrote a now familiar paper on the Nacirema (American spelled backwards). Looking at them as an anthropologist might look at traditional cultures, he describes our charm box (medicine cabinet) in our shrine room (toilet) and the magical charms it contains. He reveals our sadomasochistic practices of dental care, the priestly status accorded doctors, pharmacists, and psychotherapists, our ritual fasting (diets), breast fetishism, our belief that the body is ugly, and our strange reproduction rituals. Mol (1976, p. 152) provides an equally delightful treatment of our automobile behaviors, noting our car cleaning and driving rituals as well as the annual sacrifice of lives and money that we make to the great god Car. Such perspectives point the way to what a critical perspective on collecting in a consumer society might entail. Rather than make the strange familiar, the task of the museum in regard to consumption is to make the familiar strange so that we may see it freshly and critically. Because we are so immersed in consumer culture, we are like fish in water in being unable to appreciate it and its effects. We willingly marvel at the objects and practices of the Other, but we accept our own equally magical system of behaviors as unremarkable. To break through these accustomed views will require creative presentation and interpretation. By treating our own culture in a similar manner to others' cultures we allow for comparisons of differences in consumption ethos that remain even in an increasingly global age.

As exemplars of consumer culture, collectors themselves provide an opportunity to examine critically the benefits and problems of collecting as well as the biases that have affected prior collecting. Numerous biographies and autobiographies of collectors should facilitate such an analysis when they are not too hagiographic. Jones (1992) provides an excellent example of how this was done in an exhibition called "Gallery 33: A Meeting Ground of Cultures" at the Birmingham Museum and Art Gallery in 1990. As a part of this exhibition, the collections, collecting patterns, and biases of three collectors of the 1920s were presented: a missionary in the Solomon Islands, an officer in colonial service in Nigeria, and a private collector in Australia. While the exhibition stopped short of offering a critique of collecting and consumerism, it was able to raise questions of elitism, racism, colonialism, and relative wealth. Moreover, it went beyond the mute testimony of objects to trace how they came to the museum and what their transformation into museum objects represented. And by means of a photomontage and linguistic pastiche of the ethnic diversity of contemporary Birmingham, it brought a number of these historic issues closer to the everyday consumer lives of the community. Such an exhibition is exemplary of the application of a critical perspective to collecting.

CONCLUSION

This book began by noting that collecting is consumption writ large since it involves the perpetual pursuit of inessential luxury goods. It raised the question of whether the collector's quest for self completion and happiness in the marketplace is a realistic one. This chapter has suggested that for some people collecting is a harmful addiction, while for others it is an heroic and selfless act of love that saves unappreciated cultural treasures for future generations. For the vast majority of collectors who are neither addicted nor saviors, collecting appears to be a relatively healthy activity that invigorates consumer life with passion and purpose while it provides the collector with self-enhancing benefits that may be unavailable in their careers and households. Rather than being manipulated pawns of marketers, collectors are proactive decommoditizers of goods who creatively wrest meaning from the marketplace. I do not mean in this assessment to vindicate consumer society in general. But for the majority of collectors, their participation in consumer culture is perhaps less problematic than that of the majority of non-collectors.

At the societal level, however, collecting by individuals and especially by institutions has been found to be more problematic. Whereas individual collectors are often able to creatively reconstruct marketplace meanings, institutions in this increasingly privatized age are more likely to reiterate and celebrate these meanings, if subtly more than overtly. Moreover, museum collections have histories of elitism, colonialism, racism, and sexism that are difficult to overcome. Individual collections share some of these biases as well, but generally not to the extent of museum collections accumulated in another era. But the largest failing of institutional collections in a consumer society is their uncritical celebration of stuff. Given the ostensibly non-market perspective of museums, they would seem in a key position to begin to explore the consumer-culture relationship between people and goods. Instead, they have to date been satisfied to focus on material culture alone. If consumer goods are increasingly the focus of museums and if there is no critical analysis of what these goods mean to our lives, then we are left with the impression that the goods enshrined in our museum temples are worthy of worship. Rather than participate so fully in consumer culture, museums can still cause us to notice this culture in which we are enmeshed and to reflect on its pleasures and problems.

REFERENCES

——— •◆• ———

Abbas, Ackbar (1988), "Walter Benjamin's Collector: The Fate of Modern Experience," *New Literary History*, 20 (Autumn), 217–238.

Abbate, Janet (1993), "'People and the Computer' at the Computer Museum," *Technology and Culture*, 34 (July), 665–669.

Abelson, Elaine S. (1989), *When Ladies Go A-Thieving: Middle-Class Shoplifters in the Victorian Department Store*, New York: Oxford University Press.

Abraham, Karl (1927), *Selected Papers on Psychoanalysis*, London: Hogarth.

Ackerman, Paul H. (1990), "On Collecting: A Psychoanalytic View," *Maine Antique Digest*, May, 22A–24A.

Adams, Brooks (1994), "Industrial-Strength Warhol," *Art in America*, 9 (September), 70–77, 129, 131.

Albee, George (1977), "The Protestant Ethic, Sex, and Psychotherapy," *American Psychologist*, 32 (February), 150–161.

Alexander, Edward P. (1979), *Museums in Motion: An Introduction to the History and Functions of Museums*, Nashville, Tennessee: American Association for State and Local History.

Alpers, Svetlana (1983), *The Art of Describing: Dutch Art in the Seventeenth Century*, Chicago: University of Chicago Press.

Alsop, Joseph (1982), *The Rare Art Traditions: The History of Art Collecting and Its Linked Phenomena Wherever These Have Appeared*, New York: Harper & Row.

Ames, Michael M. (1986), *Museums, the Public and Anthropology*, Vancouver, British Columbia: University of British Columbia Press.

——(1992), *Cannibal Tours and Glass Boxes: The Anthropology of Museums*, Vancouver, British Columbia: University of British Columbia Press.

Appadurai, Arjun (1986), "Introduction: Commodities and the Politics of Value," in *The Social Life of Things: Commodities in Cultural Perspective*, Arjun Appadurai, ed., Cambridge: Cambridge University Press, 3–63.

——and Carol A. Breckenridge (1992), "Museums are Good to Think: Heritage on View in India," in *Museums and Communities*, Ivan Karp, Christine Mullen Kreamer, and Steven D. Lavine (eds), Washington, D.C.: Smithsonian Institution Press, 34–55.

Aristides, Niaholai (1988), "Calm and Uncollected," *American Scholar*, 57 (3), 327–336.

Ashton, Doris (1966), "From Achilles' Shield to Junk," in *The Man-Made Object*, Gyorgy Kepes, ed., New York: George Braziller, 192–207.

Ashworth, William B., Jr. (1991), "Remarkable Humans and Singular Beasts," in *The Age of the Marvelous*, Joy Kenseth, ed., Hanover, New Hampshire: Hood Museum of Art, Dartmouth College, 115–144.

Assendorf, Christoph (1993), *Batteries of Life: On the History of Things and Their Perception in Modernity*, Don Reneau, trans., Berkeley, California: University of California Press (original 1984, *Batterien der Lebenskraft: zur Geschichte d. Dinge u. iher Wahrnehmung im*, Giessen: Anabas).

— References —

Auchincloss, Louis (1989), *The Vanderbilt Era: Profiles of a Gilded Age*, New York: Charles Scribner's Sons.

——(1990), *J. P. Morgan: The Financier as Collector*, New York: Harry N. Abrams.

Baekeland, Frederick (1981), "Psychological Aspects of Art Collecting," *Psychiatry*, 44 (February), 45–59.

Balzac, Honoré de (1968), *Cousin Pons*, Herbert J. Hunt, trans., Harmondsworth, Middlesex: Penguin (original 1848).

Barthes, Roland (1988), "The World as Object," Richard Howard, trans., in *Calligram: Essays in New Art History from France*, Norman Bryson, ed., Cambridge: Cambridge University Press, 106–115.

——(1989), "That Old Thing, Art . . .," in *Pop Art: The Critical Dialogue*, Carol Anne Mahsun, ed., Ann Arbor, Michigan: UMI Research Press, 233–240 (original 1985, *The Responsibility of Form*, Richard Howard, trans., New York: Farrar, Straus & Giroux).

Baudrillard, Jean (1981), *For a Critique of the Political Economy of the Sign*, Charles Levin, trans., St. Louis, Missouri: Telos Press (original 1972, *Pour une Critique de l'Economie Politique du Signe*, Paris: Gallimard).

——(1988a), *Jean Baudrillard: Selected Writings*, Mark Poster, ed., Stanford, California: Stanford University Press, 119–148, 166–184.

——(1988b), "The Trompe-L'Oeil," in *Calligram: Essays in New Art History from France*, Norman Bryson, ed., Cambridge: Cambridge University Press, 53–61.

Baum, L. Frank (1900), *The Art of Decorating Show Windows and Dry Goods Interiors*, Chicago: National Windows Trimmer's Association.

——(1904), *The Land of Oz*, Chicago: Reilly & Britton.

Bayley, Stephen (1990), "Public Relations or Industrial Design? Loewy and His Legend," in *Raymond Loewy: Pioneer of American Industrial Design*, Angela Schönberger, ed., Munich: Prestel.

Bazin, Germain (1967), *The Museum Age*, Jane van Nuis Cahill, trans., New York: Universe Books.

Beaglehole, Ernest (1932), *Property: A Study in Social Psychology*, New York: Macmillan.

Bean, Susan S. (1987), "The Objects of Anthropology," *American Ethnologist*, 14 (August), 552-559.

Beaver, Patrick (1986), *The Crystal Palace: A Portrait of Victorian Enterprise*, Chichester, Sussex: Phillimore.

Becker, Howard S. (1982), *Art Worlds*, Berkeley, California: University of California Press.

Beckham, Sue Birdwell and Bradley Brooks (1989), "Mary Moody Northen and Mail Order Immortality," paper presented at American Studies Association International Convention, Toronto, November.

Bedini, Silvio A. (1965), "The Evolution of Science Museums," *Technology and Culture*, 6 (Winter), 1–29.

Behrman, S. N. (1952), *Duveen*, New York: Random House.

Belk, Russell W. (1982), "Acquiring, Possessing, and Collecting: Fundamental Processes in Consumer Behavior," in *Marketing Theory: Philosophy of Science Perspectives*, Ronald F. Bush and Shelby D. Hunt, eds., Chicago: American Marketing Association, 185–190.

——(1983), "Worldly Possessions: Issues and Criticisms," in *Advances in Consumer Research*, Vol. 10, Richard P. Bagozzi and Alice M. Tybout, eds., Ann Arbor, Michigan: Association for Consumer Research, 514–519.

——(1984), "Cultural and Historical Differences in Concepts of Self and Their Effects on Attitudes Toward Having and Giving," in *Advances in Consumer*

Research, Vol. 11, Thomas Kinnear, ed., Ann Arbor, Michigan: Association for Consumer Research, 291–297.

——(1985), "Materialism: Trait Aspects of Living in the Material World," *Journal of Consumer Research*, 12 (December), 265–280.

——(1988a), "Possessions and the Extended Self," *Journal of Consumer Research*, 15 (September), 139–168.

——(1988b), "Third World Consumer Culture," in *Marketing and Development: Toward Broader Dimensions*, Erdoğuan Kumcu and A. Fuat Firat, eds., Greenwich, Connecticut: JAI Press, 103–127.

——(1989), "Collectors and Collections," *Eclectic Collections*, Salt Lake City, Utah: Salt Lake Art Center and Opportunities Foundation.

——(1991a), "The Ineluctable Mysteries of Possessions," in *To Have Possessions: A Handbook on Ownership and Possessions*, Floyd W. Rudmin, ed., special issue of *Journal of Social Behavior and Personality*, 6 (6), 17–55.

——(1991b), "Possessions and the Sense of Past," in *Highways and Buyways: Naturalistic Research from The Consumer Behavior Odyssey*, Russell W. Belk, ed., Provo, Utah: Association for Consumer Research, 114–130.

——(1993a), "American Heroes, Fools, and Villains of Consumption," in *European Advances in Consumer Research*, W. Fred van Raiij and Gary J. Bamossy, eds., Amsterdam: Association for Consumer Research, 287–292.

——(1993b), "Materialism and the Making of the Modern American Christmas," in *Unwrapping Christmas*, Daniel Miller, ed., Oxford: Oxford University Press, 75–104.

——(forthcoming), "Studies in the New Consumer Behavior," in *Consumption as Vanguard*, Daniel Miller, ed., London: Routledge.

——and Gregory S. Coon (1993), "Gift-Giving as Agapic Love: An Alternative to the Exchange Paradigm Based on Dating Experiences," *Journal of Consumer Research*, 20 (December), 393–417.

——and Richard W. Pollay (1985), "Images of Ourselves: The Good Life in Twentieth Century Advertising," *Journal of Consumer Research*, 11 (March), 887–897.

——and Melanie Wallendorf (1990), "The Sacred Meanings of Money," *Journal of Economic Psychology*, 11 (March), 35–67.

——and Melanie Wallendorf (forthcoming), "Of Mice and Men: Gender Identity and Collecting," in *The Material Culture of Gender; The Gender of Material Culture*, Kenneth Ames and Katharine Martinez, eds., Ann Arbor, Michigan: University of Michigan Press.

——, Melanie Wallendorf, and John F. Sherry, Jr. (1989), "The Sacred and the Profane in Consumer Behavior: Theodicy on the Odyssey," *Journal of Consumer Research*, 16 (June), 1–38.

——, Melanie Wallendorf, John F. Sherry, Jr., and Morris B. Holbrook (1991), "Collecting in a Consumer Culture," in *Highways and Buyways: Naturalistic Research from The Consumer Behavior Odyssey*, Russell W. Belk, ed., Provo, Utah: Association for Consumer Research, 178–215.

——, Melanie Wallendorf, John Sherry, Morris Holbrook, and Scott Roberts (1988), "Collectors and Collections," in *Advances in Consumer Research*, Vol. 15, Michael Houston, ed., Provo, Utah: Association for Consumer Research, 548–553.

Bell, Daniel (1957), "The Impact of Advertising," *New Leader*, 6 (February), 9–11.

Bell, Whitfield J., Jr. (1967), "The Cabinet of the American Philosophical Society," in *A Cabinet of Curiosities: Five Episodes in the Evolution of American Museums*, Whitfield J. Bell, Jr., Clifford K. Shipton, John C. Ewers, Louis Leonard Tucker, and Wilcomb E. Washburn, Charlottesville, Virginia: University Press of Virginia, 1–34.

— References —

Benedict, Burton (1983), *The Anthropology of World's Fairs: San Francisco's Panama Pacific International Exposition of 1915*, Berkeley, California: Scholar Press.

Benjamin, Walter (1968a), "The Work of Art in the Age of Mechanical Reproduction," in *Illuminations*, Hannah Arendt, ed., Harry Zohn, trans., New York: Harcourt, Brace & World, 219–253 (original 1936).

——(1968b), "Unpacking My Library: A Talk About Book Collecting," in *Illuminations*, Hannah Arendt, ed., Harry Zohn, trans., New York: Harcourt, Brace & World, 59–67 (original 1955).

——(1970), "Paris, Capital of the Nineteenth Century," *Dissent*, 17, 439–447.

——(1978), "Eduard Fuchs: Collector and Historian," in *The Essential Frankfurt School Reader*, Andrew Arato and Eike Gebhardt, eds., New York: Urizen, 225–253 (original in *Zeitschrift für Sozialforschung*, Vol. 6, 1937).

Benson, Susan Porter (1979), "Palace of Consumption and Machine for Selling: The American Department Store, 1880–1940," *Radical History Review*, 21 (Fall), 199–221.

Benson, Timothy O. (1987), "Mysticism, Materialism, and the Machine in Berlin Dada," *Art Journal*, 47 (Spring), 46–55.

Benston, Margaret (1989), "Feminism and the Critique of Scientific Method," in *Feminism: From Pressure to Politics*, Angela R. Miles and Geraldine Finn, eds., Montreal: Black Rose Books, 57–76.

Berger, John, Sven Blomberg, Chris Fox, Michael Dibb, and Richard Hollis (1972), *Ways of Seeing*, London: British Broadcasting Company.

Bergler, Edmund (1959), *Money and Emotional Conflicts*, New York: Pageant Books.

Berlo, Janet Catherine, ed. (1992), *The Early Years of Native American Art History*, Seattle, Washington: University of Washington Press.

Berman, Morris (1981), *The Reenchantment of the World*, Ithaca, NY: Cornell University Press.

Berman, Phyllis and R. Lee Sullivan (1992), "Limousine Liberal," *Forbes*, 150 (October 26), 168, 172.

Bernfeld, Suzanne C. (1951), "Freud and Archaeology," *American Imago*, 8 (June), 107–128.

Berthe, Monica (1992), "Reflections on *Beni*: Red as a Key to Edo-Period Fashion," in *When Art Became Fashion: Kosode in Edo-Period Japan*, Dale Carolyn Gluckman and Sharon Sadako Taked, eds., New York: Weatherhill, 133–154.

Bodine, Sarah (1983), "Anatomy of an Exhibition," *Industrial Design*, 30 (November/December), 24–29.

Boerdam, Jaap and Warna O. Martinius (1980), "Family Photographs – A Sociological Approach," *The Netherlands' Journal of Sociology*, 16 (October), 95–119.

Boesky, Amy (1991), "'Outlandish-Fruits': Commissioning Nature for the Museum of Man," *English Literary History*, 58 (Summer), 305–330.

Bogdan, Robert (1988), *Freak Show: Presenting Human Oddities for Amusement and Profit*, Chicago: University of Chicago Press.

Boniface, Pricilla and Peter J. Fowler (1993), *Heritage and Tourism in 'The Global Village'*, London: Routledge.

Boorstin, Daniel (1973), *The Americans: The Democratic Experience*, New York: Random House.

Bourdieu, Pierre (1984), *Distinction: A Social Critique of the Judgment of Taste*, Richard Nice, trans., Cambridge, Massachusetts: Harvard University Press (original 1979, *La Distinction: Critique Sociale du Jugement*, Paris: Les Editions de Minuit).

——and Alain Darbel (1990), *The Love of Art: European Art Museums and their Public*, Caroline Beattie and Nick Merriman, trans., Stanford, California: Stanford University Press.

Bowerman, Richard (1979), "Horatio Alger, Jr.; or Adrift in the Myth of Rags and Riches," *Journal of American Culture*, 2 (Spring), 83–112.

Bowlby, Rachel (1985), *Just Looking: Consumer Culture in Dreiser, Gissing and Zola*, New York: Methuen.

Braudel, Fernand (1973), *Capitalism and Material Life, 1400–1800*, Miriam Cochan, trans., New York: Harper & Row (original 1967, *Civilisation Matérielle et Capitalisme*, Paris: Librairie Armand Colin).

——(1977), *Afterthoughts on Material Civilization and Capitalism*, Patricia M. Ranum, trans., Baltimore, Maryland: Johns Hopkins University Press.

——(1979), *The Wheels of Commerce: Civilization & Capitalism 15th–18th Century*, Vol, 2, Siân Reynolds, ed., Cambridge: Harper & Row (original 1979, *Les Juex de l'Echange*, 1979, Paris: Librarie Armand Colin).

Breckenridge, Carol A. (1989), "The Aesthetics and Politics of Colonial Collecting: India at World Fairs," *Comparative Studies in Society and History*, 31 (April), 195–216.

Briggs, Asa (1989), *Victorian Things*, Chicago: University of Chicago Press (original 1988, London: B. T. Batsford).

Brook, G. L. (1980), *Books and Book Collecting*, London: André Deutsch.

Brook, Timothy (1993), *Praying for Power: Buddhism and the Formation of Gentry Society in Late-Ming China*, Cambridge, Massachusetts: Harvard University Press.

Brookner, Anita (1971), *The Genius of the Future, Diderot, Stendhal, Baudelaire, Zola, the Brothers Goncourt, Huysmans: Studies in French Art Criticism*, London: Phaidon.

Brough, James (1963), *Auction!*, Indianapolis: Bobbs-Merrill.

Bruner, Jerome S. (1951), "Personality Dynamics and the Process of Perceiving," in *Perception: An Approach to Personality*, R. R. Blake and G. V. Ramsey, eds., New York: Ronald Press, 121–147.

Bryant, John (1989), "Stamp and Coin Collecting," in *Handbook of American Popular Culture*, 2nd ed., Vol. 3, Thomas Inge, ed., New York: Greenwood Press, 1329–1365.

Buchloh, H. D. (1983), "The Museum Fictions of Marcel Broodthaers," in *Museums by Artists*, A. A. Bronson and Peggy Gale, eds., Toronto: Art Metropole, 45–56.

Buck, Louisa and Philip Dodd (1991), *Relative Value or What's Art Worth?*, London: BBC Books.

Bunn, James H. (1980), "The Aesthetics of British Mercantilism," *New Literary History*, 11 (Winter), 303–321.

Burk, Caroline F. (1900), "The Collecting Instinct," *Pedagogical Seminary*, 7 (January), 179–207.

Burns, Alvin C., Peter L. Gillett, Marc Rubinstein, and James W. Gentry (1990), "An Exploratory Study of Lottery Playing, Gambling Addiction and Links to Compulsive Consumption," in *Advances in Consumer Research*, Vol. 17, Marvin E. Goldberg, Gerald Gorn, and Richard W. Pollay, eds., Provo, Utah: Association for Consumer Research, 298–305.

Burns, Robert I. (1982), "Relic Vendors, Barefoot Friars, and Spanish Muslims: Reflections on Medieval Economic and Religious History," *Comparative Study of Society and History*, 24 (1), 153–163.

Butsch, Richard (1984), "The Commodification of Leisure: The Case of the Model Airplane Hobby and Industry," *Qualitative Sociology*, 7 (Fall), 217–235.

Cabanne, Pierre (1963), *The Great Collectors*, London: Cassell (original 1961, *Le Roman des Grands Collectionneurs*, Paris: Opera Mundi).

Calinescu, Matei (1987), *Five Faces of Modernity: Modernism, Avant-Garde, Decadence, Kitsch, Postmodernism*, 2nd ed., Durham, North Carolina: Duke University Press.

Cameron, Duncan F. (1971), "The Museum, a Temple or the Forum," *Curator*, 14 (1), 11–24.

Campbell, Colin (1987), *The Romantic Ethic and the Spirit of Modern Consumerism*, Oxford: Basil Blackwell.

Carnegie, Andrew (1889), "Wealth," *North American Review*, 148 (June), 653–664.

Carpenter, Edmund (1983), "Introduction," in *In the Middle, Qitinganituk: The Eskimo Today*, Stephen Guion Williams, Boston: David R. Godine.

Carson, Gary (1978), "Doing History with Material Culture," in *Material Culture and the Study of American Life*, Ian M. Quimby, ed., New York: W. W. Norton, 41–64.

Cassullo, Joanne L. (1988), "The Fine Art of Corporate Collecting," *Harvard Business Review*, 66 (November–December), 137–141.

Castle, Terry (1986), *Masquerade and Civilization: The Carnivalesque in Eighteenth-Century English Culture and Fiction*, Stanford, California: Stanford University Press.

Caxton Publishing (1974), *The Pleasures of Collecting*, Lindsay Hamilton, trans., London: Derbibooks (original 1971, L'Esperto).

Chagy, Gideon (1973), *The New Patrons of the Arts*, New York: Harry N. Abrams.

Chalfen, Richard (1987), *Snapshot Versions of Life*, Bowling Green, Ohio: Bowling Green State University Popular Press.

Chamberlin, Russell (1983), *Loot! The Heritage of Plunder*, London: Thames & Hudson.

Chapman, Christine (1990), "Power and Patronage," *Art News*, 89 (March), 139–141.

Chastel, André (1963), *The Age of Humanism: Europe 1480–1530*, New York: McGraw-Hill.

Chatwin, Bruce (1989), *Utz*, New York: Viking.

Chernow, Ron (1990), *The House of Morgan: An American Banking Dynasty and the Rise of Modern Finance*, New York: Atlantic Monthly Press.

Christ, Edwin A. (1965), "The 'Retired' Stamp Collector: Economic and Other Functions of a Systematized Leisure Activity," in *Older People and their Social World: The Subculture of Aging*, Arnold M. Rose and Warren A. Peterson, eds., Philadelphia, Pennsylvania: F. A. Davis Company, 93–112.

Clark, Kenneth (1963), "Introduction," in *Great Private Collections*, Douglas Cooper, ed., New York: Macmillan, 13–19.

——(1970), "Art and Society," in *The Sociology of Art and Literature*, Milton C. Albrecht, James H. Barnett, and Mason Griff, eds., New York: Praeger, 635–650.

Clark, T. J. (1985), *The Painting of Modern Life: Paris in the Art of Manet and His Followers*, Oxford: Blackwell.

Clifford, James (1985), "Objects and Selves – An Afterword," in *Objects and Others: Essays on Museums and Material Culture*, George W. Stocking, Jr., ed., Madison, Wisconsin: University of Wisconsin Press, 236–246.

——(1990), "On Collecting Art and Culture," in *Out There: Marginalization and Contemporary Cultures*, Russell Ferguson, Martha Gever, Trinh T. Minh-ha, and Cornel West, eds., Cambridge, Massachusetts: MIT Press, 141–169.

Clunas, Craig (1991a), *Superfluous Things: Material Culture and Social Status in Early Modern China*, Urbana, Illinois: University of Illinois Press.

——(1991b), "The Art of Social Climbing in Sixteenth-Century China," *Burlington Magazine*, 133 (1059), 368–375.

Cohen, Jeffrey H. (1989), "Museo Shan-Dany: Packaging the Past to Promote the Future," *Folklore Forum*, 22 (1/2), 15–26.

Cole, Douglas (1985), *Captured Heritage: The Scramble for Northwest Coast Artifacts*, Seattle, Washington: University of Washington Press.

Connell, Evan S., Jr. (1974), *The Connoisseur*, New York: Alfred E. Knopf.

Corn, Joseph J. (1989), "The Automobile in American Life," *Journal of American History*, 76 (June), 221–224.

Cornfield, Betty and Owen Edwards (1983), *Quintessence: The Quality of Having It*, New York: Crown.

Costa, Janeen Arnold and Gary Bamossy (forthcoming), "Culture and the 'Marketing of Culture': The Museum Retail Context", in *Marketing in a Multicultural World: Ethnicity, Nationalism, and Cultural Identity*, Janeen Arnold Costa and Gary Bamossy, eds., Newbury Park, California: Sage.

Cotter, Holland (1988), "Haim Steinbach: Shelf Life," *Art in America*, 76 (May), 156–163, 201.

Cowell, F. Richard (1964), *Cicero and the Roman Republic*, 3rd ed., Baltimore, Maryland: Penguin Books.

Crabbe, Anthony (1990), "Museums of Fine Art and Their Public," in *Readings in Popular Culture: Trivial Pursuits?*, Gary Day, ed., New York: St. Martin's Press, 208–215.

Crimp, Douglas (1993), *On the Museum's Ruins*, Cambridge, Massachusetts: MIT Press.

Crispell, Diane (1988), "Collecting Memories," *American Demographics, 60* (November), 38–41.

Csikszentmihalyi, Mihaly and Eugene Rochberg-Halton (1981), *The Meaning of Things: Domestic Symbols and the Self*, Cambridge: Cambridge University Press.

Culver, Stuart (1988), "What Manikens Want: The Wonderful World of Oz and the Art of Decorating Dry Goods Windows," *Representations*, 21 (Winter), 97–116.

Currie, Barton (1931), *Fishers of Books*, Boston: Little, Brown.

Dalby, Liza Crihfield (1993), *Kimono: Fashioning Culture*, New Haven, Connecticutt: Yale University Press.

Danet, Brenda and Tamar Katriel (1986), "Books, Butterflies, and Botticellis: A Life-Span Perspective on Collecting," paper presented at the Sixth International Conference on Culture & Communication, Philadelphia, Pennsylvania, October.

——(1988), "Stamps, Erasers, Table Napkins, 'Rebbe Cards': Childhood Collecting in Israel," paper presented at the Eighteenth Annual Meeting of the Popular Culture Association, New Orleans, Louisiana, March.

——(1989), "No Two Alike: The Aesthetics of Collecting," *Play and Culture* 2 (3), 253–277.

Danilov, Victor J. (1976), "European Science and Technology Museums," *Museum News*, 54 (July/August), 34–37, 71–72.

——(1986), "Museum Pieces," *Public Relations Journal*, 42 (August), 12–16, 30-31.

Dannefer, Dale (1980), "Rationality and Passion in Private Experience: Modern Consciousness and the Social World of Old-Car Collectors," *Social Problems*, 27 (April), 392–412.

——(1981), "Neither Socialization Nor Recruitment: The Avocational Careers of Old-Car Enthusiasts," *Social Forces*, 60 (December), 395–413.

Danto, Arthur C. (1981), *The Transformation of the Commonplace*, Cambridge, Massachusetts: Harvard University Press.

——(1991), "From Matchbooks to Masterpieces: Toward a Philosophy of

Collecting," *Aperture*, 124 (Summer), 2–3.

——(1992), *Beyond the Brillo Box: The Visual Arts in Post-Historical Perspective*, New York: Farrar, Straus & Giroux.

Davies, Robertson (1991), *The Cornish Trilogy*, London: Penguin Books.

Davis, Monte (1985), "Nasty and Brutish, Nobel and Free: Our Partisan Views of Primitive Life," *Psychology Today*, 19 (January), 60–64.

Davis, Shane Adler (1989), "'Fine Cloths on the Altar': The Commodification of Late-Nineteenth-Century France," *Art Journal*, 48 (Spring), 85–89.

Dawson, Scott and Gary Bamossy (1991), "If 'We Are What We Have,' What Are We When We Don't Have?: An Exploratory Study of Materialism Among Expatriate Americans," *To Have Possessions: A Handbook on Ownership and Property*, Floyd W. Rudmin, ed., special issue of *Journal of Social Behavior and Personality*, 6 (6), 363–384.

Debord, Guy (1970), *Society of the Spectacle*, Detroit, Michigan: Black and Red.

Deci, Edward L. (1971), "Effects of Externally Mediated Rewards on Intrinsic Motivation," *Journal of Personality and Social Psychology*, 18, 105–115.

Defert, Daniel (1982), "The Collection of the World: Accounts of Voyages From the Sixteenth to the Eighteenth Centuries," *Dialectical Anthropology*, 7 (September), 11–20.

deForest, Robert W. (1928), *Art in Merchandise: Notes on the Relationships of Stores and Museums*, Industrial Arts Monograph No. 4, New York: Metropolitan Museum of Art.

Delaney, Jill (1992), "Ritual Space in the Canadian Museum of Civilization: Consuming Canadian Identity," in *Lifestyle Shopping: The Subject of Consumption*, Rob Shields, ed., London: Routledge, 136–148.

De Mente, Boye and Fred Thomas Perry (1967), *The Japanese as Consumers: Asia's First Great Mass Market*, New York: Walker.

Dewhurst, C. Kurt and Marsha MacDowell (1986), "Museum for the People: Museum Bars," *Material Culture*, 18 (1), 37–50.

DiMaggio, Paul (1982a), "Cultural Entrepreneurship in Nineteenth-Century Boston: The Creation of an Organizational Base for High Culture in America," *Media, Culture and Society*, 4 (January), 33–50.

——(1982b), "Cultural Entrepreneurship in Nineteenth-Century Boston: The Classification and Framing of American Art," *Media, Culture and Society*, 4 (October), 303–322.

——(1987), "Classification in Art," *American Sociological Review*, 52 (August), 440-455.

Dixon, Donald F. (1994), "Retailing in Classical Athens: Gleanings from Contemporary Literature and Art," in *Contemporary Marketing History: Proceedings of the Sixth Conference on Historical Research in Marketing and Marketing Thought*, Jeffrey B. Schmidt, Stanley C. Hollander, Terence Nevett, and Jagdish N. Sheth, eds., East Lansing, Michigan: Michigan State University, 231–247.

Dolan, Carrie (1988), "Why Is Capt. Crunch A Little Like Zeus? The Museum Knows," *Wall Street Journal*, 118 (21), February 1, 1+.

Donato, Eugenio (1979), "The Museum's Furnace: Notes Toward a Contextual Reading of *Bouvard and Pécuchet*," in *Textual Strategies: Perspectives in Post-Structural Criticism*, Ithaca, New York: Cornell University Press, 213–238.

Dorfles, Gillo (1966), "The Man-Made Object," in *The Man-Made Object*, Gyorgy Kepes, ed., New York: George Braziller, 1–25.

——(1969), *Kitsch: The World of Bad Taste*, New York: Universe Books.

Douglas, Mary and Baron Isherwood (1979), *The World of Goods: Towards an Anthropology of Consumption*, New York: W. W. Norton.

Dowd, Maureen (1982), "In Washington: Cleaning the Nation's Attic," *Time*, 118 (February 8), 11–12.

Drakulić, Slavenka (1991), *How We Survived Communism and Even Laughed*, New York: W. W. Norton.

·Dreiser, Theodore (1981), *Sister Carrie*, Harmondsworth, Middlesex: Penguin Books (original 1900, New York: Doubleday, Page).

Drucker, Johanna (1992), "Harnett, Haberle, and Peto: Visuality and Artifice among the Proto-Modern Americans," *Art Bulletin*, 74 (March), 37–50.

Duby, Georges, ed. (1988), *A History of Private Life II, Revelations of the Medieval World*, Cambridge, Massachusetts: Belknap Press.

Dudar, Helen (1990), "The Unexpected Private Passion of Sigmund Freud," *Smithsonian*, 21 (5), 100–109.

Duncan, Hugh Dalziel (1965), *Culture and Democracy: The Struggle for Form in Society and Architecture in Chicago and the Middle West during the Life and Times of Louis H. Sullivan*, New York: Bedminister Press.

Dunlop, M. H. (1984), "Curiosities Too Numerous to Mention: Early Regionalism and Cincinnati's Western Museum," *American Quarterly*, 36 (Fall), 524–548.

Durkheim, Emile and Marcel Mauss (1963), *Primitive Classification*, Rodney Needham, trans., Chicago: University of Chicago Press (original 1903, *De Quelques Formes Primitives de Classifications: Contribution à l'Etude des Representations Collectives*, Paris: Année Sociologique).

Durost, Walter N. (1932), *Children's Collecting Activity Related to Social Factors*, New York: Bureau of Publications, Teachers College, Columbia University.

Easterlin, Richard A. (1974), "Does Economic Growth Improve the Human Lot? Some Empirical Evidence," in *Nations and Households in Economic Growth: Essays in Honor of Moses Abramovitz*, Paul A. David and Melvin Reder (eds), New York: Academic Press.

Eccles, Lord (1968), *On Collecting*, London: Longmans.

Eco, Umberto (1986), *Travels in Hyperreality: Essays*, William Weaver, ed., San Diego, California: Harcourt Brace Jovanovich.

Eisenberg, Evan (1987), *The Recording Angel: Explorations in Phonography*, New York: McGraw-Hill.

Ellen, Roy (1988), "Fetishism," *Man*, 23 (June), 213–235.

Ellenberger, Henri F. (1974), "The Mental Hospital and the Zoological Garden," in *Animals and Man in Historical Perspective*, Joseph Klaits and Barrie Klaits, eds., New York: Harper & Row, 59–92 (original "Jardin Zoologique et Hôpital Psychiatrique," in *Psychiatrie Animale*, A. Brion and Henri Ey, eds., Paris: Editions Desclée de Brouwer, 1965, 559–578).

Engelman, Edmund, ed. (1976), *Berggasse 19: Sigmund Freud's Home and Offices, Vienna 1938: The Photographs of Edmund Engelman*, New York: Basic Books.

Estes-Smith, Marilyn (1972), "Is Nothing Junk Anymore??" in *The Popular Culture Explosion*, Ray B. Browne and David Madden, eds., New York: William C. Brown, 122.

Ettema, Michael J. (1987), "History Museums and the Culture of Materialism," in *Past Meets Present: Essays about Historic Interpretation and Public Audiences*, Jo Blatti, ed., Washington, D.C.: Smithsonian Institution Press, 62–91.

Evans, John C. (1992), *Tea in China: The History of China's National Drink*, New York: Greenwood Press.

Faber, Ronald J. (1992), "Money Changes Everything: Compulsive Buying from a Biopsychosocial Perspective," *American Behavioral Scientist*, 35 (July), 809–819.

——, Thomas C. O'Guinn, and Raymond Krych (1987), "Compulsive Consumption," in *Advances in Consumer Research*, Vol. 14, Melanie Wallendorf and Paul Anderson, eds., Provo, Utah: Association for Consumer Research, 132–135.

Farb, Peter and George Armelagos (1980), *Consuming Passions: The Anthropology of Eating*, Boston: Houghton Mifflin.

Feng, Chengbo (1991), "China's Museums Reveal a Dynamic Past as Well as Future," *Museum News*, 70 (November/December), 16–19.

Ferguson, Eugene S. (1965), "Technical Museums and International Exhibitions," *Technology and Culture*, 6 (Winter), 30–46.

Fiedler, Leslie (1978), *Freaks*, New York: Simon & Schuster.

Fine, Gary Alan (1987), "Community and Boundary: Personal Experience Stories of Mushroom Collectors," *Journal of Folklore Research*, 24 (September–December), 223–240.

Finlay, Ian (1977), *Priceless Heritage: The Future of Museums*, London: Faber & Faber.

Flaubert, Gustave (1954a), *Bibliomania: A Tale*, London: Rodale Press (original 1836).

——(1954b), *Bouvard & Pécuchet*, T. W. Earp and G. W. Stonier, trans., New York: New Directions (original 1880).

Flynn, Tom (1993), *The Trouble With Christmas*, Buffalo, New York: Prometheus Books.

Folsom, Merrill (1963), *Great American Mansions and Their Stories*, New York: Hastings House.

Formanek, Ruth (1991), "Why They Collect: Collectors Reveal Their Motivations," in *To Have Possessions: A Handbook on Ownership and Property*, Floyd W. Rudmin, ed., special issue of *Journal of Social Behavior and Personality*, 6 (6), 275–286.

Forty, Adrian (1986), *Objects of Desire: Design & Society From Wedgwood to IBM*, New York: Pantheon.

Foster, George M. (1965), "Peasant Society and the Image of Limited Good," *American Anthropologist*, 67, 293–315.

——(1972), "The Anatomy of Envy: A Study of Symbolic Behavior," *Current Anthropology*, 13, 165–182.

Foster, Hal (1993), "The Art of Fetishism: Notes on Dutch Still Life," in *Fetishism as Cultural Discourse*, Emily Apter and William Pietz, eds., Ithaca, New York: Cornell University Press, 251–265.

Foucault, Michel (1970), *The Order of Things: An Archaeology of the Human Sciences*, New York: Pantheon (original 1966, *Les Mots et les Choses*).

——(1988), "Las Meninas," *Calligram: Essays in New Art History from France*, Norman Bryson, ed., Cambridge: Cambridge University Press, 91–105.

Franco, Barbara (1980), *Childhood Treasures*, Lexington, Massachusetts: Museum of Our National Heritage.

Freeman, Kathleen (1976), *The Life and Work of Solon*, New York: Arno Press.

French, Stephanie (1991), "The Corporate Art of Helping the Arts," *Public Relations Quarterly*, 36 (Fall), 25–27.

Freud, Sigmund (1914), *The Psychopathology of Everyday Life*, New York: Macmillan.

Freudenberger, Herman (1963), "Fashion, Sumptuary Laws, and Business," *Business History Review*, 37 (Spring/Summer), 37–48.

Friedel, Robert (1988), *A Material World*, Washington, D.C.: National Museum of American History, Smithsonian Institution.

Friedman, Monroe, Piet Vanden Abeele, and Koen De Vos (1993), "Boorstin's Consumption Community Concept: A Tale of Two Countries," *Journal of Consumer Policy*, 16 (1), 35–60.

Fromkin, Howard L. and C. R. Snyder (1980), "The Search for Uniqueness and Valuation of Scarcity: Neglected Dimensions of Value in Exchange Theory," in *Social Exchange Theory: Advances in Theory and Research*, Kenneth J. Gergen, Marvin S. Greenberg, and Richard H. Willis, eds., New York: Plenum Press, 57–71.

Fromm, Erich (1976), *To Have or To Be*, New York: Harper & Row.

Fuller, Robert C. (1993), "Religion and Ritual in American Wine Culture," *Journal of American Culture*, 16 (Spring), 39–45.

Gaither, Edmund Barry (1992), "'Hey! That's Mine': Thoughts on Pluralism and American Museums," in *Museums and Communities*, Ivan Karp, Christine Mullen Kreamer, and Steven D. Lavine, eds., Washington, D.C.: Smithsonian Institution Press, 56–64.

Gamwell, Lynn (1989), "The Origins of Freud's Antiquities Collection," in *Sigmund Freud and Art: His Personal Collection of Antiquities*, Lynn Gamwell and Richard Wells, eds., Binghamton, New York: State University of New York, Binghamton, 21–32.

——and Richard Wells, eds. (1989), *Sigmund Freud and Art: His Personal Collection of Antiquities*, Binghamton, New York: State University of New York, Binghamton.

Gardner, Carl and Julie Sheppard (1989), *Consuming Passion: The Rise of Retail Culture*, London: Unwin Hyman.

Gathercole, Peter (1989), "The Fetishism of Artefacts," in *Museum Studies in Material Culture*, Susan M. Pearce, ed., London: Leicester University Press, 73–81.

Gay, Peter (1989), "Introduction," in *Sigmund Freud and Art: His Personal Collection of Antiquities*, Lynn Gamwell and Richard Wells, eds., Binghamton, New York: State University of New York, Binghamton, 14–19.

Geary, Patrick (1986), "Sacred Commodities: The Circulation of Medieval Relics," in *The Social Life of Things: Commodities in Cultural Perspective*, Arjun Appadurai, ed., Cambridge: Cambridge University Press, 169–191.

Gelber, Steven M. (1991), "A Job You Can't Lose: Work and Hobbies in the Great Depression," *Journal of Social History*, 24 (Summer), 741–766.

——(1992), "Free Market Metaphor: The Historical Dynamics of Stamp Collecting," *Comparative Studies in Society and History*, 34 (October), 742–769.

Gell, Alfred (1986), "Newcomers to the World of Goods: Consumption Among the Muria Gonds," in *The Social Life of Things: Commodities in Cultural Perspective*, Arjun Appadurai, ed., Cambridge: Cambridge University Press, 110–138.

George, Gerald (1989), "Historic Property Museums: What are they Preserving?" *Preservation Forum*, 3 (Summer), 2–5.

George, Wilma (1985), "Alive or Dead: Zoological Collections in the Seventeenth Century," in *The Origins of Museums: The Cabinet of Curiosities in Sixteenth- and Seventeenth-Century Europe*, Oliver Impey and Arthur MacGregor, eds., Oxford: Clarendon Press, 179–187.

Gilborn, Craig (1982), "Pop Pedagogy: Looking at the Coke Bottle," in *Material Culture Studies in America*, Thomas J. Schlereth, ed., Nashville, Tennessee: American Association for State and Local History, 183–191.

Glasser, William (1976), *Positive Addiction*, New York: Harper & Row.

Gluckman, Dale Carolyn (1992), "Toward a New Aesthetic: The Evolution of the Kosode and Its Decoration," in *When Art Became Fashion*, Dale Carolyn Gluckman and Sharon Sadako Taked, eds., New York: Weatherhill, 65–94.

——and Sharon Sadako Taked (1992), "Introduction," in *When Art Became Fashion*, Dale Carolyn Gluckman and Sharon Sadako Taked, eds., New York: Weatherhill, 1–42.

Godfrey, Stephen (1991), "Sponsorships Essential, ROM Says," *Globe and Mail* (Toronto), November 9, C1, C4.

Goldberg, Herb and Robert T. Lewis (1978), *Money Madness: The Psychology of Saving, Spending, Loving, and Hating Money*, New York: William Morrow.

Goodman, Jordan (1993), *Tobacco in History: The Cultures of Dependence*, London: Routledge.

Gordon, Jean and Jan McArthur (1985), "American Women and Domestic Consumption, 1800-1920: Four Interpretive Themes," *Journal of American Culture*, 8 (Fall), 35–46.

Grampp, William D. (1989), *Pricing the Priceless: Art, Artists, and Economics*, New York: Basic Books.

Granovetter, Mark (1985), "Economic Action and Social Structure: The Problem of Embeddedness," *American Journal of Sociology*, 91 (November), 481–510.

Grasskamp, Walter (1983), "Les Artistes et les Autres Collectioneurs," in *Museums by Artists*, A. A. Bronson and Peggy Gale, eds., Toronto: Art Metropole, 129–148.

Green, Nicholas (1989), "Circuits of Production, Circuits of Consumption: The Case of Mid-Nineteenth-Century French Art Dealing," *Art Journal*, 48 (Spring), 29–89.

Greenberg, Clement (1957), "Avant-Garde and Kitsch," in *Mass Culture: The Popular Arts in America*, Bernard Rosenberg and David M. White, eds., Glencoe, Illinois: The Free Press, 98–110 (original 1946, *The Partisan Reader*, 378–389).

Greenblatt, Stephen (1991), *Marvelous Possessions: The Wonder of the New World*, Chicago: University of Chicago Press.

Greenspan, Stuart (1988), "Am I Good Enough to Own This Painting?" *Avenue*, 12 (February), 88–94.

Gregory, Neal and Janice Gregory (1980), *When Elvis Died*, Washington, D.C.: Communications Press.

Gulerce, Aydan (1991), "Transitional Objects: A Reconsideration of the Phenomena," in *To Have Possessions: A Handbook on Ownership and Property*, Floyd W. Rudmin, ed., special issue of *Journal of Social Behavior and Personality*, 6 (6), 187–208.

Guth, Christine (1989), "The Tokugawa as Patrons and Collectors of Painting," in *The Tokugawa Collection, the Japan of the Shoguns*, Denise L. Bissonnette, co-ordinator, Montreal: Montreal Museum of Fine Arts, 41–51.

Hall, G. Stanley (1907), *Aspects of Child Life and Education*, Boston: Ginn.

Halle, David (1993), *Inside Culture: Art and Class in the American Home*, Chicago: University of Chicago Press.

Hallowell, Edmund M. and William J. Grace, Jr. (1991), "Money Styles," in *Money and Mind*, Sheila Klebanow and Eugene L. Lowenkopf, eds., New York: Plenum Press, 15–26.

Halverson, John (1987), "Art for Art's Sake in the Paleolithic," *Current Anthropology*, 18 (February), 63–89.

Hamilton, Gary G. (1977), "Chinese Consumption of Foreign Commodities: A Comparative Perspective," *American Sociological Review*, 42 (December), 877–891.

Handler, Richard (1986), "Authenticity," *Anthropology Today*, 2 (February), 2–4.

Handy, Bruce (1988), "Sweet Savage Teapot: The Rapid Rise of Yuppie Porn," *Utne Reader*, 26 (March/April), 108–112 (original, *Spy*, December, 1987).

Hansen, Flemming (1966), "Developments in Penetration of Special Collector Products," in *Readings in Danish Theory of Marketing*, Max Kjær-Hansen, ed., København: Einar Harcks, 309–316.

Harrah, William Fisk (1984), "My Personal Memoirs of Cars, Car Collecting, and Car People," *Automobile Quarterly*, 22 (3), 240–257.

Harris, Neil (1962), "The Gilded Age Revisited: Boston and the Museum Movement," *American Quarterly*, 14 (Winter).

——(1978), "Museums, Merchandising, and Popular Taste: The Struggle for Influence," in *Material Culture and the Study of American Life*, Ian M. Quimby, ed., New York: W. W. Norton, 140–174.

——(1987), "Collective Possession: J. Pierpont Morgan and the American Imagination," in *J. Pierpont Morgan, Collector*, Linda H. Roth, ed., Hartford, Connecticut: Wadsworth Athenium, 43–57.

——(1990), "Museums: The Hidden Agenda," in Neil Harris, *Cultural Excursions: Marketing Appetites and Cultural Tastes in Modern America*, Chicago: University of Chicago Press, 132–147 (original 1987, in *Midwest Museum News*, 46 [Spring], 17–21).

Haskell, Francis (1976), *Rediscoveries in Art: Some Aspects of Taste, Fashion and Collecting in England and France*, London: Phaidon.

Hathaway, Baxter (1968), *Marvels and Commonplaces: Renaissance Literary Criticism*, New York: Random House, p. 160.

Hattox, Ralph (1985), *Coffee and Coffeehouses: The Origins of a Social Beverage in the Medieval Near East*, Seattle, Washington: University of Washington Press.

Hauser, William B. (1992), "A New Society: Japan Under Tokugawa Rule," in *When Art Became Fashion*, Dale Carolyn Gluckman and Sharon Sadako Taked, eds., New York: Weatherhill, 43–64.

Hayashiya, Seizo and Henry Trubner (1977), *Chinese Ceramics from Japanese Collections*, New York: Asia House Gallery.

Helms, Mary W. (1988), *Ulysses' Sail: An Ethnographic Odyssey of Power, Knowledge, and Geographical Distance*, Princeton, New Jersey: Princeton University Press.

Hendon, William S. (1979), *Analyzing an Art Museum*, New York: Praeger.

Herrmann, Frank (1972), *The English as Collectors: A Documentary Chrestomathy*, London: Chatto & Windus.

Hertz, Louis H. (1969), *Antique Collecting for Men*, New York: Galahad Books.

Hinsley, Curtis M. (1990), "The World as Marketplace: Commodification of the Exotic at the World's Columbian Exposition, Chicago, 1893," in *Exhibiting Cultures*, Ivan Karp and Steven D. Lavine, eds., Washington, D.C.: Smithsonian Institution Press, 344–353.

Hirschman, Elizabeth C. (1992), "The Consciousness of Addiction: Toward a General Theory of Compulsive Consumption," *Journal of Consumer Research*, 19 (September), 155–179.

——and Morris B. Holbrook (1982), "Hedonic Consumption: Emerging Concepts, Methods, and Propositions," *Journal of Marketing*, 46 (Summer), 92–101.

Ho, Wai-Kam (1987), "Late Ming Literati: Their Social and Cultural Ambience," in *The Chinese Scholar's Studio: The Artistic Life in the Late Ming Period*, Chu-Tsing Li and James C. Y. Watt, eds., New York: Thames & Hudson, 23–36.

Hodgen, Margaret T. (1964), *Early Anthropology in the Sixteenth and Seventeenth Centuries*, Philadelphia: University of Pennsylvania Press.

Hoffer, Eric (1951), *The True Believer: Thoughts on the Nature of Mass Movements*, New York: Harper & Row.

Holdengräber, Paul (1987), "'A Visible History of Art': The Forms and Preoccupations of the Early Museum," in *Studies in Eighteenth-Century Culture*, Vol. 17, John Yolton and Leslie Ellen Brown, eds., East Lansing, Michigan: Colleagues Press, 107–117.

Hollander, Stanley C. (1984), "Sumptuary Legislation: Demarketing by Edict," *Journal of Macromarketing*, 4 (Spring), 4–16.

Holt, Elizabeth Gilmore (1979), *The Triumph of Art for the Public: The Emerging Role of Exhibitions and Critics*, Garden City, New York: Anchor Books.

Hooper-Greenhill, Eilean (1992), *Museums and the Shaping of Knowledge*, London: Routledge.

Horne, Donald (1984), *The Great Museum: The Re-Presentation of History*, London: Pluto Press.

——(1992), *The Intelligent Tourist*, McMahons Point, New South Wales: Margaret Gee.

Horowitz, Daniel (1985), *The Morality of Spending: Attitudes Toward the Consumer in America, 1875–1940*, Baltimore, Maryland: Johns Hopkins University Press.

Horrigan, Brian (1992), "'A Material World' At the National Museum of American History," *Technology and Culture*, 33 (January), 132–139.

Howarth, Patrick (1951), *The Year is 1851*, London: White Lion.

Hughes, Diane Owen (1983), "Sumptuary Law and Social Relations in Renaissance Italy," in *Disputes and Settlements: Law and Human Relations in the West*, John Bossy, ed., Cambridge: Cambridge University Press, 69–99.

——(1986), "Distinguishing Signs: Ear-Rings, Jews and Franciscan Rhetoric in the Italian Renaissance City," *Past & Present*, 112 (August), 3–59.

Hughes, Robert (1987), "How to Start a Museum," *Time*, 130, August 10, 48–50.

Humphrey, N. K. (1979), "The Biological Basis of Collecting," *Human Nature*, February, 44–47.

Hunt, John Dixon (1985), "'Curiosities to Adorn Cabinets and Gardens,'" in *The Origins of Museums: The Cabinet of Curiosities in Sixteenth- and Seventeenth-Century Europe*, Oliver Impey and Arthur MacGregor, eds., Oxford: Clarendon Press, 193–202.

Hunter, Michael (1985), "The Cabinet Institutionalized: The Royal Society's 'Repository' and Its Background," in *The Origins of Museums: The Cabinet of Curiosities in Sixteenth- and Seventeenth-Century Europe*, Oliver Impey and Arthur MacGregor, eds., Oxford: Clarendon Press, 159–168.

Hurley, Frank (1923), *Pearls and Savages*, New York: Putnam.

Hurlock, Elizabeth B. (1929), *The Psychology of Dress: An Analysis of Fashion and Its Motive*, New York: Ronald Press.

Hutter, Mark (1987), "The Downtown Department Store as a Social Force," *Social Science Journal*, 24 (3), 239–246.

Hyde, Charles K. (1989), "'The Automobile in American Life,' An Exhibit at Henry Ford Museum, Dearborn, Michigan," *Technology and Culture*, 30 (January), 105–111.

Hyde, Lewis (1983), *The Gift: Imagination and the Erotic Life of Property*, New York: Random House.

Ihamon, W. T., Jr. (1976), "Horatio Alger and American Modernism: The One Dimensional Social Formula," *American Studies*, 12 (Spring), 11–27.

Jackson, Douglas N. (1976), "Is Achievement a Unitary Construct?" *Journal of Research in Personality*, 10, 1–21.

Jackson, Holbrook (1989), *The Anatomy of Bibliomania*, Savannah, Georgia: Frederic Beil (original 1930).

Jacobson, Michael F. and Ronald K. L. Collins (1992), "How Non-Profits Can Stay Clear of Commercialism's Tentacles," *Chronicle of Philanthropy*, July 28.

Janus, Elizabeth (1992), "Material Girl," *Art Forum*, 30 (May), 79–81.

Jensen, Jens (1963), "Collector's Mania," *Acta Psychiatrica Scandinavia*, 39 (4), 606–618.

Jhally, Sut (1987), *The Codes of Advertising: Fetishism and the Political Economy* of *Meaning in the Consumer Society*, New York: St. Martin's Press.

Joeslit, David (1988), "Investigating the Ordinary," *Art in America*, 76 (May), 149–156.

Johnson, Jed (1988), "Inconspicuous Consumption," in *The Andy Warhol Collection, Contemporary Art*, Vol. 5, Sotheby's, n.p.n.

Johnson, Ragnar (1986), "Accumulation and Collecting: An Anthropological Perspective," *Art History*, 9 (March), 63–83.

Johnston, Susanna (1986), "Introduction," in *Collecting: The Passionate Pastime*, Susanna Johnston and Tim Beddow, eds., New York: Harper & Row, 13–15.

——and Tim Beddow, eds. (1986), *Collecting: The Passionate Pastime*, New York: Harper & Row.

Joline, Adrian H. (1902), *Meditations of an Autograph Collector*, New York: Harper & Brothers.

Jonaitis, Aldona (1992), "Franz Boas, John Swanton, and the New Haida Sculpture at the American Museum of Natural History," in *The Early Years of Native American Art History*, Janet Catherine Berlo, ed., Seattle, Washington: University of Washington Press, 22–61.

Jones, Ernest (1955), *The Life and Work of Sigmund Freud*, Vol. 2, New York: Basic Books.

Jones, Jane Peirson (1992), "The Colonial Legacy and the Community: The Gallery 33 Project," in *Museums and Communities*, Ivan Karp, Christine Mullen Kreamer, and Steven D. Lavine, Washington, D.C.: Smithsonian Institution Press, 221–241.

Jordanova, Ludmilla (1989), "Objects of Knowledge: A Historical Perspective on Museums," in *The New Museology*, Peter Vergo, ed., London: Reaktion Books, 22–40.

Joselit, David (1988), "Investigating the Ordinary," *Art in America*, 76 (May), 149–156.

Josephson, Mathew (1934), *The Robber Barons: The Great American Capitalists, 1861–1901*, New York: Harcourt, Brace, & World.

Joy, Annamma (1993), "The Modern Medicis: Corporations as Consumers of Art," *Research in Consumer Behavior*, Vol. 6, Janeen Arnold Costz and Russell W. Belk, ed., Greenwich, Connecticut: JAI Press, 29–54.

Jung, Carl G. (1988), *Nietzsche's Zarathustra*, Princeton, New Jersey: Princeton University Press.

Kaiser, Timothy (1990), "The Antiquities Market," *Journal of Field Archaeology*, 17 (Summer), 205–210.

Karp, Ivan and Steven D. Lavine, eds, (1990), *Exhibiting Cultures: The Poetics and Politics of Museum Display*, Washington, D.C.: Smithsonian Institution Press.

Katriel, Tamar (1988/89), "*Haxlàfot*: Rules and Strategies in Children's Swapping Exchanges," *Research on Language and Social Interaction*, 22, 157–178.

Kaufman, William (1976), "Some Emotional Uses of Money," in *The Psychoanalysis of Money*, Ernest Borneman, ed., New York: Urizen, 227–251 (original 1973, Frankfurt: Suhrkamp).

Kaufmann, Thomas DaCosta (1993), *The Mastery of Nature: Aspects of Art, Science, and Humanism in the Renaissance*, Princeton, New Jersey: Princeton University Press.

Kavanagh, Gaynor (1989), "Objects as Evidence, or Not?" *Museum Studies in Material Culture*, Susan M. Pearce, ed., London: Leicester University Press, 125–137.

Kaylan, Melik (1988), "The Warhol Collection: Why Selling it is a Shame," *Connoisseur*, 915 (April), 118–128.

Keller, Evelyn Fox (1983), "Feminism and Science," in *The Signs Reader: Women,*

Gender & Scholarship, Ellizabeth Abel and Emily K. Abel, eds., Chicago: University of Chicago Press, 109–122.

Kelly, Robert F. (1987a), "Culture as Commodity: The Marketing of Cultural Objects and Cultural Experiences," *Advances in Consumer Research*, Vol. 14, Melanie Wallendorf and Paul Anderson, eds., Provo, Utah: Association for Consumer Research, 347–351.

——(1987b), "Museums as Status Symbols II: Attaining a State of Having Been," in *Advances in Nonprofit Marketing*, Vol. 2, Russell W. Belk, ed., Greenwich, Connecticut: JAI Press, 1–38.

——(1993), "Discussion: Vesting Objects and Experiences with Symbolic Meaning," *Advances in Consumer Research*, Vol. 20, Leigh McAllister and Michael L. Rothschild, eds., Provo, Utah: Association for Consumer Research, 232–234.

Kendrick, Walter (1987), *The Private Museum: Pornography in Modern Culture*, New York: Viking.

Kenseth, Joy (1991a), "The Age of the Marvelous: An Introduction," in *The Age of the Marvelous*, Joy Kenseth, ed., Hanover, New Hampshire: Hood Museum of Art, Dartmouth College, 24–59.

——(1991b), "Kunst- und Wunderkammer," in *The Age of the Marvelous*, Joy Kenseth, ed., Hanover, New Hampshire: Hood Museum of Art, Dartmouth College, 247–249.

——(1991c), "A World of Wonders in One Closet Shut," in *The Age of the Marvelous*, Joy Kenseth, ed., Hanover, New Hampshire: Hood Museum of Art, Dartmouth College, 81–101.

King, Margaret J. (1990), "Theme Park Thesis," *Museum News*, 69 (September–October), 60–62.

——(1991), "The Theme Park Experience: What Museums Can Learn from Mickey Mouse," *The Futurist*, 25 (November–December), 24–32.

Kirshenblatt-Gimblett, Barbara (1990), "Objects of Ethnography," in *Museums and Communities*, Ivan Karp, Christine Mullen Kreamer, and Steven D. Lavine, eds., Washington, D.C.: Smithsonian Institution Press, 386–418.

Klapp, Orrin E. (1991), *Inflation of Symbols: Loss of Values in American Culture*, New Brunswick, New Jersey: Transaction Publishers.

Klein, Richard (1993), *Cigarettes are Sublime*, Durham, NC: Duke University Press.

Kohák, Erazim (1992), "Ashes, Ashes . . . Central Europe After Forty Years," *Daedalus*, 121 (Spring), 197–215.

Konishi, Massatoshi (1987), "The Museum and Japanese Studies," *Current Anthropology*, 28 (August–October), S96–S101.

Kopytoff, Igor (1986), "The Cultural Biography of Things: Commoditization as Process," in *The Social Life of Things: Commodities in Cultural Perspective*, Arjun Appadurai, ed., Cambridge: Cambridge University Press, 64–91.

Kotler, Phillip and Sidney J. Levy (1969), "Broadening the Concept of Marketing," *Journal of Marketing*, 33 (January), 10–15.

Kozminski, Andrzej K. (1992), "Consumers in Transition From the Centrally Planned Economy to the Market Economy," *Journal of Consumer Policy*, 14 (4), 351–369.

Kreamer, Christine Mullen (1990), "Defining Communities Through Exhibiting and Collecting," in *Museums and Communities*, Ivan Karp, Christine Mullen Kreamer, and Steven D. Lavine, eds., Washington, D.C.: Smithsonian Institution Press, 367–381.

Kron, Joan (1983), *Home-Psych: The Social Psychology of Home and Decoration*, New York: Clarkson N. Potter.

Kubler, George (1962), *The Shape of Time: Remarks on the History of Things*, New

Haven, CT: Yale University Press.

Kulik, Gary (1989), "Designing the Past: History-Museum Exhibitions from Peale to the Present," in *History Museums in the United States: A Critical Assessment*, Warren Leon and Roy Rosenzweig, eds., Urbana, Illinois: University of Illinois Press, 3–37.

Kunzle, David (1984), "Pop Art as Consumerist Realism," *Studies in Visual Communications*, 10 (Spring), 16–33.

Lambton, Lucinda (1987), "These are a Few of My Favourite Things: A Cabinet of Curiosities," *The Listener*, 117 (19 February), 10–11.

Landa, Louis A. (1980), *Essays in Eighteenth-Century English Literature*, Princeton, New Jersey: Princeton University Press.

Land-Weber, Ellen (1980), *The Passionate Collector*, New York: Simon & Schuster.

Laquer, Thomas W. (1992) "Sexual Desire and the Market Economy during the Industrial Revolution," in *Discourses of Sexuality: From Aristotle to AIDS*, Domna C. Stanton, ed., Ann Arbor, Michigan: University of Michigan Press, 185–215.

Laurencich-Minelli, Laura (1985), "Museography and Ethnographical Collections in Bologna During the Sixteenth and Seventeenth Centuries," in *The Origins of Museums: The Cabinet of Curiosities in Sixteenth- and Seventeenth-Century Europe*, Oliver Impey and Arthur MacGregor, eds., Oxford: Clarendon Press, 17–22.

Lavine, Steven D. (1992), "Audience, Ownership, and Authority: Designing Relations between Museums and Communities," in *Museums and Communities*, Ivan Karp, Christine Mullen Kreamer, and Steven D. Lavine, eds., Washington, D.C.: Smithsonian Institution Press, 137-157.

Leach, William (1984), "Transformations in a Culture of Consumption: Women and Department Stores, 1890–1925," *Journal of American History*, 71 (2), 319–342.

——(1989), "Strategists of Display and the Production of Desire," *Consuming Visions: Accumulation and Display of Goods in America, 1880–1920*, Simon J. Bronner, ed., New York: W. W. Norton, 99–132.

——(1993), *Land of Desire: Merchants, Power, and the Rise of a New American Culture*, New York: Vintage.

Learmount, Brian (1985), *A History of the Auction*, Iver, Buckinghamshire: Barnard & Learmount.

Lears, T. J. Jackson (1983), "From Salvation to Self-Realization: Advertising and the Therapeutic Roots of the Consumer Culture, 1880–1930," in *The Culture of Consumption: Critical Essays in American History, 1880–1980*, Richard W. Fox and T. J. Jackson Lears, eds., New York: Pantheon, 1–38.

——(1984), "Some Versions of Fantasy: Toward a Cultural History of American Advertising, 1880–1930," *Prospects: An Annual Journal of American Cultural Studies*, Vol. 10, 349–405.

Lehman, Harvey C. and Paul A. Witty (1927), "The Present Status of the Tendency to Collect and Hoard," *Psychological Review*, 34, 48–56.

Lehrer, Adrienne (1983), *Wine and Conversation*, Bloomington, Indiana: Indiana University Press.

Lehrer, Jim (1990), "And Now a Word of Praise for the Pack Rats Among Us," *Smithsonian*, 20 (March), 58–67.

Leiss, William, Stephen Kline, and Sut Jhally (1986), *Social Communication in Advertising: Persons, Products, and Images of Well-Being*, Toronto: Methuen.

Levine, Joshua (1989), "Art Chic," *Forbes*, 148 (August 21), 94, 96.

Levine, Lawrence W. (1988), *Highbrow/Lowbrow: The Emergence of Cultural Hierarchy in America*, Cambridge, Massachusetts: Harvard University Press.

Lévi-Strauss, Claude (1966), *The Savage Mind*, Chicago: University of Chicago Press.

Lewis, Russell (1983), "Everything Under One Roof: World's Fairs and Department

Stores in Paris and Chicago," *Chicago History*, 12 (Fall), 28–47.

Lewis, Wilmarth (1946), *Collector's Progress*, New York: Alfred A. Knopf.

Ley, D. and K. Olds (1988), "Landscape as Spectacle: World's Fairs and the Culture of Heroic Consumption," *Environment and Planning D: Society and Space*, 6, 191–212.

Li, Chu-Tsing (1987a), "The Artistic Theories of the Literati," in *The Chinese Scholar's Studio: The Artistic Life in the Late Ming Period*, Chu-Tsing Li and James C. Y. Watt, eds., New York: Thames & Hudson, 14–22.

——(1987b), "The Literati Life," in *The Chinese Scholar's Studio: The Artistic Life in the Late Ming Period*, Chu-Tsing Li and James C. Y. Watt, eds., New York: Thames & Hudson, 37–51.

Liming, Wei (1993), "Private Collection Highlights Exhibition," *Beijing Review*, 36, October 4–10, 28–29.

Lindeman, Eduard C. (1950), *Life Stories of Men Who Shaped History, From Plutarch's Lives*, John Langhorne and William Langhorne, trans., New York: New American Library.

Lipsitz, George (1990), *Time Passages: Collective Memory and American Popular Culture*, Minneapolis, Minnesota: University of Minnesota Press.

Lowenthal, David (1988), "Classical Antiquities as National and Global Heritage," *Antiquity*, 62 (December), 726–735.

——(1989), "Pioneer Museums," in *History Museums in the United States: A Critical Assessment*, Warren Leon and Roy Rosenzweig, eds., Urbana, Illinois: University of Illinois Press, 115–127.

Lumley, Robert (1988), "Introduction," in *The Museum Time-Machine: Putting Cultures on Display*, Robert Lumley, ed., London: Routledge, 1–23.

Lupton, Ellen (1993), *Mechanical Brides: Women and Machines from Home to Office*, New York: Princeton Architectural Press.

Lurie, David R. (1986), "Consumer and Connoisseur: On the New Museum's *Damaged Goods: Desire and the Economy of the Object*," *Arts Magazine*, 61 (November), 16–18.

Lurie, Nancy Oestreich (1981), "Museumland Revisited," *Human Organization*, 40 (Summer), 180–187.

Lynes, Russell (1955), *The Tastemakers: The Shaping of American Popular Taste*, New York: Harper & Brothers.

MacCannell, Dean (1989), *The Tourist: A New Theory of the Leisure Class*, 2nd ed., London: Macmillan.

McClelland, David C. (1961), *The Achieving Society*, New York: Free Press.

McCracken, Grant (1988), *Culture and Consumption: New Approaches to the Symbolic Character of Consumer Goods and Activities*, Bloomington, Indiana: University of Indiana Press.

——(1990), "Matching Material Cultures: Person–Object Relations Inside and Outside the Ethnographic Museum," in *Advances in Nonprofit Marketing*, Vol. 3, Russell W. Belk, ed., Greenwich, Connecticut: JAI Press, 27–49.

——(1992), "Museum as a Meaning Maker/Meaning Taker: A Study of the Reciprocal Exchange of Symbolic Properties Between the Museum, Its Objects, and Its Publics," paper presented at the Association for Consumer Research Annual Conference, Vancouver, British Columbia, October.

McDaniel, Dennis K. (1989), "A Material World," *The Public Historian*, 11 (Winter), 57–59.

MacDonald, George F. (1992), "Change and Challenge: Museums in the Information Society," in *Museums and Communities*, Ivan Karp, Christine Mullen Kreamer, and Steven D. Lavine (eds), Washington, D.C.: Smithsonian Institution Press,

158–181.

Macfarlane, Allan (1978), *The Origin of English Individualism: The Family, Property and Social Transitions*, Oxford: Blackwell.

McGill, Douglas C. (1985), "Art World Subtly Shifts to Corporate Patronage," *New York Times*, February 5, C14.

McGreevy, Ann (1990), "Treasures of Children: Collections Then and Now, or Treasures of Children Revisited," *Early Child Development and Care*, 63, 33–36.

MacGregor, Arthur (1983), "Collectors and Collections of Rarities in the Sixteenth and Seventeenth Centuries," in *The Origins of Museums: The Cabinet of Curiosities in Sixteenth- and Seventeenth-Century Europe*, Oliver Impey and Arthur MacGregor, eds., Oxford: Clarendon Press, 70–97.

Mackay, Charles (1932), *Extraordinary Popular Delusions and the Madness of Crowds*, Boston: L. C. Page (original 1841, *Memoirs of Extraordinary Popular Delusions*, London: Richard Bentley).

McKay, Shona (1988), "The Manager," *Canadian Business*, 61 (November), 193–196.

McKendrick, Neil, John Brewer, and J. H. Plumb (1982), *The Birth of a Consumer Society: The Commercialization of Eighteenth-Century England*, London: Europa.

McKibbin, Ross (1983), "Work and Hobbies in Britain, 1880–1950," in *The Working Class in Modern British History: Essays in Honour of Henry Pelling*, Jay Winter, ed., Cambridge: Cambridge University Press, 142–145.

McMurtry, Larry (1982), *Cadillac Jack*, New York: Simon & Schuster.

Macpherson, C. B. (1962), *The Political Theory of Possessive Individualism*, Oxford: Clarendon Press.

Maine, Barry (1991), "Late Nineteenth-Century *Trompe L'Oeil* and Other Performances of the Real," *Prospects: An Annual of American Cultural Studies*, Vol. 16, 281–295.

Major, J. Russell (1970), *The Age of Renaissance and Reformation: A Short History*, Philadelphia, Pennsylvania: J. B. Lippincott.

Maloney, Clarence, ed. (1976), *The Evil Eye*, New York: Columbia University Press.

Malraux, André (1967), *Museum Without Walls*, Stuart Gilbert and Francis Price, eds., Garden City, New York: Doubleday (original 1965, *Le Musée Imaginaire*, Paris: Editions Gallimard).

Mamiya, Christin J. (1992), *Pop Art and Consumer Culture: American Super Market*, Austin, Texas: University of Texas Press.

Marchand, Roland (1985), *Advertising and the American Dream: Making Way for Modernity, 1920–1940*, Berkeley, California: University of California Press.

Marcus, Leonard S. (1978), *The American Store Window*, New York: Whitney Library of Design.

Marquis, Alice Goldfarb (1991), *The Art Biz: The Covert World of Collectors, Dealers, Auction Houses, Museums, and Critics*, Chicago: Contemporary Books.

Martorella, Rosanne (1990), *Corporate Art*, New Brunswick, New Jersey: Rutgers University Press.

Mason, Peter (1994), "From Presentation to Representation: *Americana* in Europe," *Journal of the History of Collections*, 6 (1), 1–20.

Materer, Timothy (1988), "From Henry James to Ezra Pound: John Quinn and the Art of Patronage," *Paideuma*, 17 (Fall and Winter), 47–68.

Mathews, Jack (1991), "Books and Beetles," *Antioch Review*, 49 (Summer), 325-335.

Mechling, Jay (1989), "The Collecting Self and American Youth Movements," in *Consuming Visions: Accumulation and Display of Goods in America, 1889–1920*, Simon J. Bronner, ed., New York: W. W. Norton, 255–285.

Mehta, Subhash and Kan Ah Keng (1985), "Correlates of Materialism: A Study of Singaporean Chinese," in *Historical Perspective in Consumer Research: National and International Perspectives*, Chin T. Tan and Jagdish N. Sheth, eds., Singapore: Association for Consumer Research, 326–330.

Meiss, Millard (1969), *French Paintings in the Time of Jean de Berry*, 2nd ed., New York: Phaidon.

Menninger, Karl (1973), *What Ever Became of Sin?*, New York: Hawthorne Books.

Menninger, William C. (1942), "Psychological Aspects of Hobbies: A Contribution to Civilian Morale," *American Journal of Psychiatry*, 99 (July), 122–129.

Merriman, Nick (1989), "Museum Visiting as a Cultural Phenomenon," in *The New Museology*, Peter Vergo, ed., London: Reaktion Books, 149–171.

Messenger, Phyllis Mauch, ed. (1989), *The Ethics of Collecting, Whose Culture? Cultural Property, Whose Property?*, Albuquerque, New Mexico: University of New Mexico Press.

Meyer, Karl E. (1973), *The Plundered Past*, New York: Atheneum.

Mick, David Glenn and Michelle DeMoss (1990), "Self-Gifts: Phenomenological Insights from Four Contexts," *Journal of Consumer Research*, 17 (December), 322–332.

Miller, Daniel (1987), *Material Culture and Mass Consumption*, Oxford: Basil Blackwell.

Miller, Michael (1981), *The Bon Marché: Bourgeois Culture and the Department Store, 1869-1920*, Princeton, New Jersey: Princeton University Press.

Mills, Stephen F. (1990), "Disney and the Promotions of Synthetic Worlds," *American Studies International*, 28 (October), 66–79.

Miner, Horace (1956), "Body Ritual Among the Nacirema," *American Anthropologist*, 58 (3), 503–507.

Mintz, Sidney W. (1985), *Sweetness and Power: The Place of Sugar in Modern History*, New York: Viking.

Mol, Hans (1976), *Identity and the Sacred: A Sketch for a New Social-Scientific Theory of Religion*, New York: Free Press.

Morton, Alan (1988), "Tomorrow's Yesterdays: Science Museums and the Future," in *The Museum Time-Machine: Putting Cultures on Display*, Robert Lumley, ed., London: Routledge, 128–143.

Moskoff, William (1990), "The Undiminished Magic of Collecting Stamps," *Chronicle of Higher Education*, 36 (July 25), B36.

Moulin, Raymonde (1987), *The French Art Market: A Sociological View*, Arthur Goldhammer, trans., New Brunswick, New Jersey: Rutgers University Press (original 1967, *Le Marché de le Peinture en France*, Paris: Éditions de Minuit).

Moynehan, Barbara (1982), "The Legacy of Margaret Woodbury Strong," *Americana*, 10 (September–October), 82–86.

Muensterberger, Werner (1994), *Collecting, An Unruly Passion: Psychological Perspectives*, Princeton, New Jersey: Princeton University Press.

Mukerji, Chandra (1978), "Artwork: Collection and Contemporary Culture," *American Journal of Sociology*, 84, 348–365.

——(1983), *From Graven Images: Patterns of Modern Materialism*, New York: Columbia University Press.

——(1993), "Reading and Writing with Nature: A Materialist Approach to French Formal Gardens', in *Consumption and the World of Goods*, John Brewer and Roy Porter (eds), London: Routledge, 439–461.

Mullaney, Steven (1983), "Strange Things, Gross Terms, Curious Customs: The Rehearsal of Cultures in the Late Renaissance," *Representations*, 3 (Summer), 40–67.

Naifeh, Steven W. (1976), *Culture Making: Money, Success, and the New York Art*

World, Princeton, New Jersey: History Department, Princeton University.

Neal, Arminta (1980), "Collecting for History Museums: Reassembling Our Splintered Existence," *Museum News*, 58 (May/June), 24–29.

Nelson, Steve (1986), "Walt Disney's EPCOT and the World's Fair Performance Tradition," *Drama Review*, 30 (Winter), 106–146.

Neumann, Charles P. (1975), "Success Today – Achievement without Happiness," *Psychosomatics*, 16 (3), 103–106.

Newson, John and Elizabeth Newson (1968), *Four Year Old in an Urban Community*, Chicago: Aldine.

New Yorker (1992), "Stuff," *New Yorker*, 63 (April 20), 32–33.

Nicholson, Geoff (1994), *Hunters & Gatherers*, Woodstock, NY: Overlook Press.

Noorani, Arif (1992), "Teenage Wasteland," *The Varsity*, 113 (3), August 4, 7.

Nordau, Max (1896), *Degeneration*, 8th ed., translated from 2nd German edition, New York: D. Appleton.

North, Gary (1974), "The Puritan Experiment with Sumptuary Legislation," *Freeman*, 24 (June), 341–353.

Nygren, Edward J. (1988), "The Almighty Dollar: Money as a Theme in American Painting," *Winterthur Portfolio*, 23 (Summer/Autumn), 129–150.

Nyström, Bengt and Gunilla Cedrenius (1982), *Spread the Responsibility for Museum Documentation – A Programme for Contemporary Documentation at Swedish Museums of Cultural History*, Stockholm: The Stockholm Secretariat, Nordiska Museet.

Oakley, John H. and Rebecca H. Sinos (1993), *The Wedding in Ancient Athens*, Madison, Wisconsin: University of Wisconsin Press.

O'Brien, George (1981), "Living with Collections," *New York Times Magazine*, April 26, Part 2, 25–42.

O'Flynn, Paul (1990), "T-Shirts and the Coming Collapse of Capitalism," in *Readings in Popular Culture: Trivial Pursuits?*, Gary Day, ed., New York: St. Martin's Press, 68–74.

O'Guinn, Thomas C. (1991), "Touching Greatness: The Central Midwest Barry Manilow Fan Club," in *Highways and Buyways: Naturalistic Research from the Consumer Behavior Odyssey*, Russell W. Belk, ed., Provo, Utah: Association for Consumer Research, 102–111.

——and Ronald J. Faber (1989), "Compulsive Buying: A Phenomenological Exploration," *Journal of Consumer Research*, 16 (September), 147–157.

Olmi, Giuseppe (1985), "Science–Honour–Metaphor: Italian Cabinets of the Sixteenth and Seventeenth Centuries," in *The Origins of Museums: The Cabinet of Curiosities in Sixteenth- and Seventeenth-Century Europe*, Oliver Impey and Arthur MacGregor, eds., Oxford: Clarendon Press, 5–16.

Olmsted, Al D. (1988a), "Collectors and Collecting," paper presented at the Eighteenth Annual Meeting of the Popular Culture Association, New Orleans, Louisiana, March.

——(1988b), "Morally Controversial Leisure: The Social World of Gun Collectors," *Symbolic Interaction*, 11, 277–287.

——(1989), "Gun Ownership as Serious Leisure," in *The Gun Culture and Its Enemies*, William R. Tonso, ed., Columbus, Ohio: Merrill.

——(1991), "Collecting: Leisure, Investment or Obsession," in *To Have Possessions: A Handbook on Ownership and Property*, Floyd W. Rudmin, ed., special issue of *Journal of Social Behavior and Personality*, 6 (6), 287–306.

Orosz, Joel J. (1990), *Curators and Culture: The Museum Movement in America, 1740–1870*, Tuscaloosa, Alabama: University of Alabama Press.

Osgood, Charles E. and Percy H. Tannenbaum (1955), "The Principle of Congruity in the Production of Attitude Change," *Psychological Review*, 62, 42–55.

Palmer, Norman (1989), "Museums and Cultural Property," in *The New Museology*, Peter Vergo, ed., London: Reaktion Books, 172–204.

Park, Katherine and Lorraine Daston (1981), "Unnatural Conceptions: The Study of Monsters in Sixteenth- and Seventeenth-Century France and England," *Past and Present*, 92 (August), 20–54.

Parry, J. H. (1963), *The Age of Reconnaissance*, Berkeley, California: University of California Press.

Paton, W. D. M. (1988), "Bibliomania: A Clinical Case-Study, or Forty Years of Messing about with Books," *Book Collector*, 37 (Summer), 207–224.

Pavlov, Ivan Petrovitch (1928), *Lectures on Conditioned Reflexes*, Vol. 1, W. Horsley Gantt, trans., New York: International Publishers.

Pearce, Susan M. (1992), *Museums, Objects and Collections: A Cultural Study*, Leicester: Leicester University Press.

Pendergrast, Mark (1993), *For God, Country, and Coca-Cola: The Unauthorized History of the Great American Soft Drink and the Company That Makes It*, New York: Charles Scribner's Sons.

Petronius, Gaius (1944), *The Complete Work of Gaius Petronius*, Jack Lindsay, trans., New York: Wiley (original circa AD 50).

Pfeiffer, John E. (1982), *The Creative Explosion: An Inquiry into the Origins of Art and Religion*, New York: Harper & Row.

Phillips, Richard H. (1962), "The Accumulator," *Archives of General Psychiatry*, 6 (June), 96–99.

Phillips, Joana W. and Helen K. Staley (1961), "Sumptuary Legislation in Four Centuries," *Journal of Home Economics*, 53 (October), 673–677.

Piper, Dan (1972), "Dan Wittington and the Middle Class Dream of Success," in *Heroes of Popular Culture*, Ray B. Browne, Marshall Fishwick, and Michael T. Marsden, eds., Bowling Green, Ohio: Bowling Green University Popular Press, 53–59.

Pivar, Stuart (1988), "Shopping with Andy," in *The Andy Warhol Collection, Contemporary Art*, Vol. 5, Sotheby's, n.p.n.

Polhemus, Ted (1994), *Streetstyle: From Sidewalk to Catwalk*, New York: Thames and Hudson.

Pomian, Krystof (1990), *Collectors and Curiosities: Paris and Venice: 1500–1800*, Elizabeth Wiles-Portier, trans., Cambridge: Polity Press (original 1987, *Collectionneurs, Amateurs et Curieux*, Paris: Editions Gallimard).

Pope, Alexander (1931), "The Rape of the Lock," *The Poems Epistles & Satires of Alexander Pope*, London: J. M. Dent & Sons (original 1714).

Posthumus, N. W. (1929), "The Tulip Mania in Holland in the Years 1636 and 1637", *Journal of Economic and Business History*, 1 (May), 434–439.

Powers, Martin J. (1986), "Artistic Taste, The Economy and the Social Order in Former Han China," *Art History*, 9 (September), 286–310.

Praz, Mario (1971), *Conversation Pieces: A Survey of the Informal Group Portrait in Europe and America*, University Park, Pennsylvania: Pennsylvania State University Press.

Presbrey, Frank (1929), *The History and Development of Advertising*, Garden City, New York: Doubleday, Duran.

Price, Sally (1989), *Primitive Art in Civilized Places*, Chicago: University of Chicago Press.

Purcell, Rosamond Wolff and Stephen Jay Gould (1992), *Finders, Keepers: Eight Collectors*, New York: W. W. Norton.

Pynchon, Thomas (1966), *The Crying of Lot 49*, London: Jonathan Cape.

Radley, Alan (1990), "Artefacts, Memory and a Sense of the Past," in *Collective Remembering*, David Middleton and Derek Edwards, eds., London: Sage, 46–59.

Rapoport, Roger (1989), "Snap, Crackle, and Pop," *Americana*, 17 (April), 37–40.

Rash, Wayne, Jr. (1990), "Museum Quality," *Byte*, 15 (August), 286–287.

Rassuli, Kathleen M. and Stanley C. Hollander (1986), "Desire – Induced, Innate, Insatiable?", *Journal of Macromarketing*, 6 (Fall), 4–24.

Rawson, Jessica (1993), "The Ancestry of Chinese Bronze Vessels," in *History from Things: Essays on Material Culture*, Steven Lubar and W. David Kingery, eds., Washington, D. C.: Smithsonian Institution Press, 51–73.

Reekie, Gail (1993), *Temptations: Sex, Selling and the Department Store*, St. Leonards, New South Wales: Allen & Unwin.

Rehmus, James M. (1988), "The Collector's Mind," *Perspectives in Biology and Medicine*, 31 (Winter), 261–264.

Reitlinger, Gerald (1970), *The Economics of Taste: The Art Market in the 1960s*, Vol. 3, London: Barrie & Rockliff.

Revi, Albert C. (1974), *Spinning Wheel's Antiques for Men*, Hanover, Pennsylvania: Spinning Wheel Books.

Rheims, Maurice (1961), *The Strange Life of Objects: 35 Centuries of Art Collecting & Collectors*, David Pryce-Jones, trans., New York: Athenium (original 1959, *La Vie Etrange des Objets*, Paris: Librarie Plan; published in England as *Art on the Market: Thirty-Five Centuries of Collecting and Collectors from Midas to Paul Getty*, 1961).

——(1975), *The Glorious Obsession*, New York: St. Martins Press.

Ricci, Stafania (1992), *Salvatore Ferragamo: The Art of the Shoe, 1898–1960*, New York: Rizzoli.

Rice, Danielle (1992), "The 'Rocky Dilemma': Museums, Monuments, and Popular Culture in the Postmodern Era," in *Critical Issues in Public Art: Content, Context, and Controversy*, Harriet F. Senie and Sally Webster, eds., New York: Icon Editions, 228–236.

Richards, Thomas (1990), *The Commodity Culture of Victorian England: Advertising and Spectacle, 1851–1914*, Stanford, California: Stanford University Press.

Richins, Marsha L. (1987), "Media, Materialism, and Human Happiness," in *Advances in Consumer Research*, Vol. 14, Melanie Wallendorf and Paul Anderson, eds., Provo, Utah: Association for Consumer Research, 352–356.

——and Scott Dawson (1992), "A Consumer Values Orientation for Materialism and Its Measurement: Scale Development and Validation," *Journal of Consumer Research*, 19 (December), 303–316.

Rigby, Douglas and Elizabeth Rigby (1944), *Lock, Stock and Barrel: The Story of Collecting*, Philadelphia: J. B. Lippincott.

Ritvo, Harriet (1987), *The Animal Estate: The English and Other Creatures in the Victorian Age*, Cambridge, Massachusetts: Harvard University Press.

Roberts, Gwyneth (1990), "'A Thing of Beauty and a Source of Wonderment': Ornaments for the Home as Cultural Status Markers," in *Readings in Popular Culture: Trivial Pursuits?*, Gary Day, ed., New York: St. Martin's Press, 39–47.

Rochberg-Halton, Eugene (1979), "The Meaning of Personal Art Objects," in *Social Research and Cultural Policy*, Jiri Zuzanek, ed., Waterloo, Ontario: Otium, 155–181.

Rogan, Bjarne (1990), "On the Custom of Naming Artifacts," *Ethnologia Europaea*, 20, 47–60.

Rogoli, Bob (1991), "Racism in Baseball Card Collecting: Fact or Fiction?" *Human Relations*, 44 (March), 255–264.

Rook, Dennis (1985), "Body Cathexis and Market Segmentation," in *The Psychology of Fashion*, Michael R. Solomon, ed., Lexington, Massachusetts: Lexington, 233–242.

Rubenstein, Harry R. (1985), "Collecting for Tomorrow: Sweden's Contemporary Documentation Program," *Museum News*, 63 (August), 55–60.

Rudolph, Barbara (1985), "Mixing Class and Cash," *Time*, December 9, 56.

Rushing, W. Jackson (1992), "Marketing the Affinity of the Primitive and the Modern," in *The Early Years of Native American Art History*, Janet Catherine Berlo, ed., Seattle, Washington: University of Washington Press, 191–236.

Rydell, Robert W. (1984), *All the World's a Fair: Visions of Empire at America's International Expositions, 1876–1916*, Chicago: University of Chicago Press.

——(1989), "The Culture of Imperial Abundance: World's Fairs in the Making of American Culture," in *Consuming Visions: Accumulation and Display of Goods in America, 1880–1920*, Simon J. Bronner, ed., New York: W. W. Norton, 191–216.

——(1993), *World of Fairs: The Century-of-Progress Expositions*, Chicago: University of Chicago Press.

Saarinen, Aline B. (1958), *The Proud Possessors: The Lives, Times and Tastes of Some Adventurous American Art Collectors*, New York: Random House.

Sachs, Hanns (1945), *Freud: Master and Friend*, London: Imago.

Sahlins, Marshall D. (1972), *Stone Age Economics*, Chicago: Aldine.

Said, Edward W. (1978), *Orientalism*, New York: Pantheon.

Saisselin, Rémy G. (1984), *Bricabracomania: The Bourgeois and the Bibelot*, New Brunswick, New Jersey: Rutgers University Press.

Sanders, Clinton R. (1989), *Customizing the Body: The Art and Culture of Tattooing*, Philadelphia, Pennsylvania: Temple University Press.

Sandler, Carol (1989), *Margaret Woodbury: Collector*, Rochester, New York: The Strong Museum.

Sartre, Jean-Paul (1943), *Being and Nothingness: A Phenomenological Essay on Ontology*, New York: Philosophical Library.

Sayre, Shay (1992), "T-Shirt Messages: Fortune or Folly for Advertisers?" in *Advertising and Popular Culture: Studies in Variety and Versatility*, Sammy R. Danna, ed., Bowling Green, Ohio: Bowling Green State University Popular Press, 73–82.

Schama, Simon (1987), *The Embarrassment of Riches: An Interpretation of Dutch Culture in the Golden Age*, New York: Alfred A. Knopf.

Scharnhorst, Gary F. (1976), "The Boudoir Tales of Horatio Alger, Jr.," *Journal of Popular Culture*, 10 (1), 215–226.

Schiff, David (1989), "Junk Art: Some Public Firms Are Cashing In on It," *Barron's*, October 30, 14–15, 44–45.

Schiffer, Michael B., Theodore E. Downing, and Michael McCarthy (1981), "Waste Not, Want Not: An Ethnoarchaeological Study of Refuse in Tucson, Arizona," in *Modern Material Culture: The Archaeology of Us*, Michael Gould and Michael B. Schiffer, eds., New York: Academic Press, 67–86.

Schivelbusch, Wolfgang (1992), *Tastes of Paradise*, trans. David Jacobson, New York: Pantheon (original 1980, *Paradies, der Geschmack und die Vernunft*).

Schlereth, Thomas J. (1989), "Country Stores, County Fairs, and Mail-Order Catalogues: Consumption in Rural America," in *Consuming Visions: Accumulation and Display of Goods in America, 1880–1920*, Simon J. Bronner, ed., New York: W. W. Norton, 339–375.

Schmidt, Leigh Eric (1989), "'A Church-going People are a Dress-loving People': Clothes, Communication, and Religious Culture in Early America," *Church History*, 58 (March), 36–51.

Schnapper, Antoine (1986), "The King of France as Collector in the Sixteenth

Century," *Journal of Interdisciplinary History*, 17 (Summer), 185–202.

Schneider, Mark A. (1993), *Culture and Enchantment*, Chicago: University of Chicago Press.

Schoeck, Helmut (1966), *Envy: A Theory of Social Behavior*, Michael Glennyard and Betty Ross, trans., New York: Harcourt, Brace & World.

Schroeder, Fred. E. H., ed. (1981), *Twentieth-Century Popular Culture in Museums and Libraries*, Bowling Green, Ohio: Bowling Green University Popular Press.

Schroeder, Jonathon E. (1992), "Materialism and Modern Art," in *Meaning, Measure, and Morality of Materialism*, Floyd Rudmin and Marsha Richins, eds., Provo, Utah: Association for Consumer Research, 10–13.

Schudson, Michael (1984), *Advertising, The Uneasy Persuasion: Its Dubious Impact on American Society*, New York: Basic Books.

Scitovsky, Tibor (1976), *The Joyless Economy: An Inquiry into Human Satisfaction and Consumer Dissatisfaction*, New York: Oxford University Press.

Secord, Paul F. and Sidney M. Jourard (1953), "The Appraisal of Body-Cathexis: Body-Cathexis and the Self," *Journal of Consulting Psychology*, 17 (5), 343–347.

Shell, Marc (1982), *Money, Language, and Thought: Literary and Philosophical Economies from the Medieval to the Modern Era*, Berkeley, California: University of California Press.

Sherry, John F., Jr. (1991), "Postmodern Alternatives: The Interpretive Turn in Consumer Research," in *Handbook of Consumer Behavior*, Thomas S. Robertson and Harold H. Kassarjian, eds., Englewood Cliffs, New Jersey: Prentice-Hall, 548–591.

Silver, Alan (1993), "Friendship in Commercial Society: Eighteenth-Century Social Theory and Modern Sociology," *American Journal of Sociology*, 6 (May), 1474–1504.

Silverman, Debora (1986), *Selling Culture: Bloomingdale's, Diana Vreeland, and the New Aristocracy of Tastes in Reagan's America*, New York: Pantheon.

Simpson, J. A. and E. S. C. Weiner (1989),"Dilettant," *Oxford English Dictionary*, Vol. 4, 2nd ed., Oxford: Clarendon Press, 665.

Sinclair, Andrew (1981), *Corsair: The Life of J. Pierpont Morgan*, Boston: Little, Brown.

Smith, Charles W. (1989), *Auction: The Social Construction of Value*, London: Harvester Wheatsheaf.

Smith, Frederik N. (1990), "Scientific Discourse: Gulliver's Travels and the Philosophical Transactions," in *The Genres of Gulliver's Travels*, Frederik N. Smith, ed., Newark, Delaware: University of Delaware Press, 139–162.

Smith, K. C. P. and M. J. Apter (1977), "Collecting Antiques: A Psychological Interpretation," *The Antique Collector*, 48 (7), 64–66.

Smith, Roberta (1988), "Rituals of Consumption," *Art in America*, 76 (May), 164–171.

Snyder, C. R. and Howard R. Fromkin (1981), *Uniqueness: Human Pursuit of Difference*, New York: Plenum Press.

Sobol, Ken and Jule Macfie Sobol (1991), "Home-Grown Museums," *Canadian Geographic*, 11 (April/May), 74–82.

Sombart, Werner (1913), *Luxury and Capitalism*, Ann Arbor, Michigan: University of Michigan Press.

Sontag, Susan (1977), *On Photography*, New York: Farrar, Straus & Giroux.

Soroka, Michael P. (1988), "In Heaven There is No Beer, That's Why We Collect it Here," paper presented at Eighteenth Annual Meeting of the Popular Culture Association, New Orleans, March.

Soutif, Daniel (1989), "Found and Lost: On the Object in Art," *Art Forum*, 28

(October), 155–162.

Spector, Jack (1975), "Dr. Sigmund Freud, Art Collector," *Art News*, (April), 20–26.

Spence, Janet T. (1985), "Achievement American Style: The Rewards and Costs of Individualism," *American Psychologist*, 40 (December 12), 1285–1295.

Spiess, Katherine and Philip Spiess (1990), "Museum Collections," in *The Museum: A Reference Guide*, Michael Steven Shapiro, ed., New York: Greenwood Press, 141–166.

Stavenow-Hidemark, Elisabet (1985), *Home Thoughts From Abroad: An Evaluation of the SAMDOK Homes Pool*, Stockholm: The SAMDOK Secretariat, Nordiska Museet.

Stebbins, Robert A. (1979), *Amateurs: On the Margin Between Work and Leisure*, Beverly Hills, California: Sage.

——(1982), "Serious Leisure: A Conceptual Statement," *Pacific Sociological Review*, 25 (April), 251–272.

Stenross, Barbara (1987), "The Meaning of Guns: Shooters, Hunters, and Collectors," paper presented at the Association for Popular Culture Annual Meeting, Montreal, March.

Stephens, Suzanne (1986), "An Equitable Relationship?" *Art in America*, 74 (May), 116–123.

Stevenson, Robert Louis (1905), "Happy Thought," *A Child's Garden of Verses*, New York: Charles Scribner's Sons, 34.

Stewart, Susan (1984), *On Longing: Narratives of the Miniature, the Gigantic, the Souvenir, and the Collection*, Baltimore, Maryland: Johns Hopkins University Press.

Stillinger, Elizabeth (1980), *The Antiquers*, New York: Alfred A. Knopf.

Storr, Anthony (1983), "The Psychology of Collecting," *Connoisseur*, 213 (June), 35–38.

Strasser, Susan (1989), *Satisfaction Guaranteed: The Making of the American Mass Market*, New York: Pantheon.

Stuard, Susan Mosher (1985), "Medieval Workshop: Toward a Theory of Consumption and Economic Change," *Journal of Economic History*, 45 (June), 447–451.

Sudjic, Deyan (1985), *Cult Objects*, London: Paladin Books.

Sumption, Jonathon (1975), *Pilgrimage: An Image of Medieval Religion*, London: Faber & Faber.

Sutton, Peter, ed. (1988), *Dreamings: The Art of Aboriginal Australia*, New York: Viking.

Swift, Jonathan (1980), *Gulliver's Travels*, Arlington, Virginia: Great Ocean Publishers (original 1726).

Taylor, Francis Henry (1948), *The Taste of Angels: A History of Art Collecting from Ramses to Napoleon*, Boston: Little, Brown.

Taylor, Robert H. (1980), *Certain Small Works*, Princeton, New Jersey: Princeton University Press.

Tenkotte, Paul A. (1987), "International Exhibitions and the Concept of Culture-Place, 1851–1915," *American Studies*, 28 (Spring), 5–29.

Terrell, John (1991), "Disneyland and the Future of Museum Anthropology," *American Anthropologist*, 93 (March), 149–153.

Thirsk, Joan (1978), *Economic Policy and Projects: The Development of a Consumer Society in Early Modern England*, Oxford: Clarendon Press.

Thomas, Nicholas (1991), *Entangled Objects: Exchange, Material Culture, and Colonialism in the Pacific*, Cambridge, Massachusetts: Harvard University Press.

Thompson, Homer A. and R. E. Wycherley (1972), *The Agora of Athens*, Princeton,

New Jersey: American School of Classical Studies at Athens.

Thompson, Michael (1976), *Rubbish Theory*, Oxford: Oxford University Press.

Tintner, Adeline R. (1972), "'The Old Things': Balzac's *Le Curé de Tours* and James's *The Spoils of Poynton*," *Nineteenth Century Fiction*, 26 (March), 436–455.

——(1984), "The Disappearing Furniture in Maupassant's 'Qui Sait?' and *The Spoils of Poyton*," *Henry James Review*, 6 (Fall), 3–7.

——(1986), *The Museum World of Henry James*, Ann Arbor, Michigan: UMI Research Press.

Tomkins, Calvin (1970), *Merchants and Masterpieces: The Story of the Metropolitan Museum of Art*, New York: E. P. Dutton.

Tomlinson, Alan (1990), "Introduction: Consumer Culture and the Aura of the Commodity," in *Consumption, Identity, and Style: Marketing, Meanings, and the Packaging of Pleasure*, London: Routledge, 1–38.

Tooley, Kay M. (1978), "The Remembrance of Things Past: On the Collection and Recollection of Ingredients Useful in the Treatment of Disorders Resulting from Unhappiness, Rootlessness, and the Fear of Things to Come," *American Journal of Orthopsychiatry*, 48, 174–187.

Torgovnick, Mariana (1990), *Gone Primitive: Savage Intellects, Modern Lives*, Chicago: University of Chicago Press.

Trachtenberg, Alan (1982), *The Incorporation of America: Culture and Society in the Gilded Age*, New York: Hill & Wang.

Travis, Russell (1988), "Why People Collect: Motivational Tendencies and the Addiction Factor," paper presented at the Eighteenth Annual Meeting of the Popular Culture Association, New Orleans, Louisiana, March.

Treas, Charles E. and Dalton E. Brannen (1976), "The Growing Collector Market," *Proceedings*, Atlanta, Georgia: Southern Marketing Association, 234–236.

Tse, David, Russell W. Belk, and Nan Zhou (1989), "Becoming a Consumer Society: A Longitudinal and Cross-Cultural Content Analysis of Print Advertisements from Hong Kong, People's Republic of China and Taiwan," *Journal of Consumer Research*, 15 (March), 457–472.

Tuan, Yi-Fu (1982), *Segmented Worlds and Self: Group Life and Individual Consciousness*, Minneapolis, Minnesota: University of Minnesota Press.

——(1984), *Dominance & Affection: The Making of Pets*, New Haven, Connecticut: Yale University Press.

Tuchman, Mitch (1994), *Magnificent Obsessions: Twenty Remarkable Collectors in Pursuit of Their Dreams*, San Francisco, California: Chronicle Books.

Tucker, David M. (1991), *The Decline of Thrift in America: Our Cultural Shift from Saving to Spending*, New York: Praeger.

Tucker, Louis Leonard (1967), "'Ohio Show-Shop': The Western Museum of Cincinnati, 1820-1867," in *A Cabinet of Curiosities: Five Episodes in the Evolution of American Museums*, Whitfield J. Bell, Jr., Clifford K. Shipton, John C. Ewers, Louis Leonard Tucker, and Wilcomb E. Washburn (eds), Charlottesville, Virginia: University Press of Virginia, 73–105.

Turner, Jonathan (1992), "Shopping for Pop," *Art News*, 91 (September), 14.

Turner, Victor (1969), *The Ritual Process*, London: Routledge & Kegan Paul.

Unruh, David R. (1983), *Invisible Lives: Social Worlds of the Aged*, Beverly Hills, California: Sage.

Urry, John (1990), *The Tourist Gaze: Leisure and Travel in Contemporary Societies*, London: Sage.

U.S. Postal Service (1993), *The Postal Service Guide to U.S. Stamps*, 20th ed., Washington, D.C.: United States Postal Service, Item No. 8893.

Vander Gucht, Daniel (1991), "Art at Risk in the Hands of the Museum: From the

Museum to the Private Collection," *International Sociology*, 6 (September), 361–372.

Varnedde, Kirk and Adam Gopnik (1990), *High & Low: Popular Culture, Modern Art*, New York: Museum of Modern Art.

Veblen, Thorstein (1899), *The Theory of the Leisure Class*, New York: MacMillan.

Vincent, John M. (1934), "Sumptuary Legislation," in *Encyclopedia of the Social Sciences*, Vol. 14, Edwin R. A. Seligman, ed., New York: Macmillan, 464–466.

von Holst, Niels (1967), *Creators Collectors and Connoisseurs: The Anatomy of Artistic Taste from Antiquity to the Present Day*, New York: G. P. Putnam's Sons.

Wainwright, Clive (1989), *The Romantic Interior: The British Collector at Home, 1750–1850*, New Haven, Connecticut: Yale University Press.

Wallendorf, Melanie and Russell W. Belk (1987), *Deep Meaning in Possessions: Qualitative Research from the Consumer Behavior Odyssey*, video, Cambridge, Massachusetts: Marketing Science Institute.

Walls, Richard T., Roy A. Moxley, Jr., and Steven P. Gulkus (1975), "Collection Preferences of Children," *Child Development*, 46, 783–785.

Walter, Eugene (1988), *Placeways: A Theory of the Human Environment*, Chapel Hill, North Carolina: University of North Carolina Press.

Watson, Lyall (1990), *The Nature of Things: The Secret Life of Inanimate Objects*, London: Hodder & Stoughton.

Watt, James C. (1987), "The Literati Environment," in *The Chinese Scholar's Studio: The Artistic Life in the Late Ming Period*, Chu-Tsing Li and James C. Y. Watt, eds., New York: Thames & Hudson, 1–13.

Weber, William (1975), *Music and the Middle Class in Nineteenth-Century Europe*, New York: Holmes & Meier.

Weil, Stephen E. (1990), *Rethinking the Museum and Other Meditations*, Washington, D.C.: Smithsonian Institution Press.

Weisz, John R., Fred M. Rothbaum, and Thomas C. Blackburn (1984), "Standing Out and Standing In: The Psychology of Control in America and Japan," *American Psychologist*, 39 (September), 955–969.

Welch, Martin (1983), "The Ashmolean as Described by Its Earliest Visitors," in *Tradescant's Rarities: Essays on the Foundation of the Ashmolean Museum 1683 With a Catalogue of the Surviving Early Collections*, Arthur MacGregor, ed., Oxford: Clarendon Press, 59–69.

Welu, James A. (1991), "Strange New Worlds: Mapping the Heavens and Earth's Great Extent," in *The Age of the Marvelous*, Joy Kenseth, ed., Hanover, New Hampshire: Hood Museum of Art, Dartmouth College, 102–112.

Wernick, Andrew (1991), *Promotional Culture: Advertising, Ideology and Symbolic Expression*, London: Sage.

Wersig, Gernot and Petra Schuck-Wersig (1990), "A German View of Marketing in United States Museums," *Curator*, 33 (1), 72–80.

Wheelock, Arthur K., Jr. (1991), "*Trompe-l'oeil* Painting," in *The Age of the Marvelous*, Joy Kenseth, ed., Hanover, New Hampshire: Hood Museum of Art, Dartmouth College, 179-191.

White, Robert W. (1959), "Motivation Reconsidered: The Concept of Competence," *Psychological Review*, 66 (5), 297–333.

Whitley, M. T. (1929), "Children's Interest in Collecting," *Journal of Educational Psychology*, 20, 249–261.

Wicklund, Robert A. and Peter M. Gollwitzer (1982), *Symbolic Self Completion*, Hillsdale, New Jersey: Lawrence Erlbaum Associates.

Williams, Rosalind H. (1982), *Dream Worlds: Mass Consumption in Later Nineteenth-Century France*, Berkeley, California: University of California Press.

Wittlin, Alma S. (1970), *Museums: In Search of a Usable Future*, Cambridge, Massachusetts: MIT Press.

Witty, Paul A. and Harvey C. Lehman (1930), "Further Studies of Children's Interest in Collecting," *Journal of Educational Psychology*, 21, 112–127.

——and Harvey C. Lehman (1931), "Sex Differences: Collecting Interests," *Journal of Educational Psychology*, 22, 221–228.

——and Harvey C. Lehman (1933), "The Collecting Interests of Town Children and Country Children," *Journal of Educational Psychology*, 24, 170–184.

Wornum, Ralph N. (1851), "The Exhibition as a Lesson in Taste," *The Art Journal Illustrated Catalogue: The Industry of all Nations, 1851*, London: George Virtue, i-xxii.

Worrell, Estell Ansley (1980), *Children's Costume in America, 1607–1910*, New York: Charles Scribner's Sons.

Wright, John L., ed. (1992), *Possible Dreams: Enthusiasm for Technology in America*, Dearborn, Michigan: Henry Ford Museum & Greenfield Village.

Wright, Louis B. and Gordon N. Ray (1969), *The Private Collector and the Support of Scholarship*, Los Angles: University of California.

Yonemura, Ann (1989), "Splendor and Supremacy: Lacquer for the Tokugawa," in *The Tokugawa Collection, the Japan of the Shoguns*, Denise L. Bissonnette, coordinator, Montreal: Montreal Museum of Fine Arts, 75–80.

Zajonc, Robert B., Philip Shaver, C. Tavris, and D. Van Kreveid (1972), "Exposure, Satiation and Stimulus Discriminability," *Psychological Bulletin*, 81, 270–280.

Zembala, Dennis (1990), "Now, Industrial History Moves Front and Center," *Museum News*, 69 (November/December), 34–37.

Zola, Emile (1958), *Ladies' Delight*, April Fitzlyon, trans., London: Abelard-Schuman (original 1883, *Au Bonheur des Dames*, Paris: Carpentier).

Zolberg, Vera L. (1984), "American Art Museums: Sanctuary or Free-For-All," *Social Forces*, 63 (December), 377–392.

Zuckerman, Michael (1972), "The Nursery Tales of Horatio Alger," *American Quarterly*, 24 (May), 191–209.

——(1991), "Holy Wars, Civil Wars: Religion and Economics in Nineteenth-Century America," *Prospects: An Annual of American Cultural Studies*, Vol. 16, 205–240.

Zukin, Sharon (1991), *Landscapes of Power: From Detroit to Disney World*, Berkeley, California: University of California Press.

INDEX